WEBSTER'S NEW WORLD®

SPANISH GRAMMAR HANDBOOK

D1300944

WEBSTER'S NEW WORLD®

SPANISH GRAMMAR HANDBOOK

1st Edition

by Gail Stein

Wiley Publishing, Inc.

Webster's New World® Spanish Grammar Handbook

Copyright © 2005 by Wiley, Hoboken, NJ

Published by Wiley, Hoboken, NJ

Published simultaneously in Canada

For general information on our other products and services or to obtain technical support, please contact our Customer Care Department within the U.S. at 800-762-2974, outside the U.S. at 317-572-3993, or fax 317-572-4002.

Wiley also publishes its books in a variety of electronic formats. Some content that appears in print may not be available in electronic books. For more information about Wiley products, please visit our web site at www.wiley.com.

Library of Congress Cataloging-in-Publication Data is available from the publisher upon request.

ISBN-13: 978-0-7645-7897-7
ISBN-10: 0-7645-7897-9

Manufactured in the United States of America

10 9 8 7 6 5 4 3 2 1

ACKNOWLEDGMENTS

A million thanks to Roxane Cerda, my acquisitions editor, who was so instrumental in getting this book off the ground; to Kitty Jarrett, my production editor, whose excellent editing skills and suggestions made this book possible; to Paulette Waiser, whose technical expertise and input were invaluable; and to Christina Stambaugh, Kristie Rees, Linda Quigley, and all the other people at Wiley & Sons, for their patience and expertise.

DEDICATION

This book is dedicated to my husband, Douglas, for his love, support, and patience; to my son Eric, for his technical help; to my son Michael and his fiancée, Katherine Benson-Piscopo, for their encouragement; and to my parents, Sara and Jack Bernstein, for always being there for me.

TABLE OF CONTENTS

viii / Spanish Grammar Handbook

INTRODUCTION

As our society becomes increasingly multicultural, learning a foreign language becomes more and more of a necessity for all of us. *Webster's New World Spanish Grammar Handbook* is a valuable resource for those who wish to acquire proficiency in a widely spoken language whose popularity is ever-increasing. This book is for people from all walks of life: students, tourists, and businesspeople who want to be able to effectively and confidently communicate ideas, thoughts, and feelings in Spanish.

Webster's New World Spanish Grammar Handbook is an essential, comprehensive guide that is completely user friendly and was designed to carefully and clearly present all the topics and tools necessary for a complete understanding and mastery of Spanish grammar. The book is divided as follows:

- The 15 parts present all the essential elements of Spanish grammar.
- Appendix A presents verbs charts that illustrate the conjugations of regular, stem-changing, spelling-change, and irregular verbs.
- Appendix B presents thematic vocabulary that will facilitate communication.
- The Glossary lists and defines grammatical terms.

Webster's New World Spanish Grammar Handbook is organized in a thoughtful, logical manner, proceeding from the simpler elements to the more complex structural explanations and rules of Spanish grammar. Words, phrases, and expressions that are used on a daily basis in a wide variety of situations are presented at the very beginning. These are followed, part by part, in sequential order, by the elements needed to construct coherent sentences from start to finish: nouns and pronouns; simple verb tenses and moods; progressive tenses; compound tenses and moods; commands; verb infinitives; prepositions and conjunctions; interrogatives and exclamations; negatives, indefinites, and relative pronouns; reflexive verbs; adjectives, adverbs, and comparisons; and the passive voice. All topics are explored in depth, and all explanations are followed by clear, concise examples that illustrate each and every rule. More detailed grammatical points are highlighted in sidebars throughout the text. Exceptions to rules, irregularities, and rules unique to Spanish are noted, explored, discussed at length, and exemplified. Each part of the book is broken down into small, easily manageable divisions and subdivisions that will allow you to work as slowly or as quickly as you like. You can use *Webster's New World Spanish Grammar Handbook* to develop and perfect your communicative skills at a comfortable pace, one that will permit you to use the Spanish language to its best advantage.

It is absolutely essential to make use of the appendices included in *Webster's New World Spanish Grammar Handbook*. Appendix A presents a simple-to-read, comprehensive list of verb charts that will enable you to use regular, stem-changing, spelling-change, and irregular verbs with the utmost confidence and ease. Arranged by infinitives, each chart identifies the Spanish infinitive, its English meaning(s), the gerund, the past participle, and the imperative forms. Reflexive verbs, with their accompanying reflexive pronouns, are also fully illustrated. Each verb is shown in its simple and compound tenses in both the indicative and subjunctive moods.

Appendix B presents a mini-dictionary of thematic vocabulary charts that provide you with a large selection of words you can use in conjunction with the rules of grammar so that you can form creative, personalized sentences, thoughts, and ideas. These high-frequency, everyday topics include the family, the house, animals and insects, foods, quantities, parts of the body, places in town, the classroom, subjects and activities, professions, leisure time, clothing, materials, colors, jewelry, travel and transportation, car parts, countries, the continents, and weather.

Finally, the Glossary presented at the end of the book defines all the grammatical terms you'll need to know to successfully learn the material in this book.

Webster's New World Spanish Grammar Handbook explains and illustrates all that is necessary for you to successfully master the Spanish language. The rest is up to you. If you make a commitment to learn and practice a small amount each day, if you study on a regular basis, and if you persevere without getting discouraged or distracted, you will learn Spanish in a relatively short period of time. Take the time, make the effort, and before long, you'll be proficient enough to chat in both social and business situations. You can do it all with *Webster's New World Spanish Grammar Handbook*.

PART I

EVERYDAY NECESSITIES

Numbers

We use two different types of numbers on a daily basis: cardinal and ordinal numbers. Numbers are vitally important to everyday communication because they have so many applications. It is, therefore, essential to commit both sets of numbers to memory.

Writing Numbers

Numbers are written slightly differently in the Spanish-speaking world than in the English-speaking world: Put a small hook on the top of the number 1 so that it almost looks like a 7. To differentiate between a 1 and a 7, put a line through the 7, so that it looks like this: 7.

CARDINAL NUMBERS

Cardinal numbers are used for counting—1, 2, 3, 4, and so on—and we use them throughout the day, every day of our lives, to communicate prices, dates, times, ages, and personal and professional statistics. The following table lists the Spanish cardinal numbers:

Spanish	Cardinal Numeral
cero	0
uno	1
dos	2
tres	3
cuatro	4
cinco	5
seis	6
siete	7
ocho	8
nueve	9
diez	10
once	11
doce	12
trece	13
catorce	14
quince	15
dieciséis (*diez y seis*)	16
diecisiete (*diez y siete*)	17
dieciocho (*diez y ocho*)	18
diecinueve (*diez y nueve*)	19
veinte	20
veintiuno (*veinte y uno*)	21
veintidós (*veinte y dos*)	22
veintitrés (*veinte y tres*)	23
veinticuatro (*veinte y cuatro*)	24
veinticinco (*veinte y cinco*)	25
veintiséis (*veinte y seis*)	26
veintisiete (*veinte y siete*)	27
veintiocho (*veinte y ocho*)	28

Spanish	Cardinal Numeral
veintinueve (*veinte y nueve*)	29
treinta	30
cuarenta	40
cincuenta	50
sesenta	60
setenta	70
ochenta	80
noventa	90
ciento (*cien*)	100
ciento uno	101
doscientos	200
quinientos	500
mil	1.000
dos mil	2.000
cien mil	100.000
un millón	1.000.000
dos millones	2.000.000
mil millones	1.000.000.000
dos mil millones	2.000.000.000

Punctuating Numerals

In numerals and decimals, Spanish generally uses periods where English uses commas and vice versa:

Spanish	English
5.000	5,000
0,80	.80 or 0.80
$24,95	$24.95

Spanish cardinal numbers follow these rules:

- *Uno* is used when counting. Use *Un* to express "one," "a," or "an" before a masculine noun and use *una* before a feminine noun:

uno, dos, tres . . .	one, two, three . . .
un hombre y una mujer	a man and a woman
treinta y un días	thirty-one days
veintiuna semanas	twenty-one weeks

- *Uno* may also be used in the sense of a neuter pronoun:

Es uno de mis libros favoritos.	It is one of my favorite books

- Use the conjunction *y* ("and") only for numbers between 16 and 99. *Y* is not used between a number over 100 and the number that follows:

sesenta y siete	sixty-seven
trescientos noventa y nueve	three hundred ninety-nine
quinientos cuarenta y cinco	five hundred forty-five

  But:

ciento ochenta y seis	one hundred eighty-six

- The numbers 16 through 19 and 21 through 29 are generally written as one word. Put an accent on the last syllable for the numbers 16, 22, 23, and 26:

dieciséis	16
veintidós	22
veintitrés	23
veintiséis	26

  But:

diecisiete	17
veinticuatro	24

- When used before a masculine noun, *veintiún* has an accent on the last syllable:

veintiún años	twenty-one years

  But:

veintiuna semanas	twenty-one weeks

- In compounds of *ciento* (for example, *doscientos, trescientos*), there must be agreement with feminine and masculine nouns:

quinientos kilogramos	five hundred kilograms
quinientas libras	five hundred pounds

- Before nouns and before the numbers *mil* and *millones,* the *cien* form is used in place of *ciento. Ciento* is used before all other numbers:

cien pájaros	one hundred birds
cien mil flores	one hundred thousand flowers
cien millones de estrellas	one hundred million stars
doscientos pájaros	two hundred birds
quinientos mil flores	five hundred thousand flowers
novecientos millones de estrellas	nine hundred million stars

- *Un* is used before *millón* but not before *cien(to)* or *mil.* When *millón* is followed by a noun, *de* is used between *millón* and the noun:

cien segundos	one hundred seconds
ciento cuarenta minutos	one hundred forty minutes
mil horas	one thousand hours
un millón de personas	one million people

- Common arithmetic functions require the following words:

y	plus (+)
menos	minus (–)
por	times (×)
dividido por	divided by (÷)
son	equals (=)

  Examples:

Cuatro y diez son catorce	Four plus ten equals fourteen.
Quince menos cinco son diez.	Fifteen minus five equals ten.
Veinte por tres son sesenta.	Twenty times three equals sixty.
Doce dividido por tres son cuatro.	Twelve divided by three equals four.

ORDINAL NUMBERS

Ordinal numbers are used to express numbers in a series:

Spanish	Ordinal Number
primero	first
segundo	second
tercero	third
cuarto	fourth
quinto	fifth

(continues)

(continued)

Spanish	Ordinal Number
sexto	sixth
séptimo	seventh
octavo	eighth
noveno	ninth
décimo	tenth

Spanish ordinal numbers follow these rules:

- Ordinal numbers are used only through tenth. After that, cardinal numbers are used:

el séptimo día	the seventh day
su aniversario veintiuno	her twenty-first anniversary

- Ordinal numbers are masculine or feminine according to the nouns they modify. Change the final *o* of the masculine form to an *a* to arrive at the feminine form:

su segundo apartamento	her second apartment
su segunda casa	her second house

- The final *o is* dropped from *primero* and *tercero* before a masculine singular noun:

el primer piso	the first floor
el tercer ascensor	the third elevator

  But:

el siglo tercero	the third century

- The abbreviations for ordinal numbers take this form:

Ordinal Number Masc. (Fem.)	Abbreviation	Ordinal Number	Abbreviation
primero(a)	$1^{o(a)}$	*primer*	*1er*
segundo(a)	$2^{o(a)}$		
tercero(a)	$3^{o(a)}$	*tercer*	*3er*
cuarto(a)	$4^{o(a)}$		
décimo(a)	$10^{o(a)}$		

- Cardinal numbers replacing ordinal numbers are always masculine because it is presumed that *número* precedes the number:

la semana cuarenta y uno	the forty-first week

- *Primero* is the only ordinal number used in dates. In all other cases, the cardinal number is used:

el primero de enero	January 1st
el treinta y uno de octubre	October 31st

- Cardinal numbers precede ordinal numbers:

las tres primeras respuestas	the first three answers

FRACTIONS

With the exception of one half and one third, the numerator of a fraction uses a cardinal number and the denominator uses an ordinal number, through tenths:

Spanish Fraction	Alternative Expression of Fraction	Numeric Fraction
medio(a)	*la mitad de*	$\frac{1}{2}$
un tercio	*la tercera parte de*	$\frac{1}{3}$
un cuarto	*la cuarta parte de*	$\frac{1}{4}$
dos tercios	*las dos terceras partes de*	$\frac{2}{3}$
tres cuartos	*las tres cuartas partes de*	$\frac{3}{4}$
cuatro quintos	*las cuatro quintas partes de*	$\frac{4}{5}$
un sexto	*la sexta parte de*	$\frac{1}{6}$
un séptimo	*la séptima parte de*	$\frac{1}{7}$
un octavo	*la octava parte de*	$\frac{1}{8}$
un noveno	*la novena parte de*	$\frac{1}{9}$
un décimo	*la décima parte de*	$\frac{1}{10}$

After tenths, *-avo* is added to the cardinal number to form the fraction:

Spanish Fraction	Alternative Expression of Fraction	Numeric Fraction
un doceavo	*la doceava parte de*	$\frac{1}{14}$
un quinceavo	*la quinceava parte de*	$\frac{1}{15}$
un veinteavo	*la veinteava parte de*	$\frac{1}{20}$
un treintavo	*la treintava parte de*	$\frac{1}{30}$

Fractions follow these rules:

- The adjective *medio* ("half") becomes *media* before a feminine noun. The noun *la mitad (de)* expresses "half" of something:

un medio paquete	half a package
una media taza	half a cup
la mitad del postre	half of the dessert
la mitad del sándwich	half of the sandwich

- Fractions are masculine nouns. A fraction is placed either before or after a noun, depending on where it makes logical sense and sounds best:

tres y tres cuartos libras	3¾ pounds
una onza y dos tercios	1⅔ ounces

- When a quantity is divided, the fraction may be expressed with the feminine noun *parte*, except if a unit of measure is used:

un octavo (una octava parte) *de la torta*	an eighth of the pie
un octavo de una cucharadita	an eighth of a teaspoon

MULTIPLES

Multiples, which express the number of times of an event takes place, use the cardinal number followed by the feminine singular noun *vez* (*veces* in the plural):

una vez	once
dos veces	twice
cinco veces	five times

Example:

Él había olvidado mi cumpleaños *tres veces.*	He had forgotten my birthday three times.

The multiples *solo (sola)*, *doble*, *triple*, and so on may be used as adjectives, as nouns, or as adverbs:

Reservó una habitación doble.	He reserved a double room.
Yo perdí el triple de lo que Ud. perdió.	I lost three times as much as you did.
Comimos doble.	We ate twice as much.
No había una sola persona en la calle.	Not one person was in the street.

Dates and More

Expressing dates in Spanish requires knowledge of the names of the days of the week and the months of the year and a good command of cardinal numbers.

DAYS

When a person asks "*¿Qué día es hoy?*" he or she is asking for the day of the week. The appropriate answer begins with "*Hoy es . . .*" ("Today is . . .") followed by the day:

Spanish	English
lunes	Monday
martes	Tuesday
miércoles	Wednesday
jueves	Thursday
viernes	Friday
sábado	Saturday
domingo	Sunday

Using Lowercase

The Spanish days of the week and months of the year are not capitalized unless they begin a sentence. The Spanish calendar starts with Monday. Use the masculine, singular definite article *el* + singular day of the week to express "on" a particular day:

Vamos al centro el sábado.   We're going to the city on Saturday.

Use the masculine, plural definite article *los* + plural day of the week to express "on" when speaking about the day in a general sense:

Vamos al centro los sábados.   We go to the city on Saturdays.

MONTHS

The months are easy to learn because they closely resemble the names of the months in English:

Spanish	English
enero	January
febrero	February
marzo	March
abril	April
mayo	May
junio	June
julio	July
agosto	August
septiembre or *setiembre*	September
octubre	October
noviembre	November
diciembre	December

The preposition *en* expresses "in" with the name of a month:

Hace mucho frío en diciembre.   It's very cold in December.

DATES

When someone asks "*¿Cuál es la fecha de hoy?*" or "*¿A cuántos estamos?*" he or she is asking for the date. Use the following formula to give an appropriate reply:

Es (Estamos a) day + (*el*) + cardinal number (except for *primero*) + *de* + month + *de* + year

Example:

Es (Estamos a) lunes (el) nueve de   It is Monday, May 9, 2006.
mayo de dos mil seis.

The following rules pertain to dates:

• Use *Es* or *Estamos a* ("It is") + date before the date.

- Use *primero* only for the first of the month. For all other days, use cardinal numbers:

el primero de mayo	May 1st
el veintiuno de marzo	March 21st

- Use *el* to express "on" a specific date:

Te telefoneo el seis de febrero.	I'll call you (on) February 6th.

Expressing Dates

Whereas in English dates are generally expressed in hundreds, in Spanish years are expressed in thousands and hundreds:

Spanish	English	Date
mil novecientos cuarenta y siete	nineteen hundred forty-seven	1947

Dates are written with the day before the month:

Spanish	English	Date
el 11 de julio de 2006	11/7/06	July 7, 2006

Words and Expressions Pertaining to Dates

The following words and expressions will help you effectively communicate information about the date so that you can make appointments and plans:

Spanish	English
un día	a day
una semana	a week
un mes	a month
un año	a year
de hoy en una semana	a week from today
hace	ago
pasado mañana	day after tomorrow
anteayer	day before yesterday
durante	during
la víspera	eve

(continues)

(continued)

Spanish	English
desde	from
en	in
último(a)	last (in a series)
pasado(a)	last (most recent)
próximo(a)	next
por	per
hoy	today
mañana	tomorrow
mañana por la tarde	tomorrow afternoon
mañana por la mañana	tomorrow morning
mañana por la noche	tomorrow night
de mañana en dos semanas	two weeks from tomorrow
hasta	until
ayer	yesterday

The Weather

If you haven't looked out the window and are curious about the weather conditions for the day, you might ask someone "*¿Qué tiempo hace?*" ("What's the weather?").

WEATHER CONDITIONS

If you are listening to *el pronóstico* (the forecast), you will find the following weather expressions useful in helping you decide how to plan your day and what to wear so that you are comfortable:

Spanish	English
Hace mal tiempo.	It's bad weather.
Hay nubes./ Está nublado.	It's cloudy.
Hace frío.	It's cold.
Hace fresco.	It's cool.

Spanish	English
Hay niebla (neblina).	It's foggy.
Hace calor.	It's hot.
Hay humedad.	It's humid.
Hay relámpagos.	There's lightning.
Hace buen tiempo.	It's nice weather.
Está cubierto.	It's overcast.
Hay lluvias torrenciales.	It's pouring.
Hay un aguacero.	It's pouring.
Llueve./ Está lloviendo.	It's raining.
Está lluvioso.	It's showery.
Está lloviznando.	It's drizzling.
Nieva./ Está nevando.	It's snowing.
Hace sol.	It's sunny.
Está soleado.	It's sunny.
Truena.	It's thundering.
Hace viento.	It's windy.
Hay lloviznas.	There are showers.
Hay granizo.	There's hail.

TEMPERATURE

If you would like to know the temperature, you would ask, "*¿Cuál es la temperatura?*" An appropriate response would contain a cardinal number followed by the word *grados* ("degrees"). A more formal answer would be "*Hay una temperatura de* (cardinal number) *grados.*" If the weather is frigid, you use *menos* ("minus") to indicate that the temperature has dipped below zero:

veinte grados	20°
un grado	1°
menos dos grados	–2°

How to Tell the Temperature

Most Spanish-speaking countries use the Celsius scale (degrees centigrade) to tell the temperature. To convert Fahrenheit to Celsius, subtract 32 from the Fahrenheit temperature and multiply the number that remains by 5/9. To convert Celsius to Fahrenheit, multiply the degrees Celsius by 9/5 and add 32 to that number. Zero degrees Celsius is equivalent to 32° Fahrenheit. For example, 20° Celsius is equivalent to 68° Fahrenheit, and 100° Celsius is equivalent to 212° Fahrenheit.

THE SEASONS

If you would like to inquire about a season, use the preposition *en* ("in") + the definite article before the name of the season:

el invierno	winter
la primavera	spring
el verano	summer
el otoño	autumn, fall

Example:

Viajé en la primavera.	I traveled in the spring.

South of the Border

It is essential to pay careful attention to the season and weather conditions in the varying Spanish-speaking countries because south of the Equator, the seasons are opposite from those in the United States and Spain. Sunbirds would go to Argentina in the winter and to Spain in the summer.

Time

If you want to know the time, you ask, "*¿Qué hora es?*" To express the time, you use *Es la una* to say "it's one o'clock" or *Son las* + a cardinal number to express "it is" before a plural number:

Son las once.	It's eleven o'clock.

If you hear the question "*¿A qué hora . . . ?*" the speaker wants to know at what time a certain event or activity takes place. An appropriate answer begins with *a* + the definite article + a cardinal number:

a la una	at one o'clock
a las nueve	at nine o'clock

The following table lists some times in Spanish:

Spanish	Time
la una	1:00
las dos y cinco	2:05
las tres y diez	3:10
las cuatro y cuarto	4:15
las cinco y veinte	5:20
las seis y veinticinco	6:25
las siete y media	7:30
las ocho menos veinticinco	7:35
las nueve menos veinte	8:40
las diez menos cuarto	9:45
las once menos diez	10:50
las doce menos cinco	11:55
el mediodía	noon
la medianoche	midnight

Note the following about telling time in Spanish:

- To express the time after the hour (before half past), use *y* and the number of minutes:

  Son las diez y veinte.   It's 10:20.

- After half past, use the number of the next hour + *menos* + the number of minutes to express time before the next hour:

  Es la una menos diez.   It's 12:50.

- Time before the hour may also be expressed by *Faltar* + minutes + *para* + the next hour:

  Falta un minuto para la medianoche. It's 11:59.
  Faltan cinco minutos para las cinco. It's 4:55.

- Time may also be expressed by giving the hour and the number of minutes following it:

  Son las seis y cuarenta y cinco.   It's 6:45.

- *Medio* ("half") is used as an adjective and, therefore, becomes *media* to agree with *hora* ("hour"). *Cuarto* ("quarter") is used as a noun and shows no agreement:

  Son las ocho y media.   It's 8:30.
  Son las ocho y cuarto.   It's 8:15.

- *De la madrugada* expresses a.m. in the early morning hours and *de la mañana* expresses a.m. in the later morning hours:

  Son las tres de la madrugada.   It's 3 a.m.
  Son las nueve de la mañana.   It's 9 a.m.

The 24-Hour Clock

The Spanish-speaking world commonly uses the 24-hour clock for schedules and timetables. Midnight is the equivalent of the 0 hour. Numbers are expressed in their entirety:

0 h 10	*cero horas diez*	12:10 a.m.
17 horas	*diecisiete horas*	5:00 p.m.
23 h 45	*veintitrés horas cuarenta y cinco*	11:45 p.m.
20 h 35	*veinte horas treinta y cinco*	8:35 p.m.

TIME-RELATED VOCABULARY

When you speak about time, use the following words and expressions to express yourself in a precise manner:

Spanish	English
un segundo	a second
un minuto	a minute
un cuarto de hora	a quarter of an hour
una media hora	a half hour

Spanish	English
una hora	an hour
por la madrugada, por la mañana	in the morning
por la tarde	in the afternoon
por la noche	in the evening
¿a qué hora?	at what time?
a las siete en punto	at exactly 7:00
a eso de la una	at about 1:00
en una hora	in an hour
dentro de un rato	in a while
a menudo	often
hasta las tres	until 3:00
antes de las once	before 11:00
después de las cinco	after 5:00
en punto	sharp
¿desde qué hora?	since what time?
desde las nueve	since 9:00
hace dos horas	two hours ago
por hora	per hour
temprano	early
tarde	late (in time)
de retraso	late (in arriving)
a tiempo	on time
hace (time) que	ago

PART II

MARKERS, NOUNS, POSSESSION, AND PERSONAL PRONOUNS

Markers

A *marker* is usually an article or adjective that helps identify the gender (masculine or feminine) and number (singular or plural) of the noun that follows it. The most common markers in Spanish are

- Definite articles
- Indefinite articles
- Demonstrative adjectives

DEFINITE ARTICLES

A *definite article* indicates the specific person, place, thing, or idea in question. It precedes the noun it modifies and agrees with it in number and gender. Although "the" is easily expressed in English, Spanish requires four different words so that nouns are properly marked, as shown in the following table:

Definite Articles

	Masculine	Feminine
Singular	*el* muchach*o* ("the boy")	*la* muchach*a* ("the girl")
Plural	*los* muchach*os* ("the boys")	*las* muchach*as* ("the girls")

Gender and Number

Most Spanish nouns that end in *-o* are masculine in gender, while those that end in *-a* are usually feminine:

El niño y la niña están jugando al tenis.   The boy and the girl are playing tennis.

There are, however, exceptions to this rule, as explained shortly.

Most Spanish plural nouns end in *-s* or *-es*:

Los hombres y las mujeres hablan   The men and the women speak
español.   Spanish.

Using Definite Articles

Many rules govern the use of definite articles. A definite article is used before the following:

- Nouns in a general or abstract sense:

    Me gusta el chocolate.   I like chocolate.
    La riqueza no es tan importante. Wealth isn't that important.

- The cardinal number in a date:

    Es el doce de agosto.   It's August 12th.

- A cardinal number used to express time:

    Es la una.   It's one o'clock.
    Son las tres y media.   It's 3:30.

- Expressions of time:

    El mes pasado fui a Puerto Rico.   Last month I went to Puerto Rico.
    No miro la televisión por la noche.   I don't watch television at night.

- The names of seasons, except after the preposition *en* ("in"), when its use is optional:

    Voy a España en (la) primavera.   I'm going to Spain in the spring.

- The name of a day of the week, except after the verb *ser* ("to be") when giving the day of the week:

    No voy a trabajar el viernes.   I'm not going to work on Friday.
    No voy a trabajar los viernes.   I'm not going to work on Fridays.
    Hoy es viernes.   Today is Friday.

- A weight or measure to express "a," "an," or "per":

Las frutas cuestan tres dólares la libra.	The fruits cost three dollars per pound.
Las rosas cuestan treinta dólares la docena.	The roses cost $30 a dozen.

- Names of languages, except directly after *hablar, en,* and *de*:

El español es una lengua importante.	Spanish is an important language.
Hablo español con mis amigos.	I speak Spanish with my friends.
El libro está escrito en español.	The book is written in Spanish.
Mi madre es profesora de español.	My mother is a Spanish teacher.

Current Usage

In current colloquial Spanish, the definite article is often omitted after the following verbs:

aprender	to learn
enseñar	to teach
escribir	to write
estudiar	to study
leer	to read
saber	to know

Example:

Los alumnos aprenden (el) español.	The students study Spanish.

The definite article may be used before the name of a language after the verb *hablar* when it is modified:

Hablamos bien (el) español.	We speak Spanish well.

- Geographical names of rivers, mountains, and oceans; geographical names that are modified by adjectives; the names of some countries, states, and cities; the names of continents.

Geographical Names with Definite Articles

There are no hard-and-fast rules to help determine which geographical locations should be preceded by definite articles. In fact, current, colloquial usage often permits the omission of the definite article. The names that most commonly use the definite article are

los Alpes	the Alps
los Andes	the Andes
la América Central	Central America
la América del Norte	North America
la América del Sur	South America
la Argentina	Argentina
el Atlántico	the Atlantic
el Brasil	Brazil
el Canadá	Canada
el Cairo	Cairo
la China	China
el Ebro	Ebro
el Ecuador	Ecuador
el Escorial	Escorial
los Estados Unidos	the United States
la Florida	Florida
el Guadalquivir	Guadalquivir
la Habana	Havana
el Japón	Japan
el Mediterráneo	the Mediterranean
el Orinoco	the Orinoco
el Pacífico	the Pacific
el Paraguay	Paraguay
el Perú	Peru
la República Dominicana	the Dominican Republic
el Salvador	El Salvador
el Uruguay	Uruguay

Examples:

El Amazonas es un río.	The Amazon is a river.
Nací en (los) Estados Unidos.	I was born in the United States.

- Titles, except when addressing a person directly:

La señora Nuñez no está aquí.	Mrs. Nuñez isn't here.
"Buenas tardes, Señora Nuñez."	"Good afternoon, Mrs. Nuñez."

  However, the definite article is omitted before *don (doña)* and *Santo (San, Santa)*:

No veo a Doña Luisa.	I don't see Doña Luisa.

- Parts of the body or wearing apparel when the possessor is clear:

Se lava los dientes.	She brushes her teeth.
Ponga el abrigo.	Put on your coat.

- Infinitives used as nouns (the definite article is optional when the infinitive serves as the subject of the sentence):

(El) Mentir es un pecado.	Lying is a sin.

- Last names:

Los López no están aquí.	The Lopezes aren't here.

- The names of boats and ships:

La Niña *era un barco.*	The *Niña* was a boat.

Exclamations

The definite article can be used in exclamations:

¡Qué calor hace!	How hot it is!
¡El calor que hace es insoportable!	It is unbearably hot!

Omitting Definite Articles

A definite article is omitted before the following:

- Nouns in apposition (two nouns, one next to the other, that explain each other) unless they are modified or refer to a family or business relationship:

Bolívar, libertador de Colombia, era un gran hombre.	Bolívar, the liberator of Colombia, was a great man.
Marta, la hermana de Luz, es muy bonita.	Marta, Luz's sister, is very pretty.
Juan Soto, el jefe de Paco, trabaja mucho.	Juan Soto, Paco's boss, works a lot.

- Numerals used in a ruler's title:

Carlos Quinto reinó en el siglo XVI.	Carlos V reigned during the 16th century.

Contractions

The prepositions *a* ("to") and *de* ("of," "from," or "about") contract with the definite article *el* to become *al* and *del*, respectively, except when the definite article is part of a title or name:

Voy al cine.	I'm going to the movies.
Sale del teatro.	He is leaving the theater.
Nunca fui a la República Dominicana.	I never went to the Dominican Republic.
Sin embargo, fuimos a Japón.	However, we went to Japan.

The Neuter Article, *Lo*

The neuter indefinite article, *lo*, has no plural form. It is used before the following:

- A masculine or feminine adjective used as a noun to express a quality or an abstract idea:

¿Piensas lo mismo que yo?	Do you think the same as I do?
Lo peligroso le encanta.	He loves dangerous things.

- A masculine or feminine adjective or an adverb + *que* to express "how":

¿Ves lo bella que es?	Do you see how beautiful she is?
No creo lo rápido que hable.	I don't believe how fast he speaks.

Expressing "How"

The neuter indefinite article, *lo*, when preceded by the preposition *a*, means "in the manner of" or "like":

Él comía a lo bestia.	He was eating like an animal.

INDEFINITE ARTICLES

An *indefinite article* indicates "a," "an," or "one" person, place, thing, or idea that is not specifically identified. It precedes the noun it modifies and agrees with it in number and gender. Although "a," "an," and "one" are easily expressed in English, Spanish requires four different words so that nouns are properly marked, as shown in the following table:

Indefinite Articles

	Masculine	Feminine
Singular	*un* muchacho ("a boy")	*una* muchacha ("a girl")
Plural	*unos* muchachos ("some boys")	*unas* muchachas ("some girls")

Examples:

Necesito una pluma.	I need a pen.
Unos alumnos están ausentes.	Some students are absent.

Omitting Indefinite Articles

The indefinite article is omitted in the following cases:

- Before nouns in apposition, except when they are preceded by an adjective:

Cervantes, autor español, escribió Don Quijote.	Cervantes, a Spanish author, wrote *Don Quijote.*
Cervantes, un gran autor español, escribió Don Quijote.	Cervantes, a great Spanish author, wrote *Don Quijote.*

- Before an unmodified noun (a noun with no adjective to describe it) that expresses a group or a class (occupation, nationality, religion, political, and so on). When the noun is modified, the indefinite article is used:

Su abogado es colombiano.	His lawyer is Colombian.
Su abogado es un colombiano famoso.	His lawyer is a famous Colombian.

- After certain words that usually take the indefinite article in English:

Necesito otro cuchillo.	I need another knife.
En cierta ocasión, vino temprano.	On one occasion he arrived early.
Nunca dije tal cosa.	I never said such a thing.
¡Que coche tan grande!	What a big car!
Cien muchachos cantaban.	One hundred boys were singing.
Mil personas se reían.	One thousand people were laughing.

Masculine Articles with Feminine Nouns

Masculine definite and indefinite articles are used before feminine nouns that begin with stressed *a* or *ha*:

El agua está fría.	The water is cold.
Tengo un hambre de lobo.	I am ravenously hungry.

DEMONSTRATIVE ADJECTIVES

Demonstrative adjectives agree in number and gender with the nouns they modify. They are used to express "this," "that," "these," and "those," and they mark the noun according to its distance from the speaker, as shown in the following table:

Demonstrative Adjectives

	Masculine	Feminine	English	Distance
Singular	*este*	*esta*	this	near or directly concerned with the speaker
Plural	*estos*	*estas*	these	
Singular	*ese*	*esa*	that	not particularly near to or directly concerned with the
Plural	*esos*	*esas*	those	speaker
Singular	*aquel*	*aquella*	that	far from and not directly concerned with the speaker
Plural	*aquellos*	*aquellas*	those	

Examples:

Este libro es muy interesante.	This book is very interesting.
Esos coches son deportivos.	Those cars are sporty.
Aquella ciudad es grande.	That city is big.

Note the following about demonstrative adjectives:

- They are used before each noun in a series:

Este muchacho y esa muchacha son de Cuba.	This boy and that girl are from Cuba.

- They convey a pejorative meaning when they are used after the noun they modify:

Las muchachas esas no hacen nada por nadie.	Those girls do nothing for anyone.

- They may be clarified with adverbs that reinforce the location of the noun:

Este libro aquí es interesante.	This book (here) is interesting.
Quiero leer esos periódicos ahí.	I want to read those newspapers (there, but not too far).
¿Vives en aquella casa allá?	Do you live in that house (there, rather far)?

DEMONSTRATIVE PRONOUNS

A *demonstrative pronoun* replaces a demonstrative adjective and its noun and is used to make the language flow more naturally in conversation and in writing. Demonstrative pronouns are differentiated from demonstrative adjectives by an accent (although current usage allows for no accent in cases where there is no ambiguity), as shown in the following table:

	Masculine	Feminine	Neuter	English	Distance
Singular	*éste*	*ésta*	*esto*	this (one)	near to or directly concerned with the speaker
Plural	*éstos*	*éstas*		these (ones)	
Singular	*ése*	*ésa*	*eso*	that (one)	not particularly near to or directly concerned with the speaker
Plural	*ésos*	*ésas*		those (ones)	
Singular	*aquél*	*aquélla*	*aquello*	that (one)	far from and not directly concerned with the speaker
Plural	*aquéllos*	*aquéllas*		those (ones)	

Examples:

Necesito este papel y ésos.	I need this paper and those.
Estos coches y aquél son muy caros.	These cars and that one are very expensive.

Note the following about demonstrative pronouns:

- *Éste, éstos, ésta,* and *éstas* express "the former," whereas *aquél, aquéllos, aquélla,* and *aquéllas* express "the latter":

Luz y Ana son gemelas. Ésta es rubia y aquélla es morena.	Luz and Ana are twins. The former (Luz) has brown hair, and the latter (Ana) is blond.

- The neuter pronouns *esto, eso,* and *aquello* refer to ideas or concepts rather than to nouns:

Ella está enferma. Esto me preocupa.	She is sick. That worries me.
¿Qué es eso?	What is that?
Aquello no tiene importancia.	That isn't important.

Special Demonstrative Pronouns

In relative clauses, the special demonstrative pronouns *el, los, la, las,* and *lo* are used in place of the pronouns *éste, ése, aquél,* and so on when they are followed by *de* or *que*:

Yo tomo el tren de las ocho y ella toma el de las nueve.	I take the eight o'clock train and she takes the nine o'clock.
No comprendo lo que me dijiste.	I don't understand what you said to me.

Nouns

A *noun* refers to a person, a place, a thing, an idea, or a quality. Unlike in English, every Spanish noun has a gender (masculine or feminine) and a number (singular or plural), which can usually, but not always, be determined by the noun's ending.

GENDER

Nouns are generally classified as masculine or feminine according to their endings or according to certain thematic groups to which they belong.

Masculine Nouns

Most Spanish nouns that end in *-o* are masculine (except for *la mano* ["the hand"] and *la radio* ["the radio"]) and are preceded by masculine, singular markers:

el niño	the boy
un niño	a boy
este (ese, aquel) niño	this (that) boy

Nouns that end in *-aje* are masculine, singular:

el coraje	courage
el fuselaje	fuselage
el garaje	garage
el pasaje	passage
el personaje	character
el traje	suit (clothing)

Nouns that end in *-ma* or *-eta* and are derived from Greek are masculine, singular:

el clima	the climate
el drama	the drama
el idioma	the language

el poema	the poem
el problema	the problem
el programa	the program
el sistema	the system
el telegrama	the telegram
el tema	the theme
el atleta	the athlete
el cometa	the comet
el planeta	the planet
el poeta	the poet

Nouns that belong to the following thematic groups are masculine:

- Numbers:

el cinco	five
el millón	millon

- Names of days of the week:

el lunes	Monday
el martes	Tuesday

- Names of months:

el enero	January
el febrero	February

- Compass points:

el norte	north
el este	east
el sur	south
el oeste	west

- Names of trees:

el manzano	apple tree
el peral	pear tree

- Names of rivers, lakes, mountains, straits, and seas:

el Guadalquivir	the Guadalquivir
el Caribe	the Caribbean Sea

- Names of musical notes:

el do	do
el la	la

- Compound nouns:

el abrelatas	can opener
el parabrisas	windshield

Feminine Nouns

Most Spanish nouns that end in *-a* are feminine (except for *el mapa* ["the map"] and those of Greek derivation that end in *-ma,* and *-eta,* listed earlier) and are preceded by feminine, singular markers:

la niña	the girl
una niña	a girl
esta (esa, aquella) niña	this (that) girl

Nouns that end in *-ad, -ie, -ción, -sión, -ud,* and *-umbre* are generally feminine, singular:

Feminine Endings

-ad	*-ie*	*-ción*	*-sión*	*-ud*	*-umbre*
la amistad friendship	la serie series	la sensación sensation	la tensión tension	la salud health	la legumbre vegetable
la verdad truth	la especie species	la nación nation	la comisión commission	la virtud virtue	la costumbre custom
la felicidad happiness	la planicie plain	la revolución revolution	la misión mission	la aptitud aptitude	la certidumbre certainty
la caridad charity	la superficie area	la lección lesson	la procesión possession	la juventud youth	la muchedumbre crowd

Two common nouns are always feminine, despite the gender of the person being described:

la persona	the person
la víctima	the victim

Examples:

Juan es una persona muy simpática.	Juan is a very nice person.
Julio fue la víctima.	Julio was the victim.

One common noun is always masculine, despite the gender of the person being described:

    el bebé   the baby

Example:

    Marta es un bebé.   Martha is a baby.

Special Cases

Some masculine nouns that refer to people and that end in *-or, -és,* or *-n* add *-a* to form the feminine equivalent. If the masculine noun has an accented final syllable, the accent is dropped for the feminine:

Masculine	Feminine	English
el profesor	*la profesora*	the teacher
el francés	*la francesa*	the French person
el alemán	*la alemana*	the German person

The Same Noun for Both Genders

Some nouns are identical in both their masculine and feminine forms but change marker to indicate the gender:

Masculine	Feminine	English
el artista	*la artista*	the artist
el astronauta	*la astronauta*	the astronaut
el ciclista	*la ciclista*	the cyclist
el dentista	*la dentista*	the dentist
el estudiante	*la estudiante*	the student
el joven	*la joven*	the youth
el mártir	*la mártir*	the martyr
el periodista	*la periodista*	the journalist
el telefonista	*la telefonista*	the operator
el testigo	*la testigo*	the witness
el violinista	*la violinista*	the violinist

Distinct Masculine and Feminine Forms

Some nouns have different masculine and feminine forms:

Masculine	English	Feminine	English
el actor	the actor	*la actriz*	the actress
el caballo	the horse	*la yegua*	the mare
el duque	the duke	*la duquesa*	the duchess
el emperador	the emperor	*la emperatriz*	the empress
el gallo	the chicken	*la gallina*	the hen
el héroe	the hero	*la heroína*	the heroine
el hombre	the man	*la mujer*	the woman
el marido	the husband	*la esposa*	the wife
el poeta	the poet	*la poetisa*	the poet
el príncipe	the prince	*la princesa*	the princess
el rey	the king	*la reina*	the queen
el yerno	the son-in-law	*la nuera*	the daughter-in-law

Changes in Meaning

Some nouns have a different meaning, depending on their gender:

Masculine	English	Feminine	English
el capital	the capital (money)	*la capital*	the capital (of a state or country)
el cura	the priest	*la cura*	the cure
el frente	the front	*la frente*	the forehead
el guía	the male guide	*la guía*	the female guide, the guidebook
el orden	the order (succession)	*la orden*	the order (command)
el papa	the pope	*la papa*	the potato
el policía	the police officer	*la policía*	the police force, the police woman

Examples:

> *El papa comía la papa.* The pope was eating the potato.
> *El guía leía la guía.* The guide was reading the guidebook.

The Animal Kingdom

Some nouns that refer to animals, fish, reptiles, insects, and birds use the same marker and noun for animals of both sexes:

la cigüeña	stork
el mosquito	mosquito
la jirafa	giraffe
la hiena	hyena
el cóndor	condor
el murciélago	bat
la ballena	whale
la ardilla	squirrel
la serpiente	snake
la víbora	viper
la avispa	wasp
el rinoceronte	rhinoceros
la oruga	caterpillar
el tiburón	shark

NUMBER

In Spanish, just like in English, when you want to refer to more than one noun, that noun and its markers must be made plural.

To form the plural of a noun that ends in a vowel, add -*s*:

Singular	English	Plural	English
el muchacho	the boy	*los muchachos*	the boys
la muchacha	the girl	*las muchachas*	the girls
un muchacho	a boy	*unos muchachos*	some boys
una muchacha	a girl	*unas muchachas*	some girls
este muchacho	this boy	*estos muchachos*	those boys
esa muchacha	that girl	*esas muchachas*	those girls
aquel muchacho	that boy	*aquellos muchachos*	those boys

To form the plural of a noun that ends in a consonant, an accented vowel, or *y*, add -*es*:

Singular	English	Plural	English
el papel	the paper	*los papeles*	the papers
un vendedor	a salesman	*unos vendedores*	some salesmen
este rubí	this ruby	*estos rubíes*	these rubies
esa ley	that law	*esas leyes*	those laws
aquel rey	that king	*aquellos reyes*	those kings

Exceptions to the Number Rules

The following exceptions to the rules occur in Spanish:

- For some nouns that end in an accented vowel, add -*s* to form the plural:

Singular	English	Plural	English
el café	the café	*los cafés*	the cafés
la mamá	the mother	*las mamás*	the mothers
el papá	the father	*los papás*	the fathers
el sofá	the sofa	*los sofás*	the sofas

- For nouns that end in -*z*, change -*z* to -*c* before adding the -*es* plural ending:

Singular	English	Plural	English
el pez	the fish	*los peces*	the fish
esa luz	that light	*esas luces*	those lights

- For some nouns that end in -*n* or -*s*, add or delete an accent mark to maintain the original stress and the proper pronunciation of the word:

Singular	English	Plural	English
el joven	the youth	*los jóvenes*	the youths
el examen	the test	*los exámenes*	the tests
el alemán	the German	*los alemanes*	the Germans
el limón	the lemon	*los limones*	the lemons
el inglés	the Englishman	*los ingleses*	the Englishmen

- Nouns that end in an unstressed -*s* remain invariable in the plural, whereas those that end in a stressed -*s* (generally words of one syllable) require -*es* to form the plural:

Singular	English	Plural	English
el jueves	Thursday	*los jueves*	Thursdays
la crisis	the crisis	*las crisis*	the crises
el mes	the month	*los meses*	the months

- Compound nouns are invariable (that is, they do not change) in the plural:

Singular	English	Plural	English
el rascacielos	the skyscraper	*los rascacielos*	the skyscrapers
el portamonedas	the purse	*los portamonedas*	the purses

- Some nouns are always plural:

las vacaciones	vacation
las matemáticas	mathematics
las gafas	eyeglasses

Mixed Plurals

When you are referring to two nouns of different sexes of people, the masculine plural form of the noun is used:

el hijo	the son
la hija	the daughter
los hijos	the children
el señor Cruz	Mr. Cruz
la señora Cruz	Mrs. Cruz
los señores Cruz	the Cruzes

Possession

Possession shows that a noun belongs to someone or something. In English, we show possession by adding -'s or -s' after the noun that refers to the possessor. Because apostrophes are not used in Spanish, possession is shown by using the preposition *de*, by using possessive adjectives, or by using possessive pronouns.

USING THE PREPOSITION *DE*

The preposition *de* ("of") expresses possession and relationship. Whereas in English the name of the possessor comes first and is followed by the item possessed or the relationship, in Spanish the word order is reversed, with *de* joining the noun possessed with the possessor. In a sentence that contains more than one noun, it is unnecessary to repeat *de* before each noun, although *de* + the definite article is used before each noun. Note that *de* ("of") contracts with *el* ("the") to become *del* ("of the"):

El coche de Roberto es grande.	Robert's car is big.
La madre de Ana es bonita.	Ann's mother is pretty.
Los hijos de Mario e Isabel son inteligentes.	Mario and Isabel's children are smart.
Es la casa de la abuela de Juan y del tío de Javier.	It's Juan's grandmother's and Javier's uncle's house.

To ask "whose," use *¿De quién es?* for a singular response or *¿De quiénes son?* for a plural response. The verb agrees with the item possessed:

¿De quién es esa bicicleta?	Whose bicycle is that?
Es la bicicleta de María.	It's Maria's bicycle.
¿De quién son aquellos libros?	Whose books are those?
Son los libros de Paco.	They are Paco's books.
¿De quiénes es ese barco?	Whose boat is that?
Es el barco de los Gómez.	It's the Gómezes' boat.
¿De quiénes son estos coches?	Whose cars are these?
Son los coches de los Blancos.	They are the Blancoses' cars.

Avoiding Repetition

To avoid unnecessary repetition in a sentence, the noun in possession may be replaced by its corresponding definite article, according to gender and number, and the word *de*:

Mi profesora y la de mi hermano son de España.	My teacher and my brother's (teacher) are from Spain.
Su hijo y los de Carlota estudian mucho.	Your son and Carlota's (sons) study a lot.

POSSESSIVE ADJECTIVES

A *possessive adjective* agrees in number and gender with the noun it modifies (the noun possessed) and not with the possessor. Spanish possessive adjectives have short and long forms.

Short Forms

The short form of a Spanish possessive adjective is used only before each noun that it modifies. The following are the short forms of possessive adjectives:

Short Forms of Spanish Possessive Adjectives

| Before Masculine Nouns | | Before Feminine Nouns | | |
Singular	Plural	Singular	Plural	English
mi	mis	mi	mis	my
tu	tus	tu	tus	your (informal)
su	sus	su	sus	his, her, your (formal), its
nuestro	nuestros	nuestra	nuestras	our
vuestro	vuestros	vuestra	vuestras	your (informal)
su	sus	su	sus	their, your (formal)

Examples:

Su madre y mi padre son primos.   Her mother and my father are cousins.
Nuestras amigas van al campo.   Our friends are going to the country.

As mentioned previously, with parts of the body and with clothing, when the possessor is clear, the definite article replaces the possessive adjective but retains its meaning:

Él se quitó el sombrero.   He took off his hat.

Long Forms

The long form of a Spanish possessive adjective is used only after each noun that it modifies. The following are the long forms of possessive adjectives:

Long Forms of Spanish Possessive Adjectives

| After Masculine Nouns | | After Feminine Nouns | | |
Singular	Plural	Singular	Plural	English
mío	míos	mía	mías	my
tuyo	tuyos	tuya	tuyas	your (informal)
suyo	suyos	suya	suyas	his, her, your (formal), its

(continues)

Long Forms of Spanish Possessive Adjectives *(continued)*

After Masculine Nouns		After Feminine Nouns		
Singular	Plural	Singular	Plural	English
nuestro	*nuestros*	*nuestra*	*nuestras*	our
vuestro	*vuestros*	*vuestra*	*vuestras*	your (informal)
suyo	*suyos*	*suya*	*suyas*	their, your (formal)

Examples:

Olvidé el libro mío.	I forgot my book.
Unas amigas nuestras vienen.	Some of our friends are coming.

Avoiding Ambiguity

Because *su* and *sus* and *suyo* and *suyos* have several different meanings, their intended meanings can be clarified by replacing the possessive adjective with the definite article that correctly marks the noun + *de* + the pronoun that corresponds to the desired meaning (*él, ella,* or *Ud.*):

Yo tengo su pluma.	I have his (her, your) pen.
Yo tengo la pluma de él (ella, Ud.)	I have his (her, your) pen.
La madre suya es abogada.	His (Her, Your) mother is a lawyer.
La madre de él (ella, Ud.) es abogada.	His (Her, Your) mother is a lawyer.

POSSESSIVE PRONOUNS

A *possessive pronoun* replaces a possessive adjective and its accompanying noun. Like possessive adjectives, a possessive pronoun agrees in number and gender with the noun being possessed and not with the possessor. A possessive pronoun is composed of two parts: the definite article that corresponds in number and gender with the noun being possessed and the long form of the possessive adjective, as shown in the following table:

Possessive Pronouns

Replace Masculine Nouns		Replace Feminine Nouns		
Singular	**Plural**	**Singular**	**Plural**	**English**
el mío	*los míos*	*la mía*	*las mías*	mine
el tuyo	*los tuyos*	*la tuya*	*las tuyas*	yours (informal)
el suyo	*los suyos*	*la suya*	*las suyas*	his/hers/yours (formal)
el nuestro	*los nuestros*	*la nuestra*	*las nuestras*	ours
el vuestro	*los vuestros*	*la vuestra*	*las vuestras*	yours (informal)
el suyo	*los suyos*	*la suya*	*las suyas*	theirs/yours (formal)

Examples:

Tu madre es profesora y la mía es doctora.
Your mother is a teacher, and mine is a doctor.

Tu perro es pequeño. Los nuestros son grandes.
Your dog is small. Ours are big.

The definite article is generally omitted after the verb *ser*:

Este paraguas es tuyo.
This umbrella is yours.

Being Clear

For purposes of clarification, after the noun, *el suyo (la suya, los suyos, las suyos)* can be replaced by the corresponding definite article + the preposition *de*, + *Ud.* (*Uds., él, ella, ellas*):

Olvidé mi libro y el suyo.
I forgot my book and yours (his, hers)

Olvidé mi libro y el de Ud. (él, ella).
I forgot my book and yours (his, hers)

Personal Pronouns

Personal pronouns include subject pronouns, prepositional pronouns, and direct and indirect object pronouns. [*Reflexive pronouns, which serve as either direct or indirect object pronouns, are discussed in Part XIII.*]

SUBJECT PRONOUNS

A *subject pronoun* replaces a noun that performs the action of the verb. Spanish subject pronouns are not as widely used as their English counterparts (except for *Ud.* and *Uds.*) because Spanish verb endings indicate the subject. You use Spanish subject pronouns when you want to be polite, to emphasize the subject, or to be clear as to whom the subject is. Like English subject pronouns, a Spanish subject pronoun has a person and a number, as shown in the following table:

	Singular		**Plural**	
	Spanish	**English**	**Spanish**	**English**
1st Person	*yo*	I	*nosotros (nosotras)*	we
2nd Person	*tú*	you	*vosotros (vosotras)*	you
3rd Person	*usted (Ud.)*	you	*ustedes (Uds.)*	you
	él	he	*ellos*	they
	ella	she	*ellas*	they

Examples:

Ella no prestaba atención mientras Ud. hablaba.	She wasn't paying attention while you were speaking.
No diga nada. Ella tiene que explicar el problema.	Don't say anything. She has to explain the problem.
¡Pase Ud.!	Come in!

Spanish subject pronouns are not capitalized (except for the *Ud.* and *Uds.* abbreviations) unless they begin a sentence.

It is important to know the following about Spanish subject pronouns:

- *tú* **and** *Ud.*: *Tú* addresses one friend, relative, child, or pet and is the informal singular form of "you." *Ud.* shows respect to an older person, to a stranger, or to someone you do not know well. *Ud.* is the formal singular form of "you":

¿Dónde trabajas tú?	Where do you work?
¿Dónde trabaja Ud.?	Where do you live?

- *vosotros (vosotras)* **and** *Uds.*: *Vosotros* and *vosotras* are used primarily in Spain (and only rarely in Latin America) to address more than one friend, relative, child, or pet and are the informal plural forms of "you." *Vosotros* is used when speaking to a group of males or to a combined group of males and females. *Vosotras* is used only when speaking to a group of females. *Uds.* is used throughout the Spanish-speaking world to show respect to more than one older person or when speaking to strangers or people you do not know well.

Uds. is the formal plural form of "you" and replaces *vosotros (vosotras)* in Latin America. Note, however, that the *vosotros* form is widely used in Argentina:

¿Dónde trabajáis vosotros?	Where do you work?
¿Dónde trabajan Uds.?	Where do you work?

- *Él and ella:* *Él* ("he," "it") and *ella* ("she," "it") may refer to a person or to a thing:

El niño entra.	The boy enters.
El frío entra.	The cold enters.
Él entra.	He (It) enters.
La niña es grande.	The girl is big.
La falda es grande.	The skirt is big.
Ella es grande.	She (It) is big.

- *Ellos and ellas:* *Ellos* refers to more than one male or to a combined group of males and females, regardless of the number of each sex present. *Ellas* refers only to a group of females:

Juan y Luís hablan. Ellos hablan.	Juan and Luís speak. They speak.
Ana y Luz hablan. Ellas hablan.	Ann and Luz speak. They speak.
Juan y Luz hablan. Ellos hablan.	Juan and Luz speak. They speak.

- *Nosotros and nosotras:* *Nosotros* refers to more than one male or a combined group of males and females, regardless of the number of each sex present. *Nosotras* refers only to a group of females:

Nosotros (Nosotras) estudiamos.	We study.

It

The English pronoun *it* is not expressed in Spanish; however, it can be inferred from the sentence:

¿Qué es? Es un reloj.	What is it? It's a watch.
¿De dónde estâ? Es de España.	Where is it from? It's from Spain.

PREPOSITIONAL PRONOUNS

A *prepositional pronoun* follows a preposition as its object. [*A list of common prepositions can be found in the section* Common Prepositions *in Part X.*] The following pronouns are used after prepositions:

Prepositional Pronouns

Subject	Prepositional Pronoun	English
yo	*mí*	I, me
tú	*ti*	you (informal)
él	*él (sí)*	he, him, (himself)
ella	*ella (sí)*	she, her, (herself)
Ud.	*Ud.(sí)*	you, (yourself) (formal)
nosotros	*nosotros*	we, us
vosotros	*vosotros*	you (informal)
ellos	*ellos*	they, them
ellas	*ellas*	they, them
Uds	*Uds*	you (formal, plural)

Examples:

¿Vives cerca de mí?	Do you live near me?
Este regalo es para ti.	This gift is for you.

The prepositional pronouns *mí* and *ti* and the reflexive prepositional pronoun *sí* combine with the preposition *con,* respectively, to form *conmigo* ("with me"), *contigo* ("with you"), and *consigo* ("with him [her, you]"):

¿Vas a la fiesta conmigo?	Are you going to the party with me?
Por supuesto voy contigo.	Of course, I'm going with you.
Siempre lleva una tarjeta de crédito consigo.	He always takes a credit card with him.

The prepositional pronoun phrase *para sí* is used reflexively in the singular and in the plural to express "himself," "herself," "yourself," "themselves," and "yourselves":

Hacen todo para sí.	They do everything for themselves.

The neuter pronoun, *ello,* refers to a general idea:

Sueño en ello.	I dream about it.

OBJECT PRONOUNS

Object pronouns are replacement words that are used to avoid unnecessary, continuous repetition of the direct or indirect object noun. They allow for a more colloquial, free-flowing, conversational tone when speaking or writing. When using these pronouns, make sure that the conjugated verb agrees with the subject, and not with the object.

Direct Object Pronouns

A *direct object* is a noun or pronoun that tells what or whom the subject is acting on; it may refer to people, places, things, or ideas. Direct objects ordinarily receive or are in some way affected by the action of the verb. Direct object nouns may be replaced by the pronouns shown in the following table:

Direct Object Pronouns

Singular Pronoun	English	Plural Pronoun	English
me	me	*nos*	us
te	you (informal)	*os* (preferred in Spain)	you (familiar)
le (preferred in Spain for "him," "you")	him, you (formal)	*los*	them, you
lo (preferred in Latin America for "him," "you")	him, you (formal), it	*los*	them, you
la	her, it, you (formal)	*las*	them, you

Examples:

Nosotros preparamos la cena.	We prepare the dinner.
Nosotros la preparamos.	We prepare it.
Yo no veo a Roberto.	I don't see Robert.
Yo no le veo.	I don't see him. (in Spain)
Yo no lo veo.	I don't see him. (in Latin America)

Verbs That Require Direct Objects

The following verbs require direct objects in Spanish, even though they require indirect objects in English:

buscar	to look for
escuchar	to listen to
esperar	to wait for, to hope for
llamar	to call
pagar	to pay for (something)
mirar	to look at, to watch

Examples:

Yo lo llama frecuentemente.	I call him frequently.
¿Las faldas? ¿Cuánto las pagaste?	The skirts? How much did you pay for them?

The Personal *A*

The personal *a* has no English equivalent and is used only before a direct object noun to indicate that the direct object noun refers to a person (or persons), a pet, an indefinite person, or an unmodified geographic name (although this usage is becoming obsolete). The personal *a* is not used with the verb *tener* (to have):

¿Invitaste a Jorge y a su hermana?	Did you invite George and his sister?
Adora a su perro.	She adores her dog.
¿Hablas a alguien?	Are you speaking to someone?
Quiero ver a Madrid.	I want to see Madrid.
Tengo un hermano.	I have a brother.

Indirect Object Pronouns

An *indirect object* is a noun or pronoun that tells "to whom" or "for whom" the subject is doing something; it refers only to people or pets. Indirect object nouns or pronouns are indirectly affected by the action of the verb. In English, indirect object nouns may be replaced by indirect object pronouns. In Spanish, however, the indirect object pronoun is used even when the noun is mentioned. The preposition *a (al, a los, a las)* is usually an indicator that an indirect object is called for. It is important to distinguish between the prepositional *a* (meaning "to" or "for") and the personal *a* (which has no meaning in English). Generally, you use *a él, a ella*, and *a Ud.* immediately after the verb to clarify to whom you are referring. In certain cases, to maintain a complete thought, these tags may come at the end of the thought.

Note that *me, te, nos,* and *os* serve as both direct and indirect object pronouns. Spanish indirect object pronouns are shown in the following table:

Indirect Object Pronouns

Singular Pronoun	English	Plural Pronoun	English
me	to me	*nos*	to us
te	to you (informal)	*os*	to you (informal)
le	to him, to her, to you, to it	*les*	to them, to you

Examples:

Leo el libro a mis hijas.	I read the book to my daughters.
Les leo el libro.	I read the book to them.
Le escribo.	I write to him (her, you).
Le escribo una carta a él (a ella, a Ud.).	I write a letter to him (her, you).
Él nos compra regalos a nosotros.	He buys gifts for us.

Verbs That Require Indirect Objects

The following verbs require indirect objects in Spanish (because "to" or "for" is implied), regardless of the object used in English:

aconsejar	to advise
contar	to relate, to tell
contestar	to answer
dar	to give
decir	to say, to tell
devolver	to return
enviar	to send
escribir	to write
explicar	to explain
mandar	to send
ofrecer	to offer
pagar	to pay ([to] someone)
pedir	to ask
*perdonar**	to forgive
preguntar	to ask
prestar	to lend
prohibir	to forbid
prometer	to promise
*recordar**	to remind
regalar	to give a gift
telefonear	to phone

*These verbs take an indirect object only when a direct object is also present in the sentence.

Examples:

Digo la verdad a mis amigos.	I tell my friends the truth.
Les digo la verdad.	I tell them the truth.
La recuerdo.	I remember her.
Le recuerdo mi número de teléfono.	I remind her of my phone number.

Gustar and Similar Verbs

Gustar ("to please," "to be pleasing to") and a few other Spanish verbs use indirect objects to express the subjects of their English counterparts. The following table lists the most common of those verbs:

Verb	English
aburrir	to bore
agradar	to please, to be pleased with
bastar	to be enough
caer bien	to like
convenir	to be suitable, to be convenient
disgustar	to upset, to displease
doler	to be painful
encantar	to adore
entusiasmar	to enthuse, to love
faltar	to lack, to need
fascinar	to fascinate
fastidiar	to annoy, to bother
hacer daño	to harm
importar	to be important
interesar	to interest
molestar	to bother
parecer	to seem
quedar	to remain to someone, to have left
resultar	to result
sentar bien	to appreciate
sentar mal	to upset
sobrar	to be left over
sorprender	to surprise
tocar	to be one's turn

To use these verbs, follow these rules:

- The Spanish indirect object is the subject of the English sentence:

Me gustan los perros.	I like dogs.
Le interesan los coches.	Cars interest him.

- The third person singular of the verb is used with one or more infinitives:

No nos aburre jugar al tenis.	Playing tennis doesn't bore us.
Me encanta cocinar y leer.	I adore cooking and reading.

- The indirect object pronoun may be preceded by the preposition *a* + the indirect object noun or the prepositional pronoun that corresponds to the indirect object pronoun for stress or clarification:

A Elena le toca poner la mesa.	It's Elena's turn to set the table.
A mí me faltan cien dólares.	I need one hundred dollars.
Les place trabajar con Ud.	They are pleased to work with you.

The Neuter Pronoun, *Lo*

The neuter pronoun, *lo*, refers to an idea or a concept and can substitute for an adjective, an adjectival phrase, a prepositional phrase, or a subordinate clause:

Ella es inteligente, ¿no? Sí, lo es.	She's intelligent, right? Yes, she is.
¿Sabes a qué hora van a llegar?	Do you know what time they are
No lo sé.	going to arrive? No, I don't.

Positioning of Object Pronouns

Direct and indirect object pronouns are normally placed before the verb:

Yo lo quiero.	I want it.
Él no me habló.	He didn't speak to me.

In a construction that uses a gerund or an infinitive, the direct or indirect object may precede the verb that is conjugated, or it may follow and be attached to the infinitive or the gerund. When the pronoun is attached to the gerund, you add an accent to the stressed vowel by counting back three vowels from the end of the word:

Lo quiero escuchar. or *Quiero escucharlo.*	I want to listen to it.
Les estoy escribiendo. or	I'm writing to them.
Estoy escribiéndoles.	

An object pronoun is placed after an affirmative command and attached to it. In a negative command, however, an object pronoun precedes the verb. In an affirmative command, when the pronoun is attached to the imperative form, you generally add an accent to the stressed vowel by counting back three vowels from the end of the word:

Léala.	Read it.
No la lea.	Don't read it.

Double Object Pronouns

A sentence may contain both a direct object pronoun and an indirect object pronoun. When this occurs, the indirect object pronoun (which refers to a person or pet) precedes the direct object pronoun (which generally refers to a thing):

Él me la dió.	He gave it to me.
Yo te lo diré.	I will tell it to you.

When there are two third person object pronouns in a sentence, the indirect object pronouns *le* and *les* change to *se* before the direct object pronouns *lo, la, los,* and *las.* To avoid ambiguity, the phrases *a Ud. (Uds.), a él (ellos),* and *a ella (ellas)* may be used to clarify the meaning of *se*:

Yo se los ofrece a él (ella, Ud.).	I offer them to him (her, you).
Ella se la explica a ellos (ellas, Uds.).	She explains it to them (you).

The rules for the positioning of single object pronouns (with respect to infinitives, gerunds, commands, and the like) apply for double object pronouns as well. When two pronouns are added to the end of an infinitive, you generally count back three vowels and add an accent. When two pronouns are added to a gerund or an affirmative command, you generally, but not always, count back four vowels and add an accent:

¿Me lo va a enviar? or	Are you going to send it to me?
¿Va Ud. a enviármelo?	
Él nos la está contando.	He is telling it to us.
or *Él está contándonosla.*	

But:

No se lo traiga. or *Tráigaselo.*	(Don't) Bring it to him (her, you).

PART III

SIMPLE TENSES

The Present Tense

The word *tense* derives from the Latin word meaning "time" and refers to changes in the form of a verb to indicate when the action takes place. The *present tense*, as shall be pointed out later, not only refers to present time events but to customary actions and to happenings that will take place in the future.

THE PRESENT TENSE OF REGULAR VERBS

The present tense of regular Spanish verbs expresses what the subject does now. There are three main families of regular verbs: those whose infinitives end in *-ar, -er,* and *-ir*. All regular verbs that fall within a specific family follow the same rules of conjugation.

Conjugation

Conjugation refers to the act of dropping the infinitive ending and adding an ending that appropriately indicates tense (past, present, or future), voice (active or passive), or mood (indicative, conditional, subjunctive, imperative, or infinitive) and number (singular or plural) and person (first, second, or third).

To conjugate regular verbs in the present tense in Spanish, drop the infinitive ending and add the endings shown in bold in the following table:

Regular Verb Conjugations

Subject	-*ar* Verbs *hablar* ("to speak")	-*er* Verbs *comer* ("to eat")	-*ir* Verbs *vivir* ("to live")
yo	habl**o**	com**o**	viv**o**
tú	habl**as**	com**es**	viv**es**
él, ella, Ud.	habl**a**	com**e**	viv**e**
nosotros	habl**amos**	com**emos**	viv**imos**
vosotros	habl**áis**	com**éis**	viv**ís**
ellos, ellas, Uds.	habl**an**	com**en**	viv**en**

Examples:

Ellos hablan rápidamente.	They speak quickly.
No como frutas.	I don't eat fruit.
¿Vives en Acapulco.	Do you live in Acapulco?

THE PRESENT TENSE OF REFLEXIVE VERBS

An -*se* attached to the infinitive of a verb indicates that the verb is reflexive—in other words, the subject is performing the action upon itself (for example, *lavarse* ["to wash oneself"]). The difference between a regular verb and a regular reflexive verb is that a reflexive verb is conjugated in all tenses with a reflexive pronoun that serves as its direct or indirect object. Each subject pronoun has its own distinct reflexive pronoun, as shown in the following table:

Conjugating Reflexive Verbs

Reflexive Infinitive	Meaning	Subject	Reflexive Pronoun	Conjugated Verb
*bañar**se***	to bathe oneself	*yo*	*me*	*baño*
*lavar**se***	to wash oneself	*tú*	*te*	*lavas*
*levantar**se***	to get up	*él (ella, Ud.)*	*se*	*levanta*
*llamar**se***	to be named	*nosotros*	*nos*	*llamamos*
*maquillar**se***	to apply makeup	*vosotros*	*os*	*maquilláis*
*peinar**se***	to comb one's hair	*ellos (ellas, Uds.)*	*se*	*peinan*

Examples:

Ella se baña por la mañana.	She bathes in the morning.
Mis hijos se levantan tarde.	My children get up late.

In a construction that uses a gerund or an infinitive, the reflexive pronoun may precede the verb that is conjugated, or it may follow and be attached to the infinitive or the gerund. When the reflexive pronoun is attached to the gerund, you add an accent to the stressed vowel by counting back three vowels from the end of the word:

Me voy a preparar. or *Voy a prepararme.*	I'm going to prepare myself.
Se está duchando. or *Está duchándose.*	I'm writing to them.

A reflexive pronoun is placed after an affirmative command and attached to it. With a negative command, however, the object pronoun precedes the verb. With an affirmative command, when the pronoun is attached to the imperative form, you add an accent to the stressed vowel by counting back three vowels from the end of the word:

Cepíllese los dientes.	Brush your teeth.
No se enoje.	Don't get angry.

Verbs That Go Either Way

Some verbs may be reflexive or non-reflexive, depending on whom the subject is acting upon:

Nosotros nos despertamos.	We wake (ourselves) up. (reflexive)
Nosotros despertamos a los niños.	We wake the children. (non-reflexive)
Ella se mira en el espejo.	She looks at herself in the mirror. (reflexive)
Ella mira la televisión.	She looks at the television. (non-reflexive)

THE PRESENT TENSE OF SPELLING-CHANGE VERBS

A spelling change is necessary in the *yo* form of the present tense of some Spanish regular verbs in order to preserve the original sound of the verb after the *-o* ending has been added. The required changes are listed in the following table:

Verbs with Spelling Changes in the Present Tense

Infinitive Ending	Change	Verb	Present Tense
vowel + *cer*	*c→zc*	*conocer* ("to know")	*yo conozco*
vowel + *cir*	*c→zc*	*conducir* ("to drive")	*yo conduzco*
consonant + *cer*	*c→z*	*ejercer* ("to exercize")	*yo ejerzo*
consonant + *cir*	*c→z*	*esparcir* ("to spread out")	*yo esparzo*
-ger	*g→j*	*escoger* ("to choose")	*yo escojo*
-gir	*g→j*	*dirigir* ("to direct")	*yo dirijo*
-guir	*gu→g*	*distinguir* ("to distinguish")	*yo distingo*

Examples:

Yo no conozco a su hermana.   I don't know your sister.
Siempre escojo bien a mis amigos.   I always choose my friends well.

Other high-frequency verbs with spelling changes include those listed in the following tables:

Vowel + *cer*/*cir*

Spanish	English
aparecer	to appear
crecer	to grow
establecer	to establish
merecer	to deserve, to merit
nacer	to be born
obedecer	to obey
obscurecer	to darken
ofrecer	to offer
parecer	to seem
producir	to produce
reconocer	to recognize
reducir	to reduce
reproducir	to reproduce
traducir	to translate

Examples:

> *Yo ofrezco un regalo a mi amiga.*　　　I give a gift to my friend.
> *Yo no lo reconozco.*　　　I don't recognize him.

Consonant + *cer/cir*

Spanish	English
convencer	to convince
fruncir	to frown
vencer	to conquer
zurcir	to mend

Examples:

> *Siempre venzo a mis enemigos.*　　　I always conquer my enemies.
> *Lo convenzo que tengo razón.*　　　I convince him that I am right.

-*ger* Verbs

Spanish	English
coger	to seize
proteger	to protect
recoger	to gather, to pick up

Examples:

> *Yo recojo el libro del suelo.*　　　I pick up the book from the floor.
> *Yo la protejo de sus enemigos.*　　　I protect her from her enemies.

-*gir* Verbs

Spanish	English
afligir	to afflict
exigir	to demand
infligir	to inflict
surgir	to appear

Examples:

Yo no exijo nada de ti.	I don't demand anything of you.
Yo me aflijo.	I get upset.

An example of a *-guir* verb is *extinguir* ("to extinguish"):

Yo extingo el fuego.	I put out the fire.

THE PRESENT TENSE OF STEM-CHANGING VERBS

Some verbs require an internal change in the stem vowel of the *yo, tú, él (ella, Ud.)*, and *ellos (ellas, Uds.)* forms of the present tense. The *nosotros* and *vosotros* forms are conjugated without the change, as shown in the following table:

Stem Changes

Ending	Change	Verb	Present
-ar	e→ie	cerrar ("to close")	*yo cierro* *nosotros cerramos*
-ar	o→ue	recordar ("to remember")	*yo recuerdo* *nosotros recordamos*
-ar	u→ue	jugar ("to play")	*yo juego* *nosotros jugamos*
-er	e→ie	querer ("to wish," "to want")	*yo quiero* *nosotros queremos*
-er	o→ue	poder ("to be able")	*yo puedo* *nosotros podemos*
-ir	e→i	pedir ("to ask")	*yo pido* *nosotros pedimos*
-ir	e→ie	mentir ("to lie")	*yo miento* *nosotros mentimos*
-ir	o→ue	dormir (to sleep)	*yo duermo* *nosotros dormimos*
some -iar	i→í	enviar ("to send")	*yo envío* *nosotros enviamos*
some -uar	u→ú	continuar ("to continue")	*yo continúo* *nosotros continuamos*
-uir (not -guir)	add y after u	construir ("to construct")	*yo construyo* *nosotros construimos*

Examples:

*Nosotros cerramos las puertas, y ellos
    cierran las ventanas.*

*Ella duerme hasta las ocho, y nosotros
    dormimos hasta las nueve.*

We shut the doors, and they shut
    the windows.

She sleeps until eight o'clock, and
    we sleep until nine.

Other high-frequency verbs that require internal spelling changes include those listed
in the following tables:

-ar: *e→ie* Verbs

Spanish	English
atravesar	to go through
comenzar	to begin
despertar	to wake up
empezar	to begin
encerrar	to lock up, to enclose
enterrar	to bury
helar	to freeze
negar	to deny
nevar	to snow
pensar	to think
plegar	to fold
quebrar	to break, to smash
recomendar	to recommend
sentar	to seat
sosegar	to calm
temblar	to tremble
tentar	to touch, to try

Examples:

Yo me despierto temprano.

Ella piensa que él es guapo.

Ellos recomiendan ese restaurante.

I wake up early.

She thinks he's handsome.

They recommend that restaurant.

-*ar* : *o→ue* Verbs

Spanish	English
acordar	to agree
acostar	to put to bed
almorzar	to eat lunch
aprobar	to approve
colgar	to hang up
contar	to tell
costar	to cost
encontrar	to meet
forzar	to force
mostrar	to show
probar	to try (on)
sonar	to ring
soñar	to dream
tronar	to thunder

Examples:

Ellos se acuestan tarde.	They go (put themselves) to bed late.
Esos zapatos cuestan mucho.	Those shoes cost a lot.
Truena.	It's thundering.

An example of a -*gar* verb that is like *jugar* is *enjugar* ("to dry" or "to wipe away"):

Yo me enjugo las lágrimas.	I dry my tears. *or* I wipe away my tears.

-*er* : *e→ie* Verbs

Spanish	English
defender	to defend
descender	to descend
encender	to incite, to light
entender	to understand
perder	to lose

Examples:

¿Entiendes el problema?	Do you understand the problem?
¿Por qué pierde la paciencia?	Why is he losing patience?

-*er*: *o→ue* Verbs

Spanish	English
doler	to hurt
envolver	to wrap up
llover	to rain
morder	to bite
mover	to move
resolver	to resolve
revolver	to revolve
soler	to usually do something
volver	to return

Examples:

Me duelen los pies.	My feet hurt.
Ella se muerde las uñas.	She bites her nails.
Suele pasar por mi casa.	He usually comes by my house.

-*ir*: *e→ie* Verbs

Spanish	English
advertir	to warn
consentir	to allow
convertir	to convert
divertir	to amuse
herir	to wound
preferir	to prefer
referir	to refer
sentir	to feel, to regret
sugerir	to suggest

Examples:

Ella prefiere quedarse en casa.	She prefers to stay home.
Los niños se divierten mucho.	The children have a good time.
Lo siento.	I'm sorry.

An example of an *-ir* verb that has the change *o→ue* is *morir* ("to die"):

El soldado no muere.	The soldier isn't dying.

-ir: *e→i* Verbs

Spanish	English
competir	to compete
despedir	to say goodbye to
expedir	to send
gemir	to moan
medir	to measure
repetir	to repeat
servir	to serve
vestir	to clothe, to dress

Examples:

Ellos se visten elegantemente.	They dress elegantly.
¿Qué mides?	What are you measuring?
El profesor repite las reglas.	The teacher repeats the rules.

-iar Verbs Like *Enviar*

Spanish	English
confiar	to trust
criar	to rear, to raise
desviar	to divert
espiar	to spy
esquiar	to ski

Spanish	English
fiar	to trust
fotografiar	to photograph
guiar	to guide
rociar	to spray, to sprinkle
vaciar	to empty
variar	to vary

Examples:

Yo no esquío bien.   I don't ski well.
Él no se fíe de ese hombre.   He doesn't trust that man.
Ellos fotografían la ciudad.   They photograph the city.

-*uar* Verbs Like *Continuar*

Spanish	English
acentuar	to accentuate
actuar	to act
efectuar	to carry out
evaluar	to evaluate
habituar	to accustom someone to
perpetuar	to perpetuate
situar	to situate
valuar	to value

Examples:

Ellos no actúan.   They don't act.
Yo evalúo los datos.   I evaluate the data.
Ella se habitúa a la vida campestre.   She becomes accustomed to country life.

-uir Verbs Like *Construir*

Spanish	English
concluir	to conclude
contribuir	to contribute
destruir	to destroy
disminuir	to diminish
distribuir	to distribute
excluir	to exclude
huir	to flee
incluir	to include
influir	to influence
instituir	to institute
instruir	to instruct
obstruir	to obstruct
sustituir	to substitute

Examples:

¿Qué distribuyen?	What are they distributing?
Él huye a los Estados Unidos.	He is fleeing to the United States.
Ud. no influye en mi decisión.	You don't influence my decision.

Verbs with Spelling and Stem Changes

The following verbs have both spelling and stem changes in their present tense forms and must be conjugated accordingly:

Verb	English	Conjugation
colegir	to collect	***colijo, coliges, colige,*** *colegimos, colegís,* ***coligen***
corregir	to correct	***corrijo, corriges, corrige,*** *corregimos, corregís,* ***corrigen***
elegir	to elect	***elijo, eliges, elige,*** *elegimos, elegís,* ***eligen***
conseguir	to get	***consigo, consigues, consigue,*** *conseguimos, conseguís,* ***consiguen***
seguir	to follow	***sigo, sigues, sigue,*** *seguimos, seguís,* ***siguen***

THE PRESENT TENSE OF IRREGULAR VERBS

Irregular verbs follow no specific rules of conjugation. In Spanish, some verbs are irregular only in the first person singular (*yo*) form of the present tense:

Verb	English	*yo* Form of Present Tense
caber	to fit	*quepo*
caer	to fall	*caigo*
dar	to give	*doy*
hacer	to make, to do	*hago*
poner	to put	*pongo*
saber	to know a fact, to know how to	*sé*
salir	to go out	*salgo*
traer	to bring	*traigo*
valer	to be worth	*valgo*
ver	to see	*veo*

Examples:

Doy un paseo por el parque.	I go for a walk in the park.
No veo nada.	I don't see anything.

Some verbs are irregular in the *yo, tú, él (ella, Ud.),* and *ellos (ellas, Uds.)* forms but not in the *nosotros* or *vosotros* forms:

Verb	English	Conjugation
decir	to tell	*digo, dices, dice*, decimos, decís, *dicen*
estar	to be	*estoy, estás, está*, estamos, estáis, *están*
oler	to smell	*huelo, hueles, huele*, olemos, oléis, *huelen*
tener	to have	*tengo, tienes, tiene*, tenemos, tenéis, *tienen*
venir	to come	*vengo, vienes, viene*, venimos, venís, *vienen*

Examples:

Siempre digo la verdad.	I always tell the truth.
¿A qué hora vienes?	At what time are you coming?

Some verbs are irregular in most or all forms:

Verb	English	Conjugation
haber (auxiliary)	to have	*he, has, ha, hemos habéis, han*
ir	to go	*voy, vas, va, vamos, vaís, van*
oír	to hear	*oigo, oyes, oye, oímos, oís, oyen*
reír	to laugh	*río, ríes, ríe, reímos, reís, rien*
ser	to be	*soy, eres, es, somos sois, son*

Examples:

Vamos a España en el verano.	We are going to Spain in the summer.
Yo soy americana.	I am American.

USING THE PRESENT TENSE

The present tense is used in the following instances:

- To express an action happening now:

Nosotros estudiamos el español.	We are studying Spanish.
No trabajo los sábados.	I don't work on Saturdays.
Ellos van al centro.	They go (are going) to the city.

- To express a habit or custom:

Siempre haces lo necesario.	You always do what is necessary.
Bailan mucho.	They dance a lot.

- To replace the future when asking for instructions:

¿Lo repito más despacio?	Shall I repeat it more slowly?
¿Lo hacemos otra vez?	Shall we do it again?

- To replace the future when expressing an action that will take place in the near future:

Te telefoneo esta noche.	I'll call you tonight.
Nos vemos pronto.	We'll see each other soon.

- To indicate an action that started in the past and is continuing in the present by using the verb *hacer*:

¿Cuántos años hace que estudias el español? Hace un año.	How long have you been studying Spanish? It's been a year.

- To express "there is," "there are," "is there?" and "are there?" with the verb *haber*:

¿Qué hay en su bolsillo?	What's in your pocket?
No hay nada.	There's nothing.

- To show obligation with *haber* + *de*:

Hemos de lavar el coche.	We have to wash the car.

- To express an impersonal obligation with *haber* + *que*:

Hay que estudiar para salir bien.	You have to study to succeed. *or* One must study to succeed.

- To show what the subject is accustomed to doing by using the verb *soler*:

Yo suelo cenar a las siete.	I'm accustomed to eating dinner at seven.

DISTINCTIONS BETWEEN VERBS

In English one single verb may have many connotations, whereas Spanish may require using different verbs to get the different meanings. The following groups of Spanish verbs have the same English meanings but different connotations:

- *conocer* and *saber*: These verbs both mean "to know." *Conocer* is used when the words "to be acquainted with" can be substituted for "to know." Use *conocer* to express being acquainted with a person, a place, a thing, or an idea:

Yo conozco al señor Rueda.	I know Mr. Rueda.
¿Conoces la España?	Do you know (Are you acquainted with) Spain?
Conocemos ese libro.	We know that book.
Ella conoce el poema.	She knows (is acquainted with) the poem.

  Saber is used when the subject knows how to do something or knows a fact:

Yo no sé su dirección.	I don't know your address.
Él sabe bien cocinar.	He knows how to cook well.
Ella sabe el poema.	He knows the poem (by heart).

- *deber* and *tener que*: *Deber* is used to express a moral obligation, whereas *tener que* is used to express what has to be done:

Los alumnos deben estudiar.	The students must study.
Yo tengo que ir a la farmacia.	I have to go to the drugstore.

- *dejar* and *salir*: Both verbs mean "to leave," but *dejar* refers to leaving an item behind, and *salir* refers to leaving a place:

Dejo mis gafas en la biblioteca.	I leave my glasses in the library.
Yo salgo con mis amigos.	I go out with my friends.

- **estar and ser:** *Estar,* which means "to be," is used to express

  - Health:

¿Cómo estás? Estoy bien.	How are you? I'm fine.

  - Location, situation, or position:

Dónde está el museo?	Where's the museum?

  - Temporary states or conditions:

Estamos cansados.	We're tired.

  - The progressive tense:

Ella está leyendo.	She is reading.

  Ser, which also means "to be," is used to express

  - An inherent quality or characteristic:

Él es viejo.	He is old.

  - The identity of the subject:

Yo soy médico.	I'm a doctor.

  - The time, date, or place of an event:

Es la una.	It's one o'clock.
Es martes.	It's Tuesday.
¿Dónde es el baile?	Where is the dance?

  - An impersonal concept:

No es difícil hablar español.	It isn't difficult to speak Spanish.

  - The passive:

Las notas fueron copiadas por los alumnos.	The notes were copied by the students.

- **gastar and pasar:** These verbs both mean "to spend." *Gastar* refers to spending money, whereas *pasar* refers to spending time:

Ella no gasta mucho dinero.	She doesn't spend a lot of money.
Yo paso seis horas limpiando la casa.	I spend six hours cleaning the house.

- **jugar and tocar:** These verbs both mean "to play." *Jugar + a* expresses that the subject is playing a sport or a game, whereas *tocar* expresses that the subject is playing a musical instrument:

Jugamos a los naipes.	We're playing cards.
¿Juegas al golf?	Do you play golf?
Toco la guitarra.	I play the guitar.

- *llevar* and *tomar*: These verbs both mean "to take." *Llevar* expresses the idea of taking a person somewhere, of leading someone to a place, or of carrying or transporting an item, whereas *tomar* expresses picking something up in your hands and carrying it:

Llevo mi paraguas al restaurante.	I'm taking my umbrella to the restaurant.
Ella lleva a su hermano al cine.	She takes her brother to the movies.
Yo tomo su bolígrafo.	I'm taking your pen.

- *pedir* and *preguntar*: These verbs both mean "to ask." *Pedir* expresses the sense of requesting or asking *for* something, whereas *preguntar* expresses asking a question or inquiring about someone or something:

Él me pide mis consejos.	He asks me for my advice.
Ellos me preguntan si puedo ayudarlos.	They ask me if I can help them.

- *poder* and *saber*: These verbs both mean "can." *Poder* shows that the subject has the ability to perform an action, whereas *saber* shows that the subject actually knows how to perform the action:

Nosotros podemos nadar.	We can (are able to, allowed to) swim.
Nosotros sabemos nadar.	We can (know how to) swim.

- *volver* and *devolver*: These verbs both mean "to return." *Volver* expresses returning in a physical sense or coming back, whereas *devolver* indicates returning an item to its rightful owner:

Yo vuelvo a eso de las tres.	I'm coming back at about three o'clock.
Le devuelvo su coche.	I'm returning his car to him.

The Preterit

The *preterit* is a tense that expresses an action, an event, or a state of mind that occurred and was completed at a specific time in the past.

THE PRETERIT OF REGULAR VERBS

The preterit of regular verbs is formed by dropping the *-ar*, *-er*, or *-ir* infinitive endings and adding the preterit endings shown in the following table:

Subject	-*ar* Verbs *trabajar* ("to work")	-*er* Verbs *beber* ("to drink")	-*ir* Verbs *decidir* ("to decide")
yo	trabaj*é*	beb*í*	decid*í*
tú	trabaj*aste*	beb*iste*	decid*iste*
él (ella, Ud.)	trabaj*ó*	beb*ió*	decid*ió*
nosotros	trabaj*amos*	beb*imos*	decid*imos*
vosotros	trabaj*asteis*	beb*isteis*	decid*isteis*
ellos (ellas, Uds.)	trabaj*aron*	beb*ieron*	decid*ieron*

Examples:

Yo trabajé anoche.	I worked last night.
Nosotros bebimos té.	We drank tea.
Ellos decidieron ir a Puerto Rico.	They decided to go to Puerto Rico.

THE PRETERIT OF SPELLING-CHANGE VERBS

Some verbs that are regular in the present tense require spelling changes in the preterit. Some verbs that have irregularities in the present also require spelling changes in the preterit.

-CAR, -GAR, AND -ZAR VERBS

Verbs that end in -*car*, -*gar*, and -*zar* have spelling changes only in the *yo* form of the preterit, as follows:

Spelling Changes in the Preterit

Ending	Change	Verb	Preterit
-*car*	*c→qu*	*buscar* ("to look for")	*yo* bus*qué*
-*gar*	*g→gu*	*llegar* ("to arrive")	*yo* lle*gué*
-*zar*	*z→c*	*empezar* ("to begin")	*yo* empe*cé*

Examples:

Yo busqué la Avenida Sexta.	I looked for Sixth Avenue.
Yo no llegué tarde.	I didn't arrive late.
Yo empecé mi trabajo.	I began my work.

Other high-frequency verbs with spelling changes in the preterit include those listed in the following tables:

-car Verbs

Verb	English
aplicar	to apply
buscar	to look for
clarificar	to clarify
complicar	to complicate
comunicar	to communicate
confiscar	to confiscate
criticar	to criticize
educar	to educate
equivocarse	to be mistaken
explicar	to explain
identificar	to identify
indicar	to indicate
marcar	to designate, to label, to dial
notificar	to notify
platicar	to chat
practicar	to practice
sacar	to take out
significar	to mean
tocar	to touch, to play (music)
verificar	to verify

Examples:

Yo busqué a Juan.	I looked for Juan.
Yo saqué mi cartera.	I took out my wallet.
Yo toqué la guitarra.	I played the guitar.

-gar Verbs

Verb	English
apagar	to put out, to turn off
entregar	to deliver
interrogar	to interrogate
jugar	to play (a sport or game)
llegar	to arrive
pagar	to pay
rogar	to ask, to beg

Examples:

Yo apagué la luz.	I turned off the light.
Yo jugué en el parque.	I played in the park.
Yo pagué la cuenta.	I paid the bill.

-zar Verbs

Verb	English
almorzar	to eat lunch
aterrizar	to land
comenzar	to begin
cruzar	to cross
empezar	to begin
gozar	to enjoy
organizar	to organize
utilizar	to use

Examples:

Yo almorcé en casa.	I ate lunch at home.
Yo comencé la historia.	I began the story.
Yo organicé una fiesta.	I organized a party.

Verbs That Change *i* to *y*

With the exception of the verb *traer* ("to bring") and all verbs that end in *-guir*, which are regular in the preterit, verbs whose stem ends in a vowel when the infinitive *-er* or *-ir* ending is dropped change *i* to *y* in the third person singular (*él, ella, Ud.*) and third person plural (*ellos, ellas, Uds.*) forms of the preterit. For all verbs except those ending in *-uir*, the *tú, nosotros,* and *vosotros* forms replace *i* with *í* (the *yo* form ends in *í*), as shown in the following table:

i→*y* Verbs

Subject	*leer* ("to read")	*oír* ("to hear")	*construir* ("to construct")
yo	leí	oí	concluí
tú	leíste	oíste	concluiste
él, ella, Ud.	leyó	oyó	concluyó
nosotros	leímos	oímos	concluimos
vosotros	leísteis	oísteis	concluisteis
ellos, ellas, Uds.	leyeron	oyeron	concluyeron

Examples:

Todavía no leyó esa revista.	She still hasn't read that magazine.
Yo no te oí.	I didn't hear you.
¿Qué concluyeron?	What did they conclude?

Another verb like *leer* is *creer* ("to believe"):

Yo no lo creí.	I didn't believe it.

Other *-uir* verbs are listed in *The Present Tense of Stem-Changing Verbs*, earlier in this part.

THE PRETERIT OF STEM-CHANGING VERBS

Stem-changing *-ir* verbs in the present also have a stem change in the preterit. In the third person singular form (*él, ella, Ud.*) and the third person plural form (*ellos, ellas, Uds.*), *e* changes to *i* or *o* changes to *u*, as shown in the following table:

Stem-Changing -*ir* Verbs

Subject	e→*ie* in the Present e→*i* in the Preterit *mentir* ("to lie")	e→*i* in the Present e→*i* in the Preterit *pedir* ("to ask")	o→*ue* in the Present o→*u* in the Preterit *dormir* ("to sleep")
yo	mentí	pedí	dormí
tú	mentiste	pediste	dormiste
él (ella, Ud.)	mintió	pidió	durmió
nosotros	mentimos	pedimos	dormimos
vosotros	mentisteis	pedisteis	dormisteis
ellos (ellas, Uds.)	mintieron	pidieron	durmieron

Examples:

Ella mintió.	She lied.
Ellos pidieron la cuenta.	They asked for the bill.
¿Durmió Ud. al aire libre?	Did you sleep outdoors?

Reír and Sonreír

The verb *reír* ("to laugh") and its compound *sonreír* ("to smile") change *e* to *i* in the third person singular and plural forms, and they also add an accent to the *tú, nosotros,* and *vosotros* forms:

Verb	Conjugation
reír	*reí, reíste, rió, reímos, reísteis, rieron*
sonreír	*sonreí, sonreíste, sonrió, sonreímos, sonreísteis, sonrieron*

Examples:

Cuando conté la historia, ella rió.	When I told the story, she laughed.
Nosotros sonreímos.	We smiled.

THE PRETERIT OF IRREGULAR VERBS

These are the endings for most irregular verbs in the preterit:

Subject	Ending
yo	*-e*
tú	*-iste*
él, ella, Ud.	*-ió*
nosotros	*-imos*
vosotros	*-isteis*
ellos, ellas, Uds.	*-ieron*

Irregular verbs fall into the following categories:

- Those that have *i* in the preterit stem:

Verb	English	Conjugation
decir	to say	*dije, dijiste, dijo, dijimos, dijisteis, dijeron*
venir	to come	*vine, viniste, vino, vinimos, vinisteis, vinieron*
querer	to wish, to want	*quise, quisiste, quiso, quisimos, quisisteis, quisieron*
hacer	to make, to do	*hice, hiciste, hizo, hicimos, hicisteis, hicieron*
satisfacer	to satisfy	*satisfice, satisficiste, satisfizo, satisficimos, satisficisteis, satisficieron*

Examples:

Ella no dijo nada.	She didn't say anything.
¿Qué hizo Ud.?	What did you do?

- Those that have *u* in the preterit stem:

Verb	English	Conjugation
caber	to fit	*cupe, cupiste, cupo, cupimos cupisteis, cupieron*
haber (auxiliary)	to have	*hube, hubiste, hubo, hubimos, hubisteis, hubieron*
saber	to know	*supe, supiste, supo, supimos, supisteis, supieron*

Examples:

Nosotros cupimos en el coche.	We fit in the car.
Él no supo la respuesta.	He didn't know the answer.

- Those that have *uv* in the preterit stem:

Verb	English	Conjugation
andar	to walk	*and**uv**e, and**uv**iste, and**uv**o, and**uv**imos, and**uv** isteis, and**uv**ieron*
estar	to be	*est**uv**e, est**uv**iste, est**uv**o, est**uv**imos, est**uv**isteis, est**uv**ieron*

Examples:

Ellos anduvieron por el campo.	They walked in the country.
Tú no estuviste en tu oficina.	You weren't in your office.

- Those that have *j* in the preterit stem:

Verb	English	Conjugation
traer	to bring	*tra**j**e, tra**j**iste, tra**j**o, tra**j**imos, tra**j**isteis, tra**j**eron*
decir	to say, to tell	*di**j**e, di**j**iste, di**j**o, di**j**imos, di**j**isteis, di**j**eron*
conducir	to drive	*condu**j**e, condu**j**iste, condu**j**o, condu**j**imos, condu**j**isteis, condu**j**eron*

Examples:

Trajeron el correo.	They brought the mail.
¿Qué dijo Ud.?	What did you say?

All verbs that end in *-ducir* have the same change as *conducir*.

- *dar* and *ver*, which are irregular and have identical preterit endings:

Verb	English	Conjugation
dar	to give	**di, diste, dio, dimos, disteis, dieron**
ver	to see	**vi, viste, vio, vimos, visteis, vieron**

Examples:

Yo le di un regalo.	I gave him a gift.
Ellos no me vieron.	They didn't see me.

- *ser* and *ir*, which have identical preterit forms:

Verb	English	Conjugation
ser	to be	**fui, fuiste, fue, fuimos, fuisteis, fueron**
ir	to go	**fui, fuiste, fue, fuimos, fuisteis, fueron**

Examples:

No fue posible.	It wasn't possible.
¿A qué hora fue al supermercado?	At what time did you go to the supermarket?

USING THE PRETERIT

The preterit is used

- To express an action or event that began at a specific time in the past:

  | *La clase empezó a las ocho* | The class began at eight o'clock a.m. |
  | *de la mañana.* | |

- To express an action or event that was completed at a specific time in the past:

  | *Ayer jugué al tenis.* | Yesterday I played tennis. |

  - To express any other completed past action:

  | *Hice mi trabajo.* | I did my work. |

- To express a series of events that were completed within a definite time frame in the past:

  | *Fui al centro, compré un vestido,* | I went to the city, I bought a dress, |
  | *y regresé a casa.* | and I returned home. |

- To express that an action or event occurred a specific number of times:

  | *Perdí mi paraguas tres veces.* | I lost my umbrella three times. |

The Imperfect

The *imperfect* is a descriptive past tense that is used to describe scenes, settings, situations, people, or states in the past. The imperfect has no English equivalent. It expresses a continuing state or action in the past or a habitual action that was taking place or that used to happen repeatedly over an indefinite period of time.

THE IMPERFECT OF REGULAR VERBS

To form the imperfect of regular verbs, drop the -*ar*, -*er*, or -*ir* infinitive ending and add the imperfect endings shown in the following table:

The Imperfect of Regular Verbs

Subject	*-ar* Verbs *bailar* ("to dance")	*-er* Verbs *correr* ("to run")	*-ir* Verbs *permitir* ("to permit")
yo	bail**aba**	corr**ía**	permit**ía**
tú	bail**abas**	corr**ías**	permit**ías**
él, ella, Ud.	bail**aba**	corr**ía**	permit**ía**
nosotros	bail**ábamos**	corr**íamos**	permit**íamos**
vosotros	bail**abais**	corr**íais**	permit**íais**
ellos, ellas, Uds.	bail**aban**	corr**ían**	permit**ían**

Examples:

Nosotros bailábamos los domingos.	We used to dance on Sundays.
Ese niño corría mucho.	That child used to run a lot.
Su pregunta no permitía una respuesta.	His question didn't allow an answer.

THE IMPERFECT OF IRREGULAR VERBS

Only three verbs have irregular forms in the imperfect:

Verb	English	Conjugation
ir	to go	**iba, ibas, iba, íbamos, ibais, iban**
ser	to be	**era, eras, era, éramos, erais, eran**
ver	to see	**veía, veías, veía, veíamos, veíais, veían**

Examples:

Iban a la playa.	They were going to the beach.
Eran las once.	It was eleven o'clock.
No veíamos nada.	We didn't see anything.

USING THE IMPERFECT

The imperfect is a past tense that is used as follows:

- To describe actions that were ongoing or continuous in the past without regard to when they may or may not have been completed:

Jugábamos al fútbol.	We were playing tennis.

- To described actions that the subject repeated or was in the habit of doing:

Ellos iban al cine los viernes.	They used to go to the movies on Fridays.

- To describe actions that continued for an unspecified period of time:

  Yo asistía a esa universidad.   I used to attend that university.

- To describe people, places, things, conditions, states of mind, or conditions:

  Ella era muy bonita.   She was very pretty.
  Los pájaros cantaban.   The birds were singing.
  Estábamos contentos.   We were happy.

- To describe two actions that took place simultaneously:

  Yo leía mientras él dormía.   I was reading while he was sleeping.

- To describe a situation that was taking place when another action, expressed by the preterit, occurred:

  Ella estudiaba cuando el teléfono sonó.   She was studying when the phone rang.

- To describe an event or action that began and continued in the past by using the verb *hacer*:

  ¿Cuánto tiempo hacía que   How long had you been studying
  estudiabas el español? Hacía   Spanish? It had been three years.
  tres años.

THE PRETERIT AND THE IMPERFECT COMPARED

The preterit expresses a past action that occurred and was completed at a specific moment in time; it expresses what happened and was finished. The imperfect describes a past action that was taking place over an unspecified period of time; it expresses what was happening, used to happen, or would happen over time. The following table summarizes the uses of these two tenses:

The Preterit and the Imperfect Compared

Preterit	Imperfect
Expresses a past action or event that occurred at a definite time in the past, regardless of whether that time is mentioned:	Describes ongoing or continuous past actions or events, regardless of whether the action was completed:
Yo escribí una carta. I wrote a letter.	*Yo escribía una carta.* I was writing a letter.
Expresses a specific past action or event that occurred at a definite time that is mentioned:	Describes habitual or repeated past actions:
Fuimos al teatro anoche. We went to the theater last night.	*Íbamos al al teatro a menudo.* We used to go to the theater often.

(continues)

The Preterit and the Imperfect Compared *(continued)*

Preterit	Imperfect
Expresses a specific past action or event that was repeated a stated number of times:	Describes a person, place, thing, condition, or state of mind in the past:
Te telefoneé una vez. I called you once.	*El teléfono no funcionaba.* The phone wasn't working.
Expresses a series of completed past actions:	Expresses a time of day or a day of the week in the past:
Me levanté, me bañé, y me vistí. I got up, I bathed, and I got dressed.	*Era el lunes.* It was Monday. *Eran las cuatro.* It was four o'clock.
Expresses the beginning or the end of an action:	Expresses simultaneous actions in the past:
Yo empecé a hacer mis tareas a las siete. I began to do my homework at seven o'clock.	*Él reía mientras yo lloraba.* He was laughing while I was crying.

Would

When "would" expresses "used to," it is necessary to use the imperfect:

> *Cuando era joven, iba a la biblioteca los sábados.*
> When I was young, I would (used to) go to the library on Saturdays.

When "would" expresses what the subject "would do" under certain conditions, the conditional [*see Part IV*] is used:

> *Si hiciera buen tiempo, yo iría a la piscina.*
> If the weather were good, I would go to the pool.

Verbs with Different Meanings in the Preterit and Imperfect

The meaning of some verbs changes depending on whether they are used in the preterit or the imperfect:

Verb	English	Preterit	Imperfect
conocer	to know	to meet for the first time:	to know for some time:
		Los conocimos a la playa. We met them at the beach.	*Los conocían.* They knew them (for a while).
poder	to be able to	to finally be able to:	to always be able to:
		Ella pudo cocinar bien. She could finally cook well.	*Elle podía cocinar bien.* She could always cook well.

Verb	English	Preterit	Imperfect
querer	to wish, to want	to try to:	to want something for a while:
		Quisimos verlo. We wanted to see him. (tried to)	*Queríamos verlo.* We wanted to see him (for a while).
		to refuse to:	
		No quisimos verlo. We didn't want to see him. (refused to)	
saber	to know	to find out:	to know for a while:
		Yo supe el problema. I found out the problem.	*Yo sabía el problema.* I knew the problem (for a while).
tener	to have	to receive:	to carry on one's person:
		Ellos tuvieron un paquete. They had (received) a package.	*Ellos tenían un paquete.* They had a package (that they carried with them).

Words That Indicate the Preterit or the Imperfect

Certain words and expressions indicate that an action or event occurred at a specific time and then ended, whereas other words and expressions imply that an action or event was repeated in the past. The words and expressions in the following tables will help you determine whether to use the preterit or the imperfect:

Words That Indicate the Preterit

Spanish	English
anoche	last night
anteayer	day before yesterday
ayer	yesterday
ayer por (la mañana, la tarde, la noche)	last night
de repente	suddenly
el mes (año) pasado	last month (year)
el otoño(el invierno, el verano) pasado	last fall (winter, summer)
el otro día	the other day
finalmente	finally

(continues)

Words That Indicate the Preterit (continued)

Spanish	English
la primavera pasada	last spring
la semana pasada	last week
por fin	finally
primero	at first
un día	one day
una vez (dos veces)	one time (twice)

Examples:

De repente el niño se cayó.   Suddenly the child fell.
Finalmente la carta llegó.   Finally the letter arrived.

Words That Indicate the Imperfect

Spanish	English
a menudo	often
a veces	sometimes
antiguamente	formerly
cada día (semana, mes, año)	each (every) day (week, month, year)
con frequencia	frequently
de vez en cuando	from time to time
en ese momento	at that time
en general	generally
frecuentemente	frequently
generalmente	generally
habitualmente	habitually
normalmente	normally
siempre	always
todo el tiempo	all the time
todos los días (meses, años, veranos)	every day (month, year, summer)
usualmente	usually

Examples:

De vez en cuando nosotros viajábamos.　　From time to time we traveled.
Siempre quería ir a México.　　I always wanted to go to Mexico.

Either the Preterit or the Imperfect

When speaking in the past, sometimes either the preterit or the imperfect is acceptable, depending on the meaning the speaker wishes to convey:

Yo miré la televisión.　　I watched television.

Yo miraba la televisión.　　I was watching television.

The Future Tense

Future actions may be expressed in the following manner in Spanish:

- By using the present and an expression of time—for example, *más tarde* ("later"), *después* ("afterward"), *mañana* ("tomorrow"), *en un rato* ("in a while"), *dentro de poco* ("in a short time"), and *pronto* ("soon")—to indicate that the action will take place:

    Te veo más tarde.　　I'll see you later.

- By conjugating the verb *ir* ("to go") in the present [*see* The Present Tense of Irregular Verbs, *earlier in this part*] + *a* + the infinitive expressing the action, to express what the subject is going to do in the near future:

    Voy a hacer un viaje.　　I'm going to take a trip.

- By using the future tense:

    Lo ayudaré.　　I will help him.

THE FUTURE TENSE OF REGULAR VERBS

The future tense expresses what the subject will do or what action or event will occur at some future time. In Spanish, the future endings are the same for all regular and irregular verbs. There are no stem or spelling changes in this tense.

The future tense of regular verbs is formed by adding the future endings to the infinitive of the verb, as shown in the following table:

The Future of Regular Verbs

Subject	-ar Verbs tomar ("to take")	-er Verbs vender ("to sell")	-ir Verbs recibir ("to receive")
yo	tomaré	venderé	recibiré
tú	tomarás	venderás	recibirás
él, ella, Ud.	tomará	venderá	recibirá
nosotros	tomaremos	venderemos	recibiremos
vosotros	tomaréis	venderéis	recibiréis
ellos, ellas, Uds.	tomarán	venderán	recibirán

Examples:

Nosotros tomaremos el tren.　　　We will take the train.
Yo no venderé mi coche.　　　　I won't sell my car.
¿Recibirás buenas noticias?　　Will you receive good news?

THE FUTURE OF IRREGULAR VERBS

A few Spanish verbs have irregular future stems that are used in place of the infinitive. These stems end in -r or -rr. Irregular stems fall into three categories:

- Those that drop e from the infinitive ending before adding the future endings:

Infinitive	English	Future Stem Requiring Future Endings
caber	to fit	cabr-
haber (auxiliary)	to have	habr-
poder	to be able	podr-
querer	to wish, to want	querr-
saber	to know	sabr-

Examples:

¿Cabremos todos en el taxi?　　Will we all fit into the taxi?
Ellos querrán salir pronto.　　They will want to leave soon.

- Those that drop e or i from the infinitive ending and replace the dropped vowel with a d before adding the future endings:

Infinitive	English	Future Stem Requiring Future Endings
poner	to put	*pondr-*
salir	to go out	*saldr-*
tener	to have	*tendr-*
valer	to be worth	*valdr-*
venir	to come	*vendr-*

Examples:

¿Con quién saldrá Ud?	With whom will you go out?
¿Cuánto valdrá su casa?	How much will your house be worth?

- Those that are completely irregular:

Infinitive	English	Future Stem Requiring Future Endings
decir	to say	*dir-*
hacer	to make, to do	*har-*

Examples:

Él no dirá la verdad.	He won't tell the truth.
Haremos un viaje a España.	We will take a trip to Spain.

USING THE FUTURE TENSE

The future is used

- To express what will happen:

Yo saldré bien en mis exámenes.	I will do well on my exams.

- To predict a future action or event:

Hará buen tiempo mañana.	There will be nice weather tomorrow.

- To express wonder, probability, or conjecture in the present:

¿Cuántos años tendrá?	I wonder how old she is. (How old can she be?)
Serán las ocho.	It's probably eight o'clock.
¿Quién te escribió esta carta?	I wonder who wrote you this letter.
Será Ana.	It must be Ann.
Estará contento.	You must be happy.

- To express an unexpected action or result caused by something that is happening in the present:

Si Ud. trabaja muy duro, ganará mucho dinero.	If you work very hard, you will earn a lot of money.

PART IV

Simple Moods

Mood

The *mood* of a verb (also known as the *mode*) indicates the manner in which the action or state is perceived or how the speaker envisions the action or state being expressed. In Spanish there are five moods:

- The *indicative* expresses a fact or asks a question in the preterit, imperfect, present, or future tense. [*See Part III for more information about these tenses.*]
- The *conditional* expresses what the subject would do or what would happen under certain circumstances.
- The *subjunctive* expresses wishing, wanting, emotion, doubt, fear, supposition, regret, and so on.
- The *imperative* expresses a command or a suggestion. [*See Part VIII for more information about the imperative.*]
- The *infinitive* expresses the "to" form of the verb (for example, to eat, to drink, to be merry)—the form of the verb before it is conjugated into a tense. [*See Part IX for more information about infinitives.*]

Infinitives with Accents

A verb whose infinitive contains an accent drops that accent in the future tense and in the conditional mood:

reír	to laugh
oír	to hear

Examples:

Al entender eso, él no reirá.	Upon hearing that, he won't laugh.
Ellas reirían.	They would laugh.
Yo no oiré su explicación.	I won't hear his explanation.
Nosotros no sonreiríamos.	We wouldn't smile.

The Conditional

The *conditional* is generally used in Spanish in the same way it is used in English: to express actions and states that "would" occur under certain circumstances.

THE CONDITIONAL OF REGULAR VERBS

The conditional is formed by using the same stem used for all regular verbs in the future and by adding the imperfect endings used for *-er* and *-ir* regular verbs, as shown in the following table:

The Conditional of Regular Verbs

Subject	*-ar* Verbs *buscar* ("to look for")	*-er* Verbs *aprender* ("to learn")	*-ir* Verbs *asistir* ("to attend")
yo	buscaría	aprendería	asistiría
tú	buscar	aprenderías	asistirías
él, ella, Ud.	buscarías	aprendería	asistiría
nosotros	buscaríamos	aprenderíamos	asistiríamos
vosotros	buscaríais	aprenderíais	asistiríais
ellos, ellas, Uds.	buscarían	aprenderían	asistirían

Examples:

¿Buscarías una casa más grande?   Would you look for a bigger house?
No aprenderíamos el ruso.   We wouldn't learn Russian.
Yo asistiría a esa conferencia.   I would attend that conference.

THE CONDITIONAL OF IRREGULAR VERBS

Irregular verbs in the conditional are formed with the same stem used for irregular verbs in the future and add the same endings used for the conditional of regular verbs.

Spanish verbs with irregular conditional stems, which are used in place of the infinitive, are

- Those that drop *e* from the infinitive ending before adding the future endings:

Infinitive	Meaning	Conditional Stem Requiring Conditional Endings
caber	to fit	*cabr-*
haber (auxiliary)	to have	*habr-*
poder	to be able	*podr-*
querer	to wish, to want	*querr-*
saber	to know	*sabr-*

Examples:

¿Cabrían todos los invitados en la sala?	Will all the guests fit into the room?
Yo querría descansar un rato.	I would like to rest a while.

- Those that drop *e* or *i* from the infinitive ending and replace the dropped vowel with a *d* before adding the future endings:

Infinitive	Meaning	Conditional Stem Requiring Conditional Endings
poner	to put	*pondr-*
salir	to go out	*saldr-*
tener	to have	*tendr-*
valer	to be worth	*valdr-*
venir	to come	*vendr-*

Examples:

¿Valdría la pena ir al centro?	Would it be worth the effort to go to the city?
¿Tendrías ganas de viajar?	Would you want to travel? *or* Would you feel like traveling?

- Those that are completely irregular:

Infinitive	Meaning	Conditional Stem Requiring Conditional Endings
decir	to say	*dir-*
hacer	to make, to do	*har-*

Examples:

Yo no diría mentiras.	I wouldn't tell lies.
Ellos no harían el trabajo.	They wouldn't do the work.

USING THE CONDITIONAL

The conditional is used

- To express what events or actions would take place if certain hypothetical circumstances existed [see The Imperfect Subjunctive, *later in this part*]:

  Si tuviera bastante dinero, él iría   If he had enough money, he would
     a Europa.   go to Europe.

- To express an action or event that would take place in the future with respect to a past action:

  Mi amigo me dijo que nosotros   My friend told me that we would have a
     nos divertiríamos mucho al cine.   good time at the movies.

- To express wonder, probability, conjecture, or speculation that occurred in the past, regardless of whether a subordinate clause in the past tense is used or implied:

  ¿Qué tiempo haría cuando   I wonder what the weather was like
     ellos salieron?   when they went out.
  Llovería.   It must have been raining.
  Estarías triste.   You must have been sad.

- To express courtesy, kindness, or modesty:

  Me gustaría acompañarte.   I would like to go with you.
  ¿Querías tomar algo?   Would you like to drink something?

Would

Remember that when "would" means "used to (habitually did)," the imperfect is used [see The Imperfect *in Part III*]:

Iba a ese restaurante los domingos.   I would (used to) go to that restaurant
                                                         on Sundays.

When "would" means "want" or "be willing to," the preterit of *querer* is used:

Yo no quise ir al centro.   I wasn't willing (didn't want) to go
                                                         downtown.

The Present Subjunctive

The *subjunctive*, which is used far more frequently in Spanish than in English, is a mood that expresses unreal, hypothetical, theoretical, imaginary, uncorroborated, or unconfirmed conditions or situations that result from doubts, emotions, wishes, wants, needs, desires, feelings, speculations, and suppositions.

THE PRESENT SUBJUNCTIVE OF REGULAR VERBS

The present subjunctive expresses actions or events taking place in the present or the future. The present subjunctive of regular verbs is formed by dropping the *-o* from the first person singular (*yo*) form of the present tense and adding the subjunctive endings listed in the following table:

The Present Subjunctive of Regular Verbs

Subject	*-ar* Verbs *gritar* ("to shout")	*-er* Verbs *aprend* ("to learn")	*-ir* Verbs *erabir* ("to open")
present *yo* form	*grito*	*aprendo*	*abro*
yo	*grit**e***	*aprend**a***	*abr**a***
tú	*grit**es***	*aprend**as***	*abr**as***
él, ella, Ud.	*grit**e***	*aprend**a***	*abr**a***
nosotros	*grit**emos***	*aprend**amos***	*abr**amos***
vosotros	*grit**éis***	*aprend**áis***	*abr**áis***
ellos, ellas, Uds.	*grit**en***	*aprend**an***	*abr**an***

Examples:

Es importante que los niños no griten.	It is important that the children not shout.
El profesor quiere que los alumnos aprendan mucho.	The teacher wants the students to learn a lot.
Prefiero que Ud. abra las ventanas.	I prefer that you open the windows.

THE PRESENT SUBJUNCTIVE OF SPELLING-CHANGE VERBS

In the present subjunctive, *-car*, *-gar*, and *-zar* verbs have the same change that occurs in the first person singular (*yo*) form of the preterit:

- *-car* verbs change *c* to *qu*:

Infinitive	English	Preterit *yo*	Subjunctive Stem
buscar	to look for	*busqué*	*busqu-*

  Example:

  Es importante que yo busque mi libro.   It is important for me to look for my book.

- *-gar* verbs change *g* to *gu*:

Infinitive	English	Preterit *yo*	Subjunctive Stem
pagar	to pay	*pagué*	*pagu-*

  Example:

  Es increíble que él no pague la cuenta.   It's incredible that he doesn't pay the bill.

- *-zar* verbs change *z* to *c*:

Infinitive	English	Preterit *yo*	Subjunctive Stem
gozar	to enjoy	*gocé*	*goc-*

  Example:

  Es justo que gocemos de la vida.   It is right that we enjoy life.

In the present subjunctive, consonant + *-cer/-cir*, vowel + *-cer/-cir*, *-ger/-gir*, and *-guir* verbs have the same change that occurs in the first person singular (*yo*) form of the present tense:

- Consonant + *-cer/-cir* verbs change *c* to *z*:

Infinitive	English	Preterit *yo*	Subjunctive Stem
convencer	to convince	*convenzo*	*convenz-*

  Example:

  No es posible que tú me convenzas de lo contrario.   It isn't possible that you will convince me otherwise.

Infinitive	English	Preterit *yo*	Subjunctive Stem
fruncir	to frown	*frunzo*	*frunz-*

Example:

No quiero que Ud. frunza el ceño.   I don't want you to frown.

- Vowel + *-cer/-cir* verbs change *c* to *zc*:

Infinitive	English	Preterit *yo*	Subjunctive Stem
conocer	to know	cono**zc**o	*cono**zc**-*

Example:

Dudamos que él conozca a tu hermana.   We doubt that he knows your sister.

Infinitive	English	Preterit *yo*	Subjunctive Stem
traducir	to translate	*tradu**zc**o*	*tradu**zc**-*

Example:

El profesor exige que los alumnos   The teacher demands that the
traduzcan las frases.   students translate the sentences.

- *-ger/-gir* verbs change *g* to *j*:

Infinitive	English	Preterit *yo*	Subjunctive Stem
escoger	to choose	*esco**j**o*	*esco**j**-*

Example:

Es necesario que nosotros   It is necessary that we choose
escojamos bien.   well.

Infinitive	English	Preterit *yo*	Subjunctive Stem
dirigir	to direct	*diri**j**o*	*diri**j**-*

Example:

Es bueno que ellos dirijan sus pasos   It is good that they are making
hacia el banco.   their way toward the bank.

- *-guir* verbs change *-gu* to *g*:

Infinitive	English	Preterit *yo*	Subjunctive Stem
distinguir	to distinguish	*distin**g**o*	*distin**g**-*

Example:

Es importante que Uds. distingan   It is important that you distin-
entre lo bueno y lo malo.   guish between good and evil.

THE PRESENT SUBJUNCTIVE OF VERBS WITH STEM CHANGES

In the present subjunctive, stem changes occur as shown in the following table:

Stem Changes in the Present Subjunctive

Infinitive Ending [*see Part III*]	Stem Change in Present	*Verb*	*yo, tú, él, ellos* Subjunctive Stem	*nosotros/ vosotros* Subjunctive Stem
-ar	e→ie	cerrar ("to close")	cierr-	cerr-
-ar	o→ue	mostrar ("to show")	muestr-	mostr-
-er	e→ie	querer ("to wish," "to want")	quier-	quer-
-er	o→ue	poder ("to be able")	pued-	pod-
-ir	e→ie	mentir ("to lie")	mient-	mint-
-ir	o→ue	dormir (to sleep)	duerm-	durm-
-ir	e→i	servir ("to serve")	sirv-	sirv-

Examples:

No quiero que Ud. cierra la puerta.	I don't want you to shut the door.
No es necesario que me muestres tu diseño.	It isn't necessary to show me your design.
Dudo que ella quiera viajar.	I doubt she wants to travel.
Busco a una persona que pueda ayudarme.	I'm looking for a person who can help me.
Es importante que nosotros no mintamos.	It's important that we don't lie.
Es mejor que tú duermas hasta las nueve.	It is better that you sleep until nine o'clock.
Es posible que no sirvan la cena.	It's possible that they aren't serving dinner.

The Present Subjunctive of *-iar*, *-uar*, and *-uir* Verbs

Verbs that end in *-iar* [*see* The Present Tense of Stem-Changing Verbs *in Part III*] have accent marks in all present subjunctive forms except *nosotros*:

Verb	English	Conjugation
enviar	to send	*envíe, envíes, envíe, enviemos, enviéis, envíen*

Verbs that end in *-uar* [*see* The Present Tense of Stem-Changing Verbs *in Part III*] have accent marks in all present subjunctive forms except *nosotros*:

Verb	English	Conjugation
continuar	to continue	*continúe, continúes, continúe, continuemos, continuéis, continúen*

Verbs that end in *-uir* (but not *-guir* [*see* The Present Tense of Stem-Changing Verbs *in Part III*]) add a *y* after the *u* in all present subjunctive forms:

Verb	English	Conjugation
concluir	to conclude	*concluya, concluyas, concluya, concluyamos, oncluyáis, concluyan*

THE PRESENT SUBJUNCTIVE OF IRREGULAR VERBS

Verbs that are irregular in the first person singular (*yo*) form of the present tense form the present subjunctive by dropping the *o* from that irregular *yo* form and adding the appropriate subjunctive endings, as shown in the following table:

Verbs Whose Subjunctive Stem Derives from Present Tense *Yo* Form

Verb	English	*Yo* Form	Subjunctive Forms
caber	to fit	*quepo*	*quepa, quepas, quepa, quepamos, quepáis, quepan*
caer	to fall	*caigo*	*caiga, caigas, caiga, caigamos, caigáis, caigan*
decir	to say, to tell	*digo*	*diga, digas, diga, digamos, digáis, digan*
hacer	to make, to do	*hago*	*haga, hagas, haga, hagamos, hagáis, hagan*
oír	to hear	*oigo*	*oiga, oigas, oiga, oigamos, oigáis, oigan*
poner	to put	*pongo*	*ponga, pongas, ponga, pongamos, pongáis, pongan*
salir	to go out	*salgo*	*salga, salgas, salga, salgamos, salgáis, salgan*
tener	to have	*tengo*	*tenga, tengas, tenga, tengamos, tengáis, tengan*
traer	to bring	*traigo*	*traiga, traigas, traiga, traigamos, traigáis, traigan*
valer	to be worth	*valgo*	*valga, valgas, valga, valgamos, valgáis, valgan*
venir	to come	*vengo*	*venga, vengas, venga, vengamos, vengáis, vengan*
ver	to see	*veo*	*vea, veas, vea, veamos, veáis, vean*

Examples:

> *Quiero que tú me digas todo.*   I want you to tell me everything.
>
> *Es urgente que Uds. salgan.*   It's urgent that you leave.
>
> *No es necesario que traiga su chequera.*   It isn't necessary that you bring your checkbook.

Some verbs are completely irregular, and their subjunctive stems must be memorized:

Completely Irregular Verbs

Verb	English	Subjunctive Forms
dar	to give	*dé, des, dé, demos, deis, den*
estar	to be	*esté, estés, esté, estemos, estéis, estén*
haber (auxiliary)	to have	*haya, hayas, haya, hayamos, hayáis, hayan*
ir	to go	*vaya, vayas, vaya, vayamos, vayáis, vayan*
saber	to know	*sepa, sepas, sepa, sepamos, sepáis, sepan*
ser	to be	*sea, seas, sea, seamos, seáis, sean*

Examples:

> *Es improbable que la profesora*   It's improbable that the teacher
> *esté ausente.*   is absent.
>
> *Es imperativo que yo vaya a la oficina.*   It's imperative that I go to the office.
>
> *Busco a alguien que sepa reparar*   I'm looking for someone who knows
> *mi coche.*   how to repair my car.

USING THE PRESENT SUBJUNCTIVE

The present subjunctive mood is called for when all the following conditions exist in a sentence:

- The sentence contains an independent or main clause (a group of words containing a subject and a verb that can stand by itself as a sentence) and also contains a dependent or subordinate clause (a group of words containing a subject and a verb that cannot stand by itself).
- *Que* ("that") joins the two clauses and is followed by a verb in the subjunctive.
- The main clause shows, among other things, wishing, wanting, emotion, doubt, needs, necessity, feelings, commands, supposition, or speculation.
- The verb in the main clause is in the present, the future, or a command form.

Examples:

Yo insisto en que tú me lo muestres.	I insist that you show it to me.
Él saldrá tan pronto como pueda.	He will leave as soon as he can.
Déjele que hable.	Let him speak.

The Subjunctive After Impersonal Expressions

Many impersonal expressions begin with *es* ("it is") and are followed by an adjective. Others are third person singular (*él*) verb forms. *Que* ("that") then joins the clause that contains the impersonal expression with a dependent clause. If the impersonal expression shows any of the qualities of wishing, emotion, doubt, and so on, as mentioned in the preceding section, the verb in the dependent clause must be in the subjunctive. The following table lists common impersonal expressions that require the subjunctive:

Impersonal Expressions That Require the Subjunctive

Impersonal Expression	English
basta que	it is enough that
conviene que	it is advisable that
es absurdo que	it is absurd that
es aconsejable que	it is advisable that
es asombroso que	it is amazing that
es bueno que	it is good that *or* it is nice that
es conveniente que	it is fitting that
es curioso que	it is curious that
es difícil que	it is difficult that
es divertido que	it is amusing that
es dudoso que	it is doubtful that
es esencial que	it is essential that
es extraño que	it is strange that
es fácil que	it is easy that
es imperativo que	it is imperative that
es importante que	it is important that
es imposible que	it is impossible that

(continues)

Impersonal Expressions That Require the Subjunctive *(continued)*

Impersonal Expression	English
es improbable que	it is improbable that
es increíble que	it is incredible that
es indispensable que	it is indispensable that
es injusto que	it is unfair that
es interesante que	it is interesting that
es irónico que	it is ironic that
es justo que	it is fair that
es lamentable que	it is regrettable that
es lástima	it is a pity
es malo que	it is bad that
es mejor que	it is better that
es menester que	it is necessary that
es natural que	it is natural that
es necesario que	it is necessary that
es posible que	it is possible that
es preciso que	it is necessary that
es preferible que	it is preferable that
es probable que	it is probable that
es raro que	it is rare that
es sorprendiente que	it is surprising that
es suficiente que	it is enough that
es urgente que	it is urgent that
es útil que	it is useful that
importa que	it is important that
más vale que	it is better that
parece mentira que	it seems untrue that
puede ser que	it could be that

Examples:

Es dudosa que llueva.	It is doubtful that it will rain.
Es increíble que la policía esté en huelga.	It's incredible that the police are on strike.
Más vale que no salgas.	It is better if you don't go out.

Most of these expressions continue to show doubt even when negated:

No es posible que ella juegue al golf.	It isn't possible that she will play golf.
No es útil que Ud. me ayuda.	It isn't useful for you to help me.

When there is no doubt or when doubt is negated, there is no subjunctive:

No es dudoso que yo regreso pronto.	There is no doubt that I will return soon.

When an impersonal expression shows certainty, the indicative (past, present, or future) is used in the dependent clause. When certainty is negated or questioned, the subjunctive must be used. The expressions in the following table require the indicative except when negated, in which case doubt is implied:

Impersonal Expressions That Require the Indicative

Impersonal Expression	English
es cierto	it is certain, it is sure
es claro	it is clear
es evidente	it is evident
es exacto	it is exact
es obvio	it is obvious
es seguro	it is sure
es verdad	it is true
parece	it seems

Examples:

Es cierto que ella es muy inteligente.	It is certain that she is very intelligent.
Es evidente que va a nevar.	It is evident that it is going to snow.
Es obvio que tienes mucha suerte.	It is obvious that you are very lucky.

But:

No es claro que él gane el concurso.	It isn't clear that he will win the race.
¿Es evidente que ella reciba el premio.	Is it evident that she will receive the prize?

Tal Vez and *Quizás*

Tal vez and *quizás*, both meaning "perhaps," require the subjunctive when doubt or uncertainty exists. The indicative is used when there is certainty:

Tal vez (Quizás) vengamos con Uds.　　Perhaps we will come with you.

Tal vez (Quizás) tienes que ir al médico　　Perhaps you need to go to the doctor
si no estás bien.　　if you aren't well.

The Subjunctive After Certain Verbs

The subjunctive is used after the following verbs that show advice, command, demand, desire, doubt, disbelief, denial, emotion, feelings, hope, permission, preference, prohibition, request, suggestion, wishing, and wanting:

Spanish	English
aconsejar	to advise
alegrarse (de)	to be glad, to be happy
avergonzarsse de	to be ashamed of
decir	to tell (only when meaning to order)
dejar	to let, to allow
desear	to desire, to wish, to want
dudar	to doubt
enfadarse	to become angry
enojarse	to become angry
esperar	to hope
exigir	to require, to demand
hacer	to make, to cause
insistir (en)	to insist
lamentar	to regret
mandar	to command, to order
necesitar	to need
negar	to deny
ojalá que	if only

Spanish	English
ordenar	to order
pedir	to ask for, to request
permitir	to permit
preferir	to prefer
prohibir	to forbid
querer	to wish, to want
reclamar	to demand
recomendar	to recommend
requerir	to require
rogar	to beg, to request
sentir	to be sorry, to regret
solicitar	to request
sorprenderse de	to be surprised
sugerir	to suggest
suplicar	to beg, to plead
temer	to fear
tener miedo de	to fear

Examples:

La madre hace que su hija saque la basura.	The mother makes her daughter take out the garbage.
Le suplicamos que nos ayude.	We beg him to help us.
Me alegro de que tú salgas bien en tus exámenes.	I am glad that you are doing well on your tests.

Note that *dudar* and *negar* express belief or certainty when used negatively:

No dudo que él es fuerte.	I don't doubt that he is strong.
No niego que tú tienes razón.	I don't deny that you are right.

Creer and *Pensar*

The verbs *creer* ("to believe") and *pensar* ("to think") show doubt only when used negatively or interrogatively:

¿Crees que él vaya al partido de fútbol? ¿Piensas que juegue bien?

Do you believe that he is going to the soccer match? Do you think he plays well?

No creo que él vaya al partido. No pienso que juegue bien.

I don't believe he is going to the match. I don't think he plays well.

But:

Creo que él va al partido. Pienso que juega bien.

I believe he is going to the match. I think he plays well.

The Subjunctive After Certain Adjectives

The subjunctive is used in a dependent clause after an independent clause that contains the verb *estar* ("to be") and certain adjectives that show emotions or feelings + *de que*:

Spanish	English
alegre	happy
asombrado(a)	astonished, surprised
asustado(a)	afraid
avergonzado(a)	embarrassed, ashamed
contento(a)	happy
encantado(a)	delighted
enfadado(a)	displeased
enojado(a)	angry
fastidiado(a)	bothered
feliz	happy
furioso(a)	furious
infeliz	unhappy
irritado(a)	irritated
lisonjeado(a)	flattered
orgulloso(a)	proud
triste	sad

Examples:

Ella está encantada de que nosotros hagamos un viaje a España.

She is delighted that we are taking a trip to Spain.

Yo estoy furioso de que tú no me escuches.

I am furious that you aren't listening to me.

The Subjunctive After Certain Conjunctions

Some conjunctions that express time, purpose, condition, concession, negation, or fear always require the subjunctive, whereas others may take either the subjunctive or the indicative, depending on whether the speaker wishes to convey doubt or uncertainty. Note that both clauses in a subjunctive construction may have the same subject. The conjunctions listed in the following table always require the subjunctive:

Conjunctions That Always Require the Subjunctive

Spanish	English
a condición de que	on condition that
a menos que	unless
a no ser que	unless
antes de que	before
con tal que	provided that
en caso de que	in case that
para que	in order that, so that
por miedo a que	for fear that
sin que	without

Examples:

Yo te pagaré a menos que no reciba mi cheque.

I will pay you unless I don't receive my check.

Los alumnos escuchan atentamente para que el profesor no les dé muchas tareas.

The students listen attentively so that the teacher doesn't give them a lot of homework.

Some conjunctions require the subjunctive for events or actions that have not as yet occurred because future events are viewed as uncertain. These conjunctions require the indicative when they refer to past or present events because their certainty in not in question. In some instances, the subjunctive form of the verb can be translated as "may." The following conjunctions may use the subjunctive or the indicative:

Conjunctions That Require the Subjunctive or the Indicative

Spanish	English
así que	even if
aunque	although, even if, even though
cuando	when
de manera que	so that
de modo que	so that
después de que	after
en cuanto	as soon as
hasta que	until
luego que	as soon as
mientras (que)	while
tan pronto como	as soon as

Examples:

Aunque no estudie mucho, ese alumno recibirá buenas notas.	Although he doesn't (may not) study a lot, that student will receive good grades. (It is uncertain that he will, in fact, receive good grades.)
Aunque no estudió mucho, ese alumno recibió buenas notas.	Although he didn't study a lot, that student received good grades. (He received his grades, and they were, in fact, good.)
Hablaré despacio de manera que Uds. puedan comprenderme.	I will speak slowly so that you can understand me. (It is unclear whether you will understand me even if I speak slowly.)
Hablé despacio de manera que Uds. podían comprenderme.	I spoke slowly so that you could understand me. (It is clear that you understood me when I spoke slowly.)

The Subjunctive After Indefinites

The subjunctive is used after indefinites or compounds of *-quiera* or *que*:

Spanish	English
comoquiera	however
cualquier(a)	whatever, any
cuandoquiera	whenever
(a-) dondequiera	wherever
por + adjective/adverb + *que*	however, no matter how, as
quienquiera	whoever

Examples:

Cualquier que sea su problema, no hable de él con nadie.	Whatever your problem may be, don't speak about it with anyone.
Por perezosos que ellos sean, siempre terminan su trabajo.	As lazy as they are (may be), they always finish their work.

The Subjunctive in Relative Clauses

The subjunctive is used in relative clauses where the person or thing mentioned in the main clause is indefinite, nonexistent, or sought after but not as yet attained, or may or may not necessarily exist. If the person or thing mentioned clearly exists, then the indicative is used:

Busco a un hombre que pueda reparar mi televisor.	I'm looking for a man who can repair my television set. (It is unclear whether such a man exists.)
Tengo un coche que sea muy deportivo.	I have a car that is very sporty.

The Subjunctive in Third Person Commands

The subjunctive is used in third person singular or plural commands:

¡Viva la libertad!	Long live liberty!
¡Que ganen mucho!	May they earn a lot of money!

AVOIDING THE SUBJUNCTIVE

When the subject of the independent and the dependent clause are the same, *que* is omitted, and the infinitive is used in place of the subjunctive:

Yo prefiero que tú me acompañes.	I prefer that you accompany me.
Yo prefiero acompañarte.	I prefer to accompany you.

The infinitive can be used instead of the subjunctive with the verbs *dejar, hacer, madar, permitir,* and *prohibir*:

Déjeme que hable. or *Déjeme hablar.*   Let me speak.
Me manda que me vaya. or *Me manda irme.*   He orders me to go away.

When using conjunctions, if the subject of both clauses is the same, *que* is omitted, and the infinitive is used in place of the subjunctive:

Te telefonearé antes de venir a tu casa.   I will call you before coming to your house.
¿Va Ud. a esperar hasta terminar el trabajo?   Are you going to wait until you finish thework?

In relative clauses, awkward sentences may be avoided by using simpler constructions:

Quiero encontrar un hombre que sea sensible. (Quiero encontrar un hombre sensible.)   I want to meet a man who is sensitive. (I want to meet a sensitive man.)

The Imperfect Subjunctive

The *imperfect subjunctive* is a mood that has the same applications as the present subjunctive in that it, too, expresses unreal, hypothetical, theoretical, imaginary, uncorroborated, or unconfirmed conditions or situations that result from doubts, emotions, wishes, wants, needs, desires, feelings, speculations, and suppositions. The imperfect subjunctive refers to an action that has already occurred or that would or would not occur under certain circumstances.

THE IMPERFECT SUBJUNCTIVE OF ALL VERBS

The imperfect subjunctive of all verbs is formed by dropping the *-ron* from the third person plural (*ellos*) form of the preterit tense and adding either the *-ra* or *-se* imperfect subjunctive endings listed in the following table:

Forming the Imperfect Subjunctive

Infinitive	English	Third Person Plural Preterit	Imperfect -*ra* Form	Subjunctive -*se* Form
hablar	to speak	*hablaron*	*hablara*	*hablase*
			hablaras	*hablases*
			hablara	*hablase*
			habláramos	*hablásemos*
			hablarais	*hablaseis*
			hablaran	*hablasen*
comer	to eat	*comieron*	*comiera*	*comiese*
			comieras	*comieses*
			comiera	*comiese*
			comiéramos	*comiésemos*
			comierais	*comieseis*
			comieran	*comiesen*
recibir	to receive	*recibieron*	*recibiera*	*recibiese*
			recibieras	*recibieses*
			recibiera	*recibiese*
			recibiéramos	*recibiésemos*
			recibierais	*recibieseis*
			recibieran	*recibiesen*
dormir	to sleep	*durmieron*	*durmiera*	*durmiese*
			durmieras	*durmieses*
			durmiera	*durmiese*
			durmiéramos	*durmiésemos*
			durmierais	*durmieseis*
			durmieran	*durmiesen*
servir	to serve	*sirvieron*	*sirviera*	*sirviese*
			sirvieras	*sirvieses*
			sirviera	*sirviese*
			sirviéramos	*sirviésemos*
			sirvierais	*sirvieseis*
			sirvieran	*sirviesen*
ir	to go	*fueron*	*fuera*	*fuese*
ser	to be		*fueras*	*fueses*
			fuera	*fuese*
			fuéramos	*fuésemos*
			fuerais	*fueseis*
			fueran	*fuesen*

(continues)

Forming the Imperfect Subjunctive *(continued)*

Infinitive	English	Third Person Plural Preterit	Imperfect -*ra* Form	Subjunctive -*se* Form
hacer	to make, to do	hicieron	hiciera	hiciese
			hicieras	hicieses
			hiciera	hiciese
			hiciéramos	hiciésemos
			hicierais	hicieseis
			hicieran	hiciesen
traer	to bring	trajeron	trajera	trajese
			trajeras	trajeses
			trajera	trajese
			trajéramos	trajésemos
			trajerais	trajeseis
			trajeran	trajesen
leer	to read	leyeron	leyera	leyese
			leyeras	leyeses
			leyera	leyese
			leyéramos	leyésemos
			leyerais	leyeseis
			leyeran	leyesen

USING THE IMPERFECT SUBJUNCTIVE

The imperfect subjunctive is used in a dependent clause in the same way and in the same instances as the present subjunctive except that the verb in the main clause is in the imperfect, preterit, or conditional:

Yo insistí en que tú me lo mostrara (mostrase). I insisted that you show it to me.

Él salió tan pronto como pudiera (pudiese). He left as soon as he could.

No dejaría que hablara (hablase). He wouldn't allow him to speak.

Being Polite

To be extremely polite or to make a sentence softer, the imperfect subjunctive form with the *-ra* ending is often substituted for the conditional of *deber* ("to have to"), *querer* ("to wish," "to want"), and *poder* ("to be able to"):

Debieras estudiar más.	You should study more.
Quisiera verte a menudo.	I would like to see you often.
Pudiera sentarse.	You may sit.

The imperfect subjunctive is used after the expression *como si* to express "as if":

Me miraba como si fuera estúpido.	He was looking at me as if I were stupid.

The imperfect subjunctive is used after *ojalá que* to express "I wish," "I hope," or "if only" when referring to a hypothetical situation:

Ojalá que mi madre supiera cocinar.	If only my mother knew how to cook.

PART V

GERUNDS AND PROGRESSIVE TENSES

Gerunds

A *gerund* (*un gerundio*) is a verbal: a word that is derived from a verb but used as an adjective or as a noun. In Spanish, as in English, the gerund may be an adjective ending in *-ing*. The gerund may also be the equivalent of the English "by" or "while" + the present participle:

Yo estoy escuchando música.	I am listening to music.
El muchacho quien está gritando es mi primo.	The boy who is shouting is my cousin.
Trabajando duro puede hacerse rico.	By working hard you can become rich.

Unlike in English, the Spanish gerund is never used as a noun subject. The infinitive is used instead:

Jugar al tenis es un deporte muy divertido.	Playing tennis is a very enjoyable sport.

FORMING THE GERUND OF REGULAR VERBS

To form the gerund of regular verbs

- Drop the *-ar* infinitive ending and add *-ando*.
- Drop the *-er* or *-ir* infinitive ending and add *-iendo*.

The following table illustrates how this is done:

Forming the Gerund of Regular Verbs

Ending	Verb	English	Gerund	English
-ar	hablar	to speak	hab**lando**	speaking
-er	correr	to run	corr**iendo**	running
-ir	discutir	to discuss	discut**iendo**	discussing

Examples:

Los alumnos están hablando español.   The students are speaking Spanish.
El niño está corriendo por el parque.   The child is running through the park.
Estamos discutiendo sus proyectos.   We are discussing his plans.

Stems That End in Vowels

When an -er or -ir verb stem ends in a vowel, i becomes y before -endo:

Verb	English	Gerund
caer	to fall	ca**y**endo
creer	to believe	cre**y**endo
distribuir	to distribute	distribu**y**endo
leer	to read	le**y**endo
oír	to hear	o**y**endo
traer	to bring	tra**y**endo

Examples:

Los niños están distribuyendo folletos.   The children are distributing brochures.

Estoy leyendo un libro muy interesante.   I'm reading a very interesting book.

FORMING THE GERUND OF STEM-CHANGING AND IRREGULAR VERBS

To form the gerund of stem-changing -ir verbs with e to ie stem changes or with e to i stem changes, change the stem vowel from e to i. Those with o to ue stem changes undergo an o to u change in the gerund, as shown in the following table:

Stem Changes in the Gerund

Verb	English	Gerund
colegir	to collect	*coligiendo*
conseguir	to get	*consiguiendo*
corregir	to correct	*corrigiendo*
decir	to say, to tell	*diciendo*
divertir	to divert, to have fun	*divirtiendo*
dormir	to sleep	*durmiendo*
elegir	to elect	*eligiendo*
mentir	to lie	*mintiendo*
morir	to die	*muriendo*
pedir	to ask	*pidiendo*
preferir	to prefer	*prefiriendo*
referir	to refer	*refiriendo*
repetir	to repeat	*repitiendo*
seguir	to follow	*siguiendo*
sentir	to feel	*sintiendo*
servir	to serve	*sirviendo*
sugerir	to suggest	*sugiriendo*
venir	to come	*viniendo*
vestir	to dress	*vistiendo*

Examples:

Ella está mintiendo.　　　　　　　　She is lying.
El profesor está corrigiendo los exámenes.　　The teacher is correcting the tests.
Los niños están durmiendo.　　　　　The children are sleeping.

How?

The gerund answers the question "How?" or "In what way?":

¿Cómo pasa Ud. el verano?　　　How do you spend the summer?
Lo pasa viajando.　　　　　　　I spend it traveling.

Three Spanish verbs have irregular gerunds:

Verb	English	Gerund
ir	to go	*yendo* (has very limited use)
poder	to be able	*pudiendo* (has very limited use)
reír	to laugh	*riendo*

Example:

> *Las muchachas están riendo.* The girls are laughing.

Progressive Tenses

The gerund is used primarily after the verb *estar* ("to be"), but it is also used after the verbs *andar* ("to walk"), *continuar* ("to continue"), *ir* ("to go," "to continue"), *llegar* ("to arrive"), *quedarse* ("to remain," "to continue"), *salir* ("to go out"), *seguir* ("to follow," "to continue"), and *venir* ("to come") to show that an action or event is, was, will, or would be in progress or continuing at any given moment in time.

THE PRESENT PROGRESSIVE

The present tense in Spanish shows what the subject habitually or generally does now. The *present progressive* shows what the subject is doing at present:

> *Yo leo novelas.* I read novels.
> *Yo estoy leyendo una novela.* I am reading a novel.

The present progressive is most often formed by taking the present tense of the verb *estar (estoy, estás, está, estamos, estáis, están)* or any of the verbs of motion listed above [*see* The Present Tense *in Part III for the present tense conjugations of these verbs*] and adding the gerund expressing the action or event that is occurring:

> *Ellos están preparando la comida.* They are preparing the meal.
> *Yo ando buscando mi perro.* I'm walking along looking for my dog.
> *El niño continúa llorando.* The child continues crying.
> *Sus ideas van cambiando.* Her ideas are changing.
> *¿Por qué llegas sonriendo?* Why do you arrive smiling?
> *Los muchachos se quedan jugando.* The boys continue playing.
> *Ella sale riendo.* She leaves laughing.
> *Nosotros seguimos estudiando.* We continue studying.
> *Ellas vienen corriendo.* They come running.

Verbs Not Used in the Progressive

The *gerunds* of the verbs of motion listed on page 112 are not used to form any of the progressive tenses of those verbs. Instead, the appropriate tense or mood is used:

Ellos andan por la ciudad.	They are walking through the city.
Las muchachas iban al cine.	The girls were going to the movies.
Yo seguiré el proceso	I will be monitoring the process.
Ella no vendría sola.	She wouldn't be coming alone.

THE PAST PROGRESSIVE

The preterit tense in Spanish expresses what the subject did or what action or event took place and was completed at a specific moment in time. The imperfect tense in Spanish describes what the subject "would" or "used to" do, or it describes an action or event that continued in the past over an indefinite period of time. The preterit progressive expresses what the subject was doing or what action or event was taking place at a specific moment in time. The imperfect progressive describes what the subject was doing or what action or event was taking place for an indefinite period of time:

Yo estuve estudiando en la biblioteca ayer por la tarde.	I was studying in the library yesterday afternoon.
Yo estaba estudiando con Carlos.	I was studying with Carlos.

The *past progressive* is most often formed by taking the preterit tense of the verb *estar* (*estuve, estuviste, estuvo, estuvimos, estuvisteis, estuvieron*) or the imperfect of the verb *estar* (*estaba, estabas, estaba, estábamos, estabais, estaban*) or the preterit or the imperfect of any of the verbs of motion listed on page 112 [*see* The Preterit Tense *in Part III for the preterit and the imperfect tense conjugations of these verbs*] and adding the gerund expressing the action or event that was occurring:

Estuvieron trabajando toda la tarde.	They were working all afternoon.
Todavía estaban trabajando a las dos.	They were still working at two o'clock.
Ella coninuó bailando hasta la medianoche.	She continued dancing until midnight.
Ella continuaba bailando con su novio.	She continued dancing with her boyfriend.
Salió aplaudiendo.	He left clapping.
Salía hablando de la obra.	He was leaving speaking of the work.

THE FUTURE PROGRESSIVE

The future tense in Spanish shows what the subject will do or what action or event will happen in the future. The *future progressive* shows what the subject will be doing or what actions or events will be occurring in the future:

> *Nosotros viajaremos durante*   We will travel during the winter.
> *el invierno.*
> *Nosotros estaremos viajando durante*   We will be traveling during the winter.
> *el invierno.*

The future progressive is most often formed by taking the future tense of the verb *estar* (*estaré, estarás, estará, estaremos, estaréis, estarán*) or any of the verbs of motion listed on page 112 [*see* The Future Tense *in Part III for the future tense conjugations of these verbs*] and adding the gerund expressing the action or event that will be occurring:

> *Ella tocará el piano por la mañana.*   She will play the piano in the morning.
> *Ella estará tocando el piano toda*   She will be playing the piano all morning.
> *la mañana.*
> *Yo estudiaré el español.*   I will study Spanish.
> *Yo seguiré estudiando el español.*   I will be continuing to study Spanish.
> *Él traerá un regalo a mi casa.*   He will bring a gift to my house.
> *Él vendrá a mi casa trayendo*   He will come to my house bringing a gift.
> *un regalo.*

THE CONDITIONAL PROGRESSIVE

The conditional mood in Spanish shows what the subject would do or what action or event would happen in certain situations. The *conditional progressive* shows what the subject would be doing or what actions or events would be occurring in certain situations:

> *Si hiciera buen tiempo, yo jugaría*   If it were nice weather, I would play
> *al golf.*   golf.
> *Si hiciera buen tiempo, yo estaría*   If it were nice weather, I would be
> *jugando más al golf.*   playing golf more.

The conditional progressive is most often formed by taking the conditional of the verb *estar* (*estaría, estarías, estaría, estaríamos, estaríis, estarían*) or any of the verbs of motion listed on page 112 [*see* The Conditional *in Part IV for the conditional conjugations of these verbs*] and adding the gerund expressing the action or event that would be occurring in certain situations. The situation in the clause that follows *si* ("if") is hypothetical and requires a verb in the imperfect subjunctive [*see* The Imperfect Subjunctive *in Part IV*]:

Si tuviera más dinero yo compraría un coche nuevo ahora.	If I had more money, I would buy a new car now.
Si tuviera más dinero, yo estaría comprando un coche nuevo ahora.	If I had more money, I would be buying a new car now.
Si hubiera un huracán, no trabajaría.	If there were a hurricane, I wouldn't work.
Si hubiera un huracán, no iría trabajando.	If there were a hurricane, I wouldn't be working.
Si tuviera buena fortuna, cantaría.	If he had good fortune, he would sing.
Si tuviera buena fortuna, llegaría cantando.	If he had good fortune, he would arrive singing.

The Gerund in Commands

The gerund commonly follows command forms of the verbs *seguir* and *continuar*:

Sigan Uds. tocando la guitarra.	Continue playing the guitar.
No sigue hablando.	Don't continue to speak.
Continúe Ud. estudiando.	Continue studying.
No continúes leyendo.	Do not continue to read.

PRONOUNS AND GERUNDS

When using a direct object [*see* Direct Object Pronouns *in Part II*], indirect object [*see* Indirect Object Pronouns *in Part II*], or reflexive pronoun [*see* Reflexive Pronouns *in Part III*] with a gerund, follow these rules for the placement of the pronoun and any necessary accent marks:

- One pronoun may be placed before the conjugated verb of motion or may follow and be attached to the gerund. When the pronoun is attached to the gerund, count back three vowels and add an accent:

La estoy buscando. or *Estoy buscándola.*	I am looking for her.
Nos seguían hablando. or *Seguían hablándonos.*	They were continuing to speak to us.
Se continuó bañando hasta las dos. or *Continuó bañándose hasta las dos.*	She continued bathing until two o'clock.

- Two pronouns may be placed before the conjugated verb of motion or may follow and be attached to the gerund. When the pronouns are attached to the gerund, count back four vowels and add an accent:

Él me lo está leyendo. or *Él está leyéndomelo.*	He is reading it to me.
Se la continuaré escribiendo. or *Continuaré escribiéndosela.*	I will continue to write it to him.
Ella se los seguía repitiendo. or *Ella seguía repitiéndoselos.*	She continued repeating them to herself.

PART VI

COMPOUND TENSES

Simple vs. Compound Tenses

Verb tenses and moods are classified as either simple or compound. A *simple tense or mood* requires just one verb form to express the event or action: when it takes places and what it is. A *compound tense* consists of two verb forms to express "when" and "what": an auxiliary, or helping, verb, which indicates the time period or the mood in which the action or event takes place, and a past participle, which indicates what action or event is taking place.

Spanish has four simple verb tenses and three simple moods, each of which has a corresponding compound tense or mood. To form a compound, conjugate the helping verb, *haber* ("to have"), in the parallel simple tense and add the past participle, as shown in the following table:

Simple vs. Compound Tenses and Moods

Simple Tenses and Moods	Compound Tenses and Moods
Present (do/does; am/are/is) *Ella entra.*　　She enters.	Present perfect (have + past participle) *Ella ha entrado.*　　She has entered.
Preterit (did) *Ella entró.*　　She entered.	Preterit perfect (had + past participle) *Ella hubo entrado.*　　She had entered.
Imperfect (was, used to) *Ella entraba.*　　She was entering.	Pluperfect (had + past participle) *Elle había entrado.*　　She had entered.
Future (will) *Ella entrará.*　　She will enter.	Future perfect (will have + past participle) *Elle habrá entrado.*　　She will have entered.
Conditional (would) *Ella entraría.*　　She would enter.	Conditional perfect (would have + past participle) *Ella habría entrado.*　　She would have entered.
Present subjunctive (may) . . . *que ella entre* . . . that she may enter	Perfect (past) subjunctive (may have + past participle) . . . *que ella haya entrado.* . . that she may have entered
Imperfect subjunctive (might) . . . *que ella entrara (entrase)* . . . that she might enter	Pluperfect subjunctive (might have + past participle) . . . *que ella hubiera (hubiese) entrado* . . . that she might have entered

The Past Participle

The *past participle* is a verb form that expresses what action or event took place in one of the perfect tenses or moods:

> *Él ha llegado.*   He has arrived.
> *Habíamos conducido a la fiesta.*   We had driven to the party.
> *¿Habrás terminado antes el mediodía?*   Will you have finished before noon?

PAST PARTICIPLES OF REGULAR VERBS

To form the past participle of regular verbs

- Drop the *-ar* infinitive ending and add *-ado*.
- Drop the *-er* or *-ir* infinitive ending and add *-ido*.

The following table illustrates how past participles are formed:

Past Participles of Regular Verbs

Ending	Verb	English	Past Participle	English
-ar	trabajar	to work	trabajado	worked
-er	comer	to eat	comido	eaten
-ir	decidir	to decide	decidido	decided

Examples:

> *Ellos han trabajado mucho.*   They have worked a lot.
> *No habíamos comido nada.*   We hadn't eaten anything.
> *¿Qué habría Ud. decidido?*   What would you have decided?

If a vowel precedes an *-er* or *-ir* verb ending, add an accent to that vowel. If the verb ends in an accented vowel, maintain that accent, as shown in the following table:

Past Participles That Require Accents

Verb	English	Past Participle	English
caer	to fall	caído	fallen
creer	to believe	creído	believed
leer	to read	leído	read
oír	to hear	oído	heard

Verb	English	Past Participle	English
reír	to laugh	*reído*	laughed
sonreír	to smile	*sonreído*	smiled
traer	to bring	*traído*	brought

Examples:

El niño ha caído.	The child has fallen.
No me habrían creído.	They wouldn't have believed me.
Yo había reído.	I had laughed.

IRREGULAR PAST PARTICIPLES

Stem-changing and spelling-change verbs have regular past participles. The verbs listed in the following table have irregular past participles, even though some of them are regular in the simple tenses:

Irregular Past Participles

Verb	English	Past Participle	English
abrir	to open	*abierto*	opened
cubrir	to cover	*cubierto*	covered
decir	to tell, to say	*dicho*	said
escribir	to write	*escrito*	written
freír	to fry	*frito*	fried
hacer	to make	*hecho*	made
morir	to die	*muerto*	died
poner	to put	*puesto*	put
proveer	to provide	*provisto*	provided
resolver	to resolve	*resuelto*	resolved
romper	to break	*roto*	broken
satisfacer	to satisfy	*satisfecho*	satisfied
ver	to see	*visto*	seen
volver	to return	*vuelto*	returned

Examples:

Él ha abierto la puerta.	He has opened the door.
Habían hecho un viaje.	They had taken a trip.
Habría visto esa película.	I would have seen that film.

USING THE PAST PARTICIPLE

When used as a verbal, the past participle is invariable, always ends in *-o*, and cannot be separated from the helping verb:

Nosotros hemos resuelto el problema.	We have resolved the problem.
La muchacha había roto el juguete.	She had broken the toy.
No se lo habría dicho.	I wouldn't have said it to him.

When used as an adjective, the past participle agrees in number (singular or plural) and gender (masculine or feminine) with the noun it modifies:

El señor Gómez es un hombre educado.	Mr. Gómez is an educated man.
Veo una puerta cerrada.	I see a closed door.
Leo libros escritos en español.	I read books written in Spanish.
Hay montañas cubiertas de nieve.	There are mountains covered with snow.

Reflexive Verbs

In compound tenses, reflexive pronouns are always placed before the conjugated form of *haber*:

Roberto se ha afeitado.	Robert has shaved.
Nos habíamos divertido.	We had had fun.

The Present Perfect

The *present perfect* expresses an action that began in the past and continues up to the present or an action that was completed at an unspecified time in the past but is somehow connected to the present:

Hemos comido en ese restaurante recientemente.	We have eaten in that restaurant recently.
No he leído esa novela.	I haven't read that novel.
¿Has visto esa película?	Have you seen that film?

FORMING THE PRESENT PERFECT

The present perfect is formed by joining the present tense of the helping verb, *haber*, and the past participle of the action that took place, as shown in the following table:

Forming the Present Perfect

Subject + Present Tense of *Haber*	Sample Past Participle	English
Yo **he**	cantado.	I have sung.
Tú **has**	respondido.	You have responded.
Él (Ella, Ud.) **ha**	aplaudido.	He (she, you) has/have clapped.
Nosotros **hemos**	olvidado.	We have forgotten.
Vosotros **habéis**	reído.	You have laughed.
Ellos (Ellas, Uds.) **han**	vuelto.	They (you) have returned.

Examples:

Ellos han ido a casa de sus abuelos.	They have gone to their grandparents' house.
¿Has hecho un viaje a Uruguay?	Have you taken a trip to Uruguay?
Ella me ha dado un regalo.	She has given me a gift.

USING THE PRESENT PERFECT

The present perfect is used to express what the subject has done or what action or event has occurred. The helping verb, *haber*, must always be used in the present perfect, even if an English translation does not contain the word *has* or *have*:

He leído muchos libros interesantes.	I (have) read many interesting books.
Ya ha terminado el verano.	The summer (has) already ended.
Han disfrutado de vacaciones maravillosas.	They (have) enjoyed a marvelous vacation.

The Preterit Perfect

The *preterit perfect* expresses an action or event that had ended in the past:

Cuando el presidente hubo terminado su discurso, todo el mundo aplaudió.	When the president had finished his speech, everyone clapped.
En cuanto hube llegado a casa preparé la cena.	As soon as I arrived home, I prepared dinner.

> *Apenas se hubieron despertado*   They had hardly awakened when
>   *cuando su amigo llamó.*   their friend called.

FORMING THE PRETERIT PERFECT

The preterit perfect is formed by joining the preterit tense of the helping verb, *haber*, and the past participle of the action that took place, as shown in the following table:

Forming the Preterit Perfect

Subject + Preterit Tense of *Haber*	Sample Past Participle	English
Yo **hube**	cantado.	I had sung.
Tú **hubes**	respondido.	You had responded.
Él (Ella, Ud.) **hubo**	aplaudido.	He (she, you) had clapped.
Nosotros **hubimos**	olvidado.	We had forgotten.
Vosotros **hubistéis**	reído.	You had laughed.
Ellos (Ellas, Uds.) **hubieron**	vuelto.	They (you) had returned.

Examples:

> *Apenas yo hube abierto la puerta, cuando*   I had hardly opened the door,
>   *una mosca entró.*   when a fly flew in.
> *Tan pronto él hubo entendido todo,*   As soon as he had heard everything,
>   *comprendió el problema.*   he understood the problem.
> *Luego que se hubo dormido,*   As soon as she had fallen asleep,
>   *el teléfono sonó.*   the telephone rang.

USING THE PRETERIT PERFECT

The preterit perfect is used mainly in literary and historic works to express what the subject had done or what action or event had just occurred. The helping verb, *haber*, must always be used in the preterit perfect, even if an English translation does not contain the word *had*:

> *En cuanto hube salido, empezó a llover.*   As soon as I had gone out, it began to
>   rain.
> *Así que los alumnos hubieron*   As soon as the students had finished
>   *terminado su trabajo, el profesor*   their work, the teacher corrected
>   *lo corrigió.*   it.

Después de que nosotros hubimos vuelto, tuvimos que preparar la cena.

After we had arrived, we had to prepare dinner.

To express "had" in conversational and informal writing, the pluperfect or the simple preterit replaces the preterit perfect.

Expressions Indicating the Preterit Perfect

The preterit perfect is generally used after the following expressions:

Spanish	English
apenas	hardly, scarcely
cuando	when
después (de) que	after
así que	as soon as
en cuanto	as soon as
luego que	as soon as
tan pronto como	as soon as

The Pluperfect

The *pluperfect* describes an action or event that was completed in the past before another action or event occurred, whether or not it is specifically mentioned:

Ella había limpiado la casa (antes de salir).

She had cleaned the house (before going out).

Cuando era alumno, había estudiado mucho.

When I was a student, I had studied a lot.

Te habían llamado después de llegar a casa.

They had called you after arriving home.

FORMING THE PLUPERFECT

The pluperfect is formed by joining the imperfect tense of the helping verb, *haber*, and the past participle of the action that had taken place, as shown in the following table:

Forming the Pluperfect

Subject + Imperfect Tense of *Haber*	Sample Past Participle	English
Yo **había**	cantado.	I had sung.
Tú **habías**	respondido.	You had responded.
Él (Ella, Ud.) **había**	aplaudido.	He (she, you) had clapped.
Nosotros **habíamos**	olvidado.	We had forgotten.
Vosotros **habíais**	reído.	You had laughed.
Ellos (Ellas, Uds.) **habían**	vuelto.	They (you) had returned.

Examples:

Nunca había comido paella antes.	I had never eaten paella before.
Cuando ella era joven, había vivido en España.	When she was young, she had lived in Spain.
Cuando salimos de nuestra casa, ya habíamos cenado.	When we left our house, we had already eaten dinner.

USING THE PLUPERFECT

The pluperfect is used to describe an action or event that had occurred further in the past than any action or event expressed in the preterit. Because the pluperfect is used in relationship to another past action, that action either is not expressed or is expressed by the preterit or the imperfect:

Cuando llegamos tarde al aeropuerto, el vuelo ya había despegado.	When we arrived late at the airport, the flight had already taken off.
Cuando íbamos al supermercado, ya había empezado a nevar.	When we were going to the supermarket, it had already started to snow.
Cuando él se durmió, ya había terminado su trabajo.	When he fell asleep, he had already finished his work.

The Future Perfect

The *future perfect* expresses an action or event that will have occurred and been completed in the past:

Antes de acostarse, María habrá terminado sus tareas.	Before going to bed, María will have finished her homework.
Antes el fin de la semana yo habré, pintado mi dormitorio.	Before the end of the week, I will have painted my bedroom.
Después de estudiar mucho, ellos habrán aprendido todas las reglas de gramática.	After having studied a lot, they will have learned all the grammar rules.

FORMING THE FUTURE PERFECT

The future perfect is formed by joining the future tense of the helping verb, *haber,* and the past participle of the action that will take place, as shown in the following table:

Forming the Future Perfect

Subject + Future Tense of *Haber*	Sample Past Participle	English
Yo **habré**	*cantado.*	I will have sung.
Tú **habrás**	*respondido.*	You will have responded.
Él (Ella, Ud.) **habrá**	*aplaudido.*	He (she, you) will have clapped.
Nosotros **habremos**	*olvidado.*	We will have forgotten.
Vosotros **habréis**	*reído.*	You will have laughed.
Ellos (Ellas, Uds.) **habrán**	*vuelto.*	They (you) will have returned.

Examples:

Antes el fin del mes, ella habrá pagado todas sus cuentas.	Before the end of the month, she will have paid all her bills.
Antes el siete de la mañana, yo habré hecho muchas cosas.	Before seven o'clock in the morning, I will have done many things.
Después de un año en España, los alumnos habrán aprendido mucho.	After a year in Spain, the students will have learned a lot.

USING THE FUTURE PERFECT

The future perfect expresses what the subject will have done or what action or event will have occurred in the past before another action will take place (expressed by the future):

Para las ocho de la mañana, ya habré comido y podré salir.	By eight o'clock in the morning, I will have already eaten and I will be able to go out.

Antes el fin del día, ya habremos es tudiado mucho y querremos divertirnos.

Before the end of the day, we will already have studied a lot and we'll want to have fun.

Después de una hora en la biblioteca, él habrá aprendido mucho y escribirá su artículo.

After an hour in the library, he will have learned a lot and will write his article.

The future perfect is also used to express probability or conjecture in the past:

¿Quién habrá hecho todos estos errores?

Who has made all these mistakes? *or* I wonder who has made all these mistakes.

¿Habrá vuelto?

Has he returned? *or* I wonder if he has returned.

Habrán olvidado su cumpleaños.

They have probably forgotten your birthday. *or* They must have forgotten your birthday.

Deber De

Deber de + the perfect infinitive [*see* The Perfect Infinitive *in Part IX*] may replace the future perfect to express probability in the past:

Deben de haber llegado tarde.   They must have arrived late.

Debe de haber tomado otro vuelo.   He must have taken a different flight.

PART VII

COMPOUND MOODS

The Conditional Perfect

The *conditional perfect* expresses an action or event that would have occurred and been completed in the past:

Yo te habría dicho todo.	I would have told you everything.
Ella la habría ayudado.	She would have helped her.
Ellos no me habrían dicho mentiras.	They wouldn't have lied to me.

FORMING THE CONDITIONAL PERFECT

The conditional perfect is formed by joining the conditional tense of the auxiliary (helping) verb, *haber,* and the past participle of the action that will take place, as shown in the following table:

Forming the Conditional Perfect

Subject + Conditional of *Haber*	Sample Past Participle	English
Yo **habría**	*cantado.*	I would have sung.
Tú **habrías**	*respondido.*	You would have responded.
Él (Ella, Ud.) **habría**	*aplaudido.*	He (she, you) would have clapped.
Nosotros **habríamos**	*olvidado.*	We would have forgotten.
Vosotros **habríais**	*reído.*	You would have laughed.
Ellos (Ellas, Uds.) **habrían**	*vuelto.*	They (you) would have returned.

Examples:

Ellos no le habrían dado mucho dinero.	They wouldn't have given her a lot of money.
Mi abuela habría tenido cien años.	My grandmother would have been one hundred years old.
Te habríamos ayudado.	We would have helped you.

USING THE CONDITIONAL PERFECT

The conditional perfect expresses what the subject would have done or what action or event would have occurred in the past if (*si*) another situation had taken place (expressed by the pluperfect subjunctive [*see* The Pluperfect Subjunctive, *later in this part*]):

Si hubiera hecho buen tiempo, yo habría conducido a la playa.	If it had been nice weather, I would have driven to the beach.
Nosotros nos habríamos viajado por el mundo si hubiéramos tenido mucho dinero.	We would have traveled around the world if we had had a lot of money.
Si hubiera ganado la lotería, ella se habría comprado un castillo en España.	If she had won the lottery, she would have bought herself a castle in Spain.

The conditional perfect is also used to express probability or conjecture in the past:

¿Quién habría hecho todos estos errores?	Who had made all these mistakes? *or* I wonder who had made all these mistakes.
¿Habría vuelto?	Had he returned? *or* I wonder if he had returned.
Habrían olvidado su cumpleaños.	They had probably forgotten your birthday. *or* They must have forgotten your birthday.
Habría sido la medianoche cuando llegaron.	It was probably midnight when they returned.

The Present Perfect Subjunctive

The *present perfect subjunctive* expresses an action or event that occurred and was completed in the past in the dependent clause before the action of the main clause took place:

Yo dudo que ellos me hayan entendido.	I doubt that they understood me.
Es imposible que él ya no haya llegado.	It's impossible that he hasn't arrived yet.
El profesor no cree que los alumnos hayan estudiado bastante.	The teacher doesn't believe that the students studied enough.

FORMING THE PRESENT PERFECT SUBJUNCTIVE

The present perfect subjunctive is formed by joining the present subjunctive of the helping verb, *haber,* and the past participle of the action that took place, as shown in the following table:

Forming the Present Perfect Subjunctive

Subject + Present Subjunctive of *Haber*	Sample Past Participle	English
Yo **haya**	*cantado.*	I (may) have sung.
Tú **hayas**	*respondido.*	You (may) have responded.
Él (Ella, Ud.) **haya**	*aplaudido.*	He (she, you) (may) have clapped.
Nosotros **hayamos**	*olvidado.*	We (may) have forgotten.
Vosotros **hayáis**	*reído.*	You (may) have laughed.
Ellos (Ellas, Uds.) **hayan**	*vuelto.*	They (you) (may) have returned.

Examples:

Es natural que nosotros hayamos estudiado para el examen.	It is natural that we studied for the test.
No creo que ellas hayan llegado.	I don't believe they arrived.
Espero que Ud. haya enviado los documentos.	I hope you sent the documents.

USING THE PRESENT PERFECT SUBJUNCTIVE

The present perfect subjunctive is used in the same manner as the present subjunctive. The present perfect subjunctive, however, expresses what the subject may have done or what action or event may have occurred in the past before another action took place:

Yo no creo que el tren haya llegado a tiempo.	I don't believe that the train arrived on time.
Es bueno que nosotros hayamos hecho una reservación en ese restaurante.	It is good that we made a reservation in that restaurant.
Es extraño que tú no hayas traído su libro en clase.	It is strange that you didn't bring your book to class.

The Pluperfect Subjunctive

The *pluperfect subjunctive* expresses an action or event that occurred and was completed in the past:

El jefe esperaba que los obradores lo hubieran (hubiesen) entendido.	The boss hoped that the workers had understood him.
Yo no creía que él hubiera (hubiese) muerto.	I didn't believe that he had died.
Ella no estaba segura de que él la hubiera (hubiese) querido.	She wasn't sure that he had loved her.

FORMING THE PLUPERFECT SUBJUNCTIVE

The pluperfect subjunctive is formed by joining the imperfect subjunctive of the helping verb, *haber,* and the past participle of the action that took place, as shown in the following table:

Forming the Pluperfect Subjunctive

Subject + Imperfect Subjunctive of *Haber*	Sample Past Participle	English
Yo **hubiera (hubiese)**	*cantado.*	I (might) have sung.
Tú **hubieras (hubieses)**	*respondido.*	You (might) have responded.
Él (Ella, Ud.) **hubiera (hubiese)**	*aplaudido.*	He(she, you) (might) have clapped.
Nosotros **hubiéramos (hubiésemos)**	*olvidado.*	We (might) have forgotten.
Vosotros **hubierais (hubieseis)**	*reído.*	You (might) have laughed.
Ellos(Ellas,Uds.) **hubieran (hubiesen)**	*vuelto.*	They (you) (might) have returned.

Examples:

Ella insistía en que los niños no hubieran (hubiesen) tomado demasiado chocolate.	She insisted that the children hadn't eaten too much chocolate.
El médico lo examinó antes de que él le hubiera (hubiese) explicado sus síntomas.	The doctor examined him before he had explained his symptoms.
Yo temía que Ud. no me hubiera (hubiese) dado bastante información.	I was afraid that you hadn't given me enough information.

USING THE PLUPERFECT SUBJUNCTIVE

The pluperfect subjunctive is used in the same manner as the imperfect subjunctive. The pluperfect subjunctive, however, expresses what the subject might have done or what action or event might have occurred in the past:

¿CreeríaUd. que ellos no hubieran (hubiesen) venido a la conferencia?	Would you believe that they hadn't come to the conference?
No pensaba que Ud. lo hubiera (hubiese) hablado.	I didn't think that you had spoken to him.
Buscábamos a una persona que hubiera (hubiese) hecho ese viaje.	We were looking for a person who had taken that trip.

The pluperfect subjunctive is used after the expression *como si* to express "as if":

Me hablaban como si no hubiera entendido nada.	They were speaking to me as if I hadn't understood anything.

The pluperfect subjunctive is used after *ojalá que* to express "I wish," "I hope," or "if only" when referring to a contrary-to-fact situation:

Ojalá que ellos me hubieran (hubiesen) explicado el problema más pronto.	If only they had explained the problem to me sooner.

Sequence of Tenses in the Subjunctive

In Spanish, the tense of the verb in the main clause determines the correct subjunctive mood (present, present perfect, imperfect, or pluperfect) to use in the dependent clause. The following table shows the rules that are followed:

Sequence of Tenses in the Subjunctive

Verb in Main Clause	Verb in Dependent Clause
Present indicative, present perfect, future, *or* command	Present subjunctive *or* present perfect subjunctive
Preterit, imperfect, conditional, *or* pluperfect	Imperfect subjunctive *or* pluperfect subjunctive

Examples:

El profesor manda que los alumnos hablen solamente español.	The teacher orders that the students speak only Spanish.
El profesor ha mandado que los alumnos hablen solamente español.	The teacher has ordered that the students speak only Spanish.
El profesor mandará que los alumnos hablen solamente español.	The teacher will order that the students speak only Spanish.
Mande Ud. que los alumnos hablen solamente español.	Order that the students speak only Spanish.
No pienso que los alumnos hayan hablado solamente español.	I don't think that the students have spoken only Spanish.
El profesor mandó que los alumnos hablaran solamente español.	The teacher ordered that the students speak only Spanish.
El profesor mandaba que los alumnos hablaran solamente español.	The teacher ordered (was ordering, used to order) that the students speak only Spanish.
El profesor mandaría que los alumnos hablaran solamante español.	The teacher would order that the students speak only Spanish.
El profesor había mandado que los alumnos hablaran solamente español.	The teacher had ordered that the students speak only Spanish.
No pensaba que los alumnos hubieran (hubiesen) hablado solamente español.	I didn't think that the students had spoken only Spanish.

Conditional Sentences

A *conditional sentence* is composed of two clauses:

- A *si* ("if") clause
- A main or result clause

In any given sentence, the *si* clause may precede or follow the main clause. The sequence of tenses used in a conditional sentence depends on whether the real conditions or contrary-to-fact conditions exist in the sentence.

REAL CONDITIONS

Real conditions describe situations that exist, that are certain, or that are likely to take place. When a real condition exists, the indicative (past, present, or future tense or the imperative) is used:

Si tú me enviaste una carta, yo no la recibí.	If you sent me a letter, I didn't receive it.
Yo iré a la piscina si hace buen tiempo.	I'll go to the pool if the weather is nice.
Si tú me acompañaras, yo haré un viaje a México.	If you will accompany me, I will take a trip to Mexico.
Dígame si Uds. vienen.	Tell me if you are coming.

CONTRARY-TO-FACT CONDITIONS

Contrary-to-fact conditions do not really exist or have not as yet occurred. When a contrary-to-fact condition exists in the present, the imperfect subjunctive (-*ra* or -*se* form) is used in the *si* clause, and the conditional or the imperfect subjunctive (the -*ra* form only) is used in the main or result clause. When a contrary-to-fact condition exists in the past, the pluperfect subjunctive (-*ra* or -*se* form) is used in the *si* clause, and the conditional perfect or the pluperfect subjunctive (-*ra* form only) is used in the main or result clause. The following table summarizes how the tenses are used:

Contrary-to-Fact Conditions

	Si Clause	Main or Result Clause
Present Time	Imperfect subjunctive (-*ra* or -*se* form)	Conditional *or* imperfect subjunctive (-*ra* form only)
Past Time	Pluperfect subjunctive (-*ra* or -*se* form)	Conditional perfect *or* pluperfect subjunctive (-*ra* form only)

Examples:

Si yo trabajara (trabajase) mucho, yo ganaría (ganara) mucho dinero.	If I worked (were to work) a lot, I would earn a lot of money.
Si yo hubiera (hubiese) trabajado mucho, yo habría (hubiera) ganado mucho dinero.	If I had worked (were to have worked) a lot, I would have earned a lot of money.

The Perfect Infinitive

The *perfect infinitive* is used after a preposition (usually *por*) and is formed by adding a past participle to the infinitive of *haber*.

Ella se enoja por no haber recibido el puesto.	She becomes angry for not having received the job.
Él se puso enfermo por haber comido demasiado. comido demasiado.	He became sick for having eaten too much.

PART VIII

THE IMPERATIVE

Formal Commands

A *formal, or polite, command* addresses people who are older or unfamiliar to the speaker and to whom respect must be shown. In English, the subject of the command, "you," is understood, and the pronoun is not used. In Spanish, the "you" subject may or may not be expressed. When the pronoun is not given, the verb ending identifies the subject. There are two formal commands in Spanish: one that uses the singular subject *Ud.* and one that uses the plural subject *Uds.*

THE IMPERATIVE OF REGULAR VERBS

To form the *Ud.* or *Uds.* formal command, use the present subjunctive of the third person singular or plural of the verb indicating the action. The present subjunctive is formed as follows:

- Drop the final *-o* from the present tense *yo* form of the verb.
- For *-ar* infinitives, add *-e* for *Ud.* and *-en* for *Uds.*
- For *-er* or *-ir* infinitives, add *-a* for *Ud.* and *-an* for *Uds.*

A negative command requires *no* before the conjugated verb.

The following table shows how to form the imperative of regular verbs:

The Imperative of Regular Verbs

Infinitive	English	Affirmative	Negative	English
hablar	to speak	*hable(n)*	*no hable(n)*	(don't) speak
correr	to run	*corra(n)*	*no corra(n)*	(don't) run
subir	to go up	*suba(n)*	*no suba(n)*	(don't) go up

Examples:

Hable (Ud.) más despacio, por favor.   Please speak more slowly.
No corran (Uds.)   Don't run.
Suba (Ud.) al segundo piso.   Go up to the second floor.

Proper Punctuation

When writing, to emphasize a command, place an inverted exclamation point at the beginning of the command and a regular exclamation point at the end of it:

¡No coman (Uds.) tanto!	Don't eat so much!
¡Escuche (Ud.)!	Listen!

THE IMPERATIVE OF SPELLING-CHANGE VERBS

All spelling-change verbs, except for those ending in *-car*, *-gar*, and *-zar*, form the affirmative and negative polite imperative by using the present subjunctive *Ud.* and *Uds.* form of the verb. Take the *yo* form of the present, drop the final *-o*, and add the correct present subjunctive endings to form the *Ud.* and *Uds.* imperative, as shown in the following table:

Formal Commands for *-er* and *-ir* Infinitive Spelling-Change Verbs

Infinitive	*Yo* Form of Present	Imperative	English
convencer	*convenzo*	*(no) convenza(n)*	(don't) convince
desobedecer	*desobedezco*	*(no) desobedezca(n)*	(don't) disobey
recoger	*recojo*	*(no) recoja(n)*	(don't) pick up
distinguir	*distingo*	*(no) distinga(n)*	(don't) distinguish
exigir	*exijo*	*(no) exija(n)*	(don't) demand
fruncir	*frunzo*	*(no) frunza(n)*	(don't) frown
traducir	*traduzco*	*(no) traduzca(n)*	(don't) translate

Examples:

¡No desobedezcan (Uds.) al profesor!	Don't disobey the teacher!
¡Recoja (Ud.) los papeles!	Pick up the papers!
¡Exija (Ud.) lo mejor!	Demand the best!

To form the imperative of *-car*, *-gar*, and *-zar* spelling-change verbs, drop the *-é* from the *yo* form of the preterit and add *-e* or *-en* for *Ud.* and *Uds.*, respectively, as shown in the following table:

Formal Commands for *-car, -gar,* and *-zar* Spelling-Change Verbs

Infinitive	*Yo* Form of Preterit	Imperative	English
buscar	busqué	(no) busque(n)	(don't) look (for)
cruzar	crucé	(no) cruce(n)	(don't) cross
llegar	llegué	(no) llegue(n)	(don't) arrive

Examples:

¡Busque (Ud.) el libro!	Look for the book!
¡No lleguen (Uds.) tarde!	Don't arrive late!
¡Crucen (Uds.) la calle!	Cross the street!

THE IMPERATIVE OF STEM-CHANGING VERBS

All stem-changing verbs form the affirmative and negative polite imperative by using the present subjunctive *Ud.* and *Uds.* form of the verb. Take the *yo* form of the present, drop the final *-o*, and add the correct present subjunctive endings to form the *Ud.* and *Uds.* imperative, as shown in the following table:

Formal Commands for Stem-Changing Verbs

Infinitive	*Yo* Form of Present	Imperative	English
cerrar	cierro	(no) cierre(n)	(don't) close
continuar	continúo	(no) continúe(n)	(don't) continue
enviar	envío	(no) envíe(n)	(don't) send
mostrar	muestro	(no) muestre(n)	(don't) show
encender	enciendo	(no) encienda(n)	(don't) light
envolver	envuelvo	(no) envuelva(n)	(don't) wrap
torcer	tuerzo	(no) tuerza(n)	(don't) twist
contribuir	contribuyo	(no) contribuya(n)	(don't) contribute
corregir	corrijo	(no) corrija(n)	(don't) correct
distinguir	distingo	(no) distinga(n)	(don't) distinguish
dormir	duermo	(no) duerma(n)	(don't) sleep
seguir	sigo	(no) siga(n)	(don't) follow
servir	sirvo	(no) sirva(n)	(don't) serve
sugerir	sugiero	(no) sugiera(n)	(don't) suggest

Examples:

¡No cierren (Uds.) las ventanas!	Don't close the windows!
¡Encienda (Ud.) la luz!	Turn on the light!
¡Siga (Ud.) hablando!	Continue speaking!

THE IMPERATIVE OF IRREGULAR VERBS

All irregular verbs, including those that have irregular present tense *yo* forms, form the affirmative and negative polite imperative by using the present subjunctive *Ud.* and *Uds.* form of the verb. Take the *yo* form of the present, drop the final *-o*, and add the correct present subjunctive endings to form the *Ud.* and *Uds.* imperative, as shown in the following table:

Formal Commands for Verbs with Irregular *Yo* Forms

Infinitive	*Yo* Form of Present	Imperative	English
caber	quepo	(no) quepa(n)	(don't) fit
caer	caigo	(no) caiga(n)	(don't) fall
decir	digo	(no) diga(n)	(don't) tell, (don't) say
hacer	hago	(no) haga(n)	(don't) do, (don't) make
oír	oigo	(no) oiga(n)	(don't) hear
poner	pongo	(no) ponga(n)	(don't) put
salir	salgo	(no) salga(n)	(don't) leave, (don't) go out
tener	tengo	(no) tenga(n)	(don't) have
traer	traigo	(no) traiga(n)	(don't) bring
valer	valgo	(no) valga(n)	(don't) be worth
venir	vengo	(no) venga(n)	(don't) come
ver	veo	(no) vea(n)	(don't) see

Examples:

¡No diga (Ud.) nada!	Don't say anything!
¡Salgan (Uds.)!	Leave!
¡Tráigame (Ud.) un vaso de agua!	Bring me a glass of water!

The formal commands of irregular verbs must be memorized, as shown in the following table:

Formal Commands of Irregular Verbs

Infinitive	Command	English
dar	*(no) dé (den)*	(don't) give
estar	*(no) esté(n)*	(don't) be
ir	*(no) vaya(n)*	(don't) go
saber	*(no) sepa(n)*	(don't) know
ser	*(no) sea(n)*	(don't) be

Examples:

Déme (Ud.) una pluma, por favor.	Give me a pen, please.
No vayan (Uds.) al estadio.	Don't go to the stadium.
¡No sea (Ud.) tonto!	Don't be silly!

Informal Commands

Informal, or *familiar*, *commands* are directed to friends, peers, family members, children, pets, or someone younger than the speaker. A *tú* command, which is an informal, or familiar, singular command, is used if only one person is being addressed. A *vosotros* command, which is an informal, or familiar, plural command, is used when more than one person is being addressed. *Vosotros* commands are used primarily in Spain, whereas *Uds.* commands are used in Latin American Spanish-speaking countries.

INFORMAL *TÚ* COMMANDS

Affirmative informal *tú* commands are formed in a different way than negative informal *tú* commands, so it is important to pay attention to the type of command that is being given.

Affirmative *Tú* Commands of Most Verbs

Affirmative *tú* commands of most verbs (regular, spelling-change, and stem-changing verbs) are formed by dropping the final -*s* from the present tense *tú* form of the verb, which results in the third person singular (*él, ella, Ud.*) present tense form of the verb, as shown in the following tables:

Affirmative *Tú* Commands of Regular Verbs

Infinitive	*Tú* Form of Present	Command	English
ayudar	ayudas	ayuda (tú)	help
comer	comes	come (tú)	eat
abrir	abres	abre (tú)	open

Examples:

Ayuda a tu hermana.   Help your sister.
Come frutas.   Eat fruit.
Abre la ventana.   Open the window.

Affirmative *Tú* Commands of Spelling-Change Verbs

Infinitive	*Tú* Form of Present	Command	English
buscar	buscas	busca (tú)	look for
lanzar	lanzas	lanza (tú)	throw
llegar	llegas	llega (tú)	arrive
convencer	convences	convence (tú)	convince
desobedecer	desobedeces	desobedece (tú)	disobey
recoger	recoges	recoge (tú)	pick up
distinguir	distingues	distingue (tú)	distinguish
exigir	exiges	exige (tú)	demand
fruncir	frunces	frunce (tú)	frown
traducir	traduces	traduce (tú)	translate

Examples:

Recoge el periódico.   Pick up the newspaper.
Traduce esta frase.   Translate that sentence.
Distingue entre lo bueno y lo malo.   Distinguish between good and evil.

Affirmative *Tú* Commands of Stem-Changing Verbs

Infinitive	*Tú* Form of Present	Command	English
cerrar	cierras	cierra (tú)	close
continuar	continúas	continúa (tú)	continue
enviar	envías	envía (tú)	send
mostrar	muestras	muestra (tú)	show
encender	enciendes	enciende (tú)	light
envolver	envuelves	envuelve (tú)	wrap
torcer	tuerces	tuerce (tú)	twist
contribuir	contribuyes	contribuye (tú)	contribute
corregir	corriges	corrige (tú)	correct
dormir	duermes	duerme (tú)	sleep
seguir	sigues	sigue (tú)	follow
servir	sirves	sirve (tú)	serve
sugerir	sugieres	sugiere (tú)	suggest

Examples:

Cierra la caja.	Close the box.
Continúa escribiendo.	Continue writing.
Sirve carne.	Serve meat.

Affirmative *Tú* Commands of Irregular Verbs

A few irregular verbs have irregular affirmative informal command forms, as shown in the following table:

Affirmative *Tú* Commands of Irregular Verbs

Infinitive	Irregular Command	English
decir	di (tú)	say, tell
hacer	haz (tú)	do, make
ir	ve (tú)	go
poner	pon (tú)	put
salir	sal (tú)	leave, go out

(continues)

Affirmative *Tú* Commands of Irregular Verbs *(continued)*

Infinitive	Irregular Command	English
ser	sé (tú)	be
tener	ten (tú)	have, be
valer	val (tú)	be worth
venir	ven (tú)	come

Examples:

Di lo que vas a hacer.	Say what you are going to do.
Ten cuidado.	Be careful.
Ven conmigo.	Come with me.

Tú Commands

When issuing a singular informal command, the pronoun *tú* is generally not used in the sentence:

Repite tu nombre, por favor.	Repeat your name, please.
No pagues la cuenta.	Don't pay the bill.

Also note that the singular informal commands for *ver* ("to see") and *ir* ("to go") are identical:

Ve esa película.	See that film.
Ve a ese teatro.	Go to that theater.

Negative *Tú* Commands of Most Verbs

All verbs (regular, spelling-change, and stem-changing verbs) use the *tú* form of the present subjunctive for the negative *tú* commands, as shown in the following tables:

Negative *Tú* Commands of Regular Verbs

Infinitive	*Tú* Form of Subjunctive/Command	English
ayudar	no ayudes	don't help
comer	no comas	don't eat
abrir	no abras	don't open

Examples:

No ayudes a tu hermana.	Don't help your sister.
No comas frutas.	Don't eat fruit.
No abras la ventana.	Don't open the window.

Negative *Tú* Commands of Spelling-Change Verbs

Infinitive	*Tú* Form of Subjunctive/Command	English
buscar	*no busques*	don't look for
lanzar	*no lances*	don't throw
llegar	*no llegues*	don't arrive
convencer	*no convenzas*	don't convince
desobedecer	*no desobedezcas*	don't disobey
recoger	*no recojas*	don't pick up
distinguir	*no distingas*	don't distinguish
exigir	*no exijas*	don't demand
fruncir	*no frunzas*	don't frown
traducir	*no traduzcas*	don't translate

Examples:

No recojas el periódico.	Don't pick up the newspaper.
No traduzcas esta frase.	Don't translate that sentence.
No distingas entre lo bueno y lo malo.	Don't distinguish between good and evil.

Negative *Tú* Commands of Stem-Changing Verbs

Infinitive	*Tú* Form of Subjunctive/Command	English
cerrar	*no cierres*	don't close
continuar	*no continúes*	don't continue
enviar	*no envíes*	don't send
mostrar	*no muestres*	don't show
encender	*no enciendas*	don't light
envolver	*no envuelvas*	don't wrap
torcer	*no tuerzas*	don't twist

(continues)

Negative *Tú* Commands of Stem-Changing Verbs *(continued)*

Infinitive	*Tú* Form of Subjunctive/Command	English
contribuir	*no contribuyas*	don't contribute
corregir	*no corrijas*	don't correct
dormir	*no duermas*	don't sleep
seguir	*no sigas*	don't follow
servir	*no sirvas*	don't serve
sugerir	*no sugieras*	don't suggest

Examples:

No cierres la caja.   Don't close the box.
No contnúes escribiendo.   Don't continue writing.
No sirvas carne.   Don't serve meat.

Negative *Tú* Commands of Irregular Verbs

The few irregular verbs that have irregular affirmative informal command forms have regular negative command formation in that they use the *tú* form of the present subjunctive:

Negative *Tú* Commands of Irregular Verbs

Infinitive	Irregular Command	English
decir	*no digas*	don't say, don't tell
hacer	*no hagas*	don't do, don't make
ir	*no vayas*	don't go
poner	*no pongas*	don't put
salir	*no salgas*	don't leave, don't go out
ser	*no seas*	don't be
tener	*no tengas*	don't have, don't be
valer	*no valgas*	don't be worth
venir	*no vengas*	don't come

Examples:

No digas lo que vas a hacer.   Don't say what you are going to do.
No tengas cuidado.   Don't be careful.
No vengas conmigo.   Don't come with me.

INFORMAL *VOSOTROS* COMMANDS

Affirmative informal *vosotros* commands are formed in a different way than negative informal *vosotros* commands, so it is important to pay attention to the type of command that is being given.

Affirmative *Vosotros* Commands of All Verbs

Affirmative *vosotros* commands of all verbs (regular, spelling-change, and stem-changing verbs) are formed by dropping the final -*r* from the infinitive of the verb and adding -*d*, as shown in the following tables:

Affirmative *Vosotros* Commands of Regular Verbs

Infinitive	*Vosotros* Command	English
ayudar	ayudad (vosotros)	help
comer	comed (vosotros)	eat
abrir	abrid (vosotros)	open

Examples:

Ayudad a vuestra hermana.	Help your sister.
Comed frutas.	Eat fruit.
Abrid la ventana.	Open the window.

Affirmative *Vosotros* Commands of Spelling-Change Verbs

Infinitive	Command	English
buscar	buscad (vosotros)	look for
lanzar	lanzad (vosotros)	throw
llegar	llegad (vosotros)	arrive
convencer	convenced (vosotros)	convince
desobedecer	desobedeced (vosotros)	disobey
recoger	recoged (vosotros)	pick up
distinguir	distinguid (vosotros)	distinguish
exigir	exigid (vosotros)	demand
fruncir	fruncid (vosotros)	frown
traducir	traducid (vosotros)	translate

Examples:

Recoged el periódico.	Pick up the newspaper.
Traducid esta frase.	Translate that sentence.
Distinguid entre lo bueno y lo malo.	Distinguish between good and evil.

Affirmative *Vosotros* Commands of Stem-Changing Verbs

Infinitive	Command	English
cerrar	*cerrad (vosotros)*	close
continuar	*continuad (vosotros)*	continue
enviar	*enviad (vosotros)*	send
mostrar	*mostrad (vosotros)*	show
encender	*encended (vosotros)*	light
envolver	*envolved (vosotros)*	wrap
torcer	*torced (vosotros)*	twist
contribuir	*contribuid (vosotros)*	contribute
corregir	*corregid (vosotros)*	correct
dormir	*dormid (vosotros)*	sleep
seguir	*seguid (vosotros)*	follow
servir	*servid (vosotros)*	serve
sugerir	*sugerid (vosotros)*	suggest

Examples:

Cerrad la caja.	Close the box.
Continuad escribiendo.	Continue writing.
Servid carne.	Serve meat.

Affirmative *Vosotros* Commands of Irregular Verbs

Irregular verbs form their *vosotros* commands by dropping the final *-r* from the infinitive and adding *-d*:

Affirmative *Vosotros* Commands of Irregular Verbs

Infinitive	Irregular Command	English
decir	*decid (vosotros)*	say, tell
hacer	*haced (vosotros)*	do, make
ir	*id (vosotros)*	go
poner	*poned (vosotros)*	put
salir	*salid (vosotros)*	leave, go out
ser	*sed (vosotros)*	be
tener	*tened (vosotros)*	have, be
valer	*valed (vosotros)*	be worth
venir	*venid (vosotros)*	come

Examples:

Decid lo que vais a hacer.	Say what you are going to do.
Tened cuidado.	Be careful.
Venid conmigo.	Come with me.

Negative *Vosotros* Commands of Most Verbs

All verbs (regular, spelling-change, and stem-changing verbs) use the *vosotros* form of the present subjunctive for the negative *vosotros* commands, as shown in the following tables:

Negative *Vosotros* Commands of Regular Verbs

Infinitive	*Vosotros* Form of Subjunctive/Command	English
ayudar	*no ayudéis*	don't help
comer	*no comáis*	don't eat
abrir	*no abráis*	don't open

Examples:

No ayudéis a vuestra hermana.	Don't help your sister.
No comáis frutas.	Don't eat fruit.
No abráis la ventana.	Don't open the window.

Negative *Vosotros* Commands of Spelling-Change Verbs

Infinitive	*Vosotros* Form of Subjunctive/Command	English
buscar	no busquéis	don't look for
lanzar	no lancéis	don't throw
llegar	no lleguéis	don't arrive
convencer	no convenzáis	don't convince
desobedecer	no desobedezcáis	don't disobey
recoger	no recojáis	don't pick up
distinguir	no distingáis	don't distinguish
exigir	no exijáis	don't demand
fruncir	no frunzáis	don't frown
traducir	no traduzcáis	don't translate

Examples:

No recojáis el periódico.   Don't pick up the newspaper.
No traduzcáis esta frase.   Don't translate that sentence.
No distingáis entre lo bueno y lo malo.   Don't distinguish between good and
                                                                evil.

Negative *Vosotros* Commands of Stem-Changing Verbs

Infinitive	*Vosotros* Form of Subjunctive/Command	English
cerrar	no cerréis	don't close
continuar	no continuéis	don't continue
enviar	no enviéis	don't send
mostrar	no mostréis	don't show
encender	no encendáis	don't light
envolver	no envolváis	don't wrap
torcer	no torzáis	don't twist
contribuir	no contribuyáis	don't contribute
corregir	no corrijáis	don't correct
dormir	no dormáis	don't sleep
seguir	no sigáis	don't follow

Infinitive	*Vosotros* Form of Subjunctive/Command	English
servir	*no sirváis*	don't serve
sugerir	*no sugeráis*	don't suggest

Examples:

No cerráis la caja.	Don't close the box.
No contnuéis escribiendo.	Don't continue writing.
No sirváis carne.	Don't serve meat.

Negative *Vosotros* Commands of Irregular Verbs

Irregular verbs have regular negative command formation in that they use the *vosotros* form of the present subjunctive:

Negative *Vosotros* Commands of Irregular Verbs

Infinitive	Irregular Command	English
decir	*no digáis*	don't say, don't tell
hacer	*no hagáis*	don't do, don't make
ir	*no vayáis*	don't go
poner	*no pongáis*	don't put
salir	*no salgáis*	don't leave, don't go out
ser	*no seáis*	don't be
tener	*no tengáis*	don't have, don't be
valer	*no valgáis*	don't be worth
venir	*no vengáis*	don't come

Examples:

No digáis lo que vais a hacer.	Don't say what you are going to do.
No tengáis cuidado.	Don't be careful.
No vengáis conmigo.	Don't come with me.

Vosotros Commands

In a plural informal command, the pronoun *vosotros* is generally not used in the sentence:

Repetid vuestro nombre, por favor.	Repeat your name, please.
No pagáis la cuenta.	Don't pay the bill.

Indirect Commands

Indirect commands are expressed by *Que* ("Let") and the third person singular and plural present subjunctive:

Que prepare Elena el postre.	Let Elena prepare the dessert.
Que hablen (ellos).	Let them speak.
Que no lo vean.	Let them not see it.
Que se acueste temprano.	Let him go to bed early.

There are two ways to express "Let us" or "Let's":

- Use *vamos a* + infinitive (or noun) in the affirmative or *no vayamos a* + infinitive (or noun) in the negative:

Vamos a jugar a la pelota.	Let's play ball.
Vamos al banco.	Let's go to the bank.
No vayamos a sentarnos.	Let's not sit down.
No vayamos al cine.	Let's not go to the movies.

- Use the *nosotros* form of the subjunctive:

Comamos.	Let's eat.
Bebamos.	Let's drink.

OBJECT PRONOUNS WITH COMMANDS

Direct object, indirect object, and reflexive pronouns are attached to the verb in an affirmative command and precede the verb in a negative command:

Léelo.	Read it.
No lo leas.	Don't read it.
Pídale su número de teléfono.	Ask her for her phone number.

No le pida su dirección.	Don't ask her for her address.
Siéntense.	Sit down.
No se sienten.	Don't sit down.

Reflexive "Let's"

With a reflexive verb, the affirmative "Let's" is expressed by dropping the final *-s* of the *nosotros* ending before adding the reflexive pronoun [*see* Position of Reflexive Pronouns *in Part XIII*]:

Levantémonos.	Let's get up.
No nos levantemos.	Let's not get up.

With a reflexive verb, the affirmative *vosotros* command drops the final *-d* before adding the reflexive pronouns [*see* Position of Reflexive Pronouns *in Part XIII*]. When *-os* is added to an *-ir* reflexive verb [*see* Position of Reflexive Pronouns *in Part XIII*], an accent is added before the *-os* ending:

Sentaos.	Sit.
No os sentáis.	Don't sit.
Desvestíos.	Undress.
No os desvistáis.	Don't undress.

With indirect commands, any object pronoun always precedes the verb:

Que lo haga Jorge.	Let Jorge do it.
Que no lo haga Jorge.	Let Jorge not do it.
Que me hablen ellos.	Let them speak to me.
Que no me hablen ellos.	Let them not speak to me.
Que se sienten aquí.	Let them sit here.
Que no se sienten aquí.	Let them not sit here.

Accents

In an affirmative command, when one pronoun is attached to the conjugated verb form, count back three vowels from the end and add an accent:

Póngase (Ud.) un abrigo.	Put on an overcoat.
¡Dígannos (Uds.) la verdad!	Tell us the truth!

This is done to maintain correct stress and pronunciation.

If the command form has only one syllable, no accent is needed:

Ponlo en la mesa.	Put it on the table.
Dime tu dirección.	Give me your address.

Note that two vowels that are pronounced as one sound (diphthongs) generally count as one vowel, and the accent is placed on the second vowel in the diphthong. For instance, in the following example, the accent is placed on the *e* of the *ie* diphthong:

Siéntese.	Sit.

An exception to this rule occurs with the command form of the verb *traer* ("to bring"):

Tráiganlo.	Bring it.

When two pronouns are attached to one another, count back four vowels from the end and add an accent:

Dígamelo.	Tell it to me.
Muéstrenoslos.	Show them to us.

Again, note the exception with the verb *traer* ("to bring"):

Tráiganoslos.	Bring them to us.

PART IX

INFINITIVES

Using Infinitives

The *infinitive* is the form of the verb before it is conjugated and that expresses "to" + an action. An infinitive may be used as a noun and, less frequently, as an adjective.

INFINITIVES AS NOUNS

In Spanish, an infinitive may be used as the subject of a sentence, as the object of a verb, as a predicate noun, or as the object of a preposition.

The Infinitive as the Subject

An infinitive is used as the subject of a sentence where English uses a gerund:

Estudiar no es muy divertido.	Studying isn't a lot of fun.
Fumar es peligroso.	Smoking is dangerous.

The use of the definite article *el* before the infinitive is optional:

(La) Avaricia es un vicio.	Greed is a vice.
(El) Trabajar es necesario.	Working is necessary.

Negating an Infinitive

An infinitive is negated by placing *no* before it and any other negative words after it:

Es importante no olvidar esa fecha.	It is important not to forget that date.
Ella decide no cocinar nada.	She decides not to cook anything.

The Infinitive as the Object of a Verb

An infinitive may be used as the direct object of a verb:

Quiero ir a la fiesta.	I want to go to the party.
Espera recibir el premio.	She hopes to receive the prize.

Verbs that are followed directly by an infinitive used as an object are shown in the following table:

Verbs Followed Directly by an Infinitive

Verb	English
conseguir	to succeed in, to manage to
creer	to think, to believe
deber	should, ought to
decidir	to decide
dejar	to let, to allow
desear	to want, to wish
esperar	to hope, to expect, to wait
hacer	to make
impedir	to impede, to prevent from
intentar	to try to
lograr	to succeed in
mandar	to order
merecer	to deserve, to merit
necesitar	to need, to have to
oír	to hear
olvidar	to forget
parecer	to seem
pensar	to intend
permitir	to permit
poder	to be able to, can
preferir	to prefer

Verb	English
pretender	to attempt
procurar	to try to
prohibir	to prohibit
prometer	to promise
querer	to want
recordar	to remember
saber	to know how to
sentir	to regret, to be sorry
soler	to be used to, to be accustomed to
temer	to fear
ver	to see

Examples:

> *Ella piensa hacer un viaje.* — She intends to take a trip.
> *Yo prefiero quedarme en casa.* — I prefer to stay home.
> *Nosotros no sabemos esquíar.* — We don't know how to ski.

The Infinitive as a Predicate Noun

A *predicate noun* is a word or group of words used to complete the sense of the subject—it refers back to and modifies the subject:

> *Su problema era decirle la verdad.* — Her problem was to tell him the truth.
> *Mi sueño es llegar a ser médico.* — My dream is to become a doctor.

The Infinitive as the Object of a Preposition

An infinitive may be used as the object of the following prepositions:

- *a* ("to," "at"):

  > *Vamos a bailar.* — Let's go dancing.

- *al* ("upon"):

  > *Al llegar a casa, leí mi correo electrónico.* — Upon arriving home, I read my e-mail.

- *antes de* ("before"):

  > *Te llamo antes de venir.* — I'll call you before coming.

- *con* ("with," "to," "of," "by"):

No gana nada con mentir.	You gain nothing by lying.

- *de* ("of," "to"):

Tengo ganas de divertirme.	I feel like having a good time.

- *después de* ("after"):

Fui a casa después de ir al mercado.	I went home after going to the market.

- *en* ("in," "on," "of"):

Insistía en tomar el tren.	He insisted on taking the train.

- *en lugar de* ("instead of") and *en vez de* ("instead of"):

Mira la televisión en vez de estudiar.	He watches television instead of studying.
Nos quedamos en casa en lugar de salir.	We stay home instead of going out.

- *hasta* ("until"):

Ella trabajó hasta dormirse.	She worked until falling asleep.

- *para* ("for," "in order to"):

Va a la tienda para comprar un regalo.	She goes to the store to buy a gift.

- *sin* ("without"):

Ellos salieron sin decir nada.	They went out without saying a word.

Certain verbs in Spanish require the preposition *a, de, en,* or *con* before an infinitive, as shown in the following tables:

Verbs That Require *a* Before the Infinitive

Verb	English
acercarse	to approach
acostumbrarse	to become accustomed
animar	to encourage
aprender	to learn
apresurarse	to hurry

Verb	English
aspirar	to aspire
atreverse	to dare
ayudar	to help
comenzar	to begin
convidar	to invite
correr	to run
decidirse	to decide
dedicarse	to devote oneself
disponerse	to get ready
echarse	to lie down, to move aside
empezar	to begin
enseñar	to teach
invitar	to invite
ir	to go
llegar	to succeed in
negarse	to refuse
obligar	to force
oponerse	to oppose
ponerse	to begin
prepararse	to prepare oneself
principiar	to begin
regresar	to return
resignarse	to resign oneself
salir	to go out
venir	to come
volver	to do something (again)

Examples:

La madre le enseña a su hija a nadar.	The mother teaches her daughter to swim.
Vamos a reunirnos a las seis.	We are going to meet at six o'clock.
Ellos se preparan a ir al baile.	They prepare themselves to go to the dance.

Verbs That Require *de* Before the Infinitive

Verb	English
acabar	to have just
acordarse	to remember to
alegrarse	to be glad
arrepentirse	to regret
cansarse	to tire
cesar	to stop
dejar	to stop
disfrutar	to enjoy
encargarse	to take charge of
gozar	to enjoy
ocuparse	to deal with
olvidarse	to forget
terminar	to stop
tratar de	to try to

Examples:

Acabo de telefonearte. — I just called you.
Ellos no dejaron de reír. — They didn't stop laughing.
Ella terminó de escribir la composición. — She finished writing the composition.

Verbs That Require *en* Before the Infinitive

Verb	English
consentir	to consent to
consistir	to consist of
convenir	to agree to
empeñarse	to insist on
insistir	to insist on
pensar	to think (to reflect)
tardar	to delay in

Examples:

¿Consentirías en acompañarme al centro?	Would you agree to accompany me to the city?
Se empeñó en comprar esta falda roja.	She insisted on buying that red skirt.
¿En qué piensas?	What are you thinking about?

Verbs That Require *con* Before the Infinitive

Verb	English
amenazar	to threaten
conformarse	to be satisfied with
contar	to count on
soñar	to dream of

Examples:

Ellos amenazaron con no pagar la factura.	They threatened not to pay the bill.
El equipo cuenta con ganar el campeonato.	The team counts on winning the championship.
Ella sueña con ir a la fiesta.	She dreams about going to the party.

Using Infinitives and the Subjunctive Correctly

In the construction verb + preposition + infinitive, there are generally two clauses, each containing the same subject. If, however, there are two clauses with two different subjects, *que* is required after the preposition, and the subjunctive is used instead of the infinitive:

Consiente en vernos.	He agrees to see us.
Consiente en que nosotros lo veamos.	He agrees that we can see him.
Ella fue al banco antes de ir al supermercado.	She went to the bank before going to the supermarket.
Ella fue al banco antes de que su esposo fuera al supermercado.	She went to the bank before her husband went to the supermarket.

INFINITIVES AS ADJECTIVES

An infinitive can be used as an adjective when it is used to modify a noun:

> *Tengo mucho trabajo que hacer.*   I have a lot of work to do.

In this example, the infinitive *hacer* ("to do") is describing the noun *trabajo* ("work").

Derivations from Infinitives

Some nouns or adjectives are derived from infinitives.

NOUNS DERIVED FROM INFINITIVES

Several categories of noun endings are derived from infinitives.

Nouns from Verb Stems + -*o* or -*a*

Some *-ar* infinitives drop their ending and add *-o* or *-a* to form nouns, as shown in the following table:

Nouns from Stem + -*o* or -*a*

Infinitive	English	Noun	English
abusar	to abuse	*el abuso*	abuse
acentuar	to accentuate	*el acento*	accent
ayudar	to help	*la ayuda*	help
bañar	to bathe	*el baño*	bathroom
besar	to kiss	*el beso*	kiss
caminar	to walk	*el camino*	path
causar	to cause	*la causa*	cause
dañar	to harm	*el daño*	harm
descansar	to rest	*el descanso*	rest
faltar	to lack	*la falta*	mistake

Examples:

Necesito ayuda.	I need help.
Dame un beso.	Give me a kiss.
Haces una falta.	You are making a mistake.

Nouns That End in *-ción*

Some *-ar* infinitives drop their final *-r* and add *-ción* to form nouns, as shown in the following table:

Nouns That End in *-ción*

Infinitive	English	Noun	English
afirmar	to affirm	la afirmación	affirmation
alimentar	to feed	la alimentación	feeding
animar	to animate	la animación	animation
circular	to circulate	la circulacíon	circulation, traffic
combinar	to combine	la combinación	combination
declarar	to declare	la declaración	declaration
destinar	to destine	la destinación	destination
fascinar	to fascinate	la fascinación	fascination
limitar	to limit	la limitación	limitation
reconciliar	to reconcile	la reconciliación	reconciliation

Examples:

Hablaban con animación.	They were speaking with animation.
Hay mucha circulación.	There's a lot of traffic.
Miran el espectáculo con fascinación.	They watch the spectacle with fascination.

Nouns That End in *-miento*

Some *-ar*, *-er*, and *-ir* infinitives drop their final *-r* and add *-miento* to form nouns, as shown in the following table:

Nouns That End in *-miento*

Infinitive	English	Noun	English
acercar	to approach	el acercamiento	approach
alojar	to accommodate	el alojamiento	accommodation
compartir	to share	el compartimiento	compartment

(continues)

Nouns That End in -*miento (continued)*

Infinitive	English	Noun	English
comportar	to behave	el comportamiento	behavior
embotellar	to bottle	el embotellamiento	traffic jam
enfrentar	to set against	el enfrentamiento	confrontation
enterrar	to bury	el enterramiento	burial
equipar	to equip	el equipamiento	equipment
mover	to move	el movimiento	movement (motion)
sufrir	to suffer	el sufrimiento	suffering

Examples:

Les dieron alojamiento.	They put them up (gave them accommodations).
Su comportamiento me sorprende.	His behavior surprises me.
El mecáncio puso en movimiento el motor.	The mechanic put the motor in motion.

Verbs That End in -*cer*

Verbs that end in -*cer* and the verb *mover* change the final -*e* from the infinitive ending to -*i* before adding -*miento*:

Verb	English	Noun	English
conocer	to know	el conocimiento	acquaintance
crecer	to grow	el crecimiento	growth
establecer	to establish	el establecimiento	establishment

Nouns That End in -*encia*

Some -*ar,* -*er,* and -*ir* infinitives drop their ending and add -*encia* to form nouns, as shown in the following table (note that *c* is followed by *i* and that *t* becomes *c* where necessary to maintain the proper sound):

Nouns That End in *-encia*

Infinitive	English	Noun	English
coexistir	to coexist	la coexistencia	coexistence
coincidir	to coincide	la coincidencia	coincidence
competer	to compete	la competencia	competence
complacer	to please	la complaciencia	pleasure
corresponder	to correspond	la correspondencia	correspondence
depender	to depend	la dependencia	dependence
impacientar	to grow impatient	la impaciencia	impatience
inferir	to infer	la inferencia	inference
subsistir	to subsist	la subsistencia	subsistence
sugerir	to suggest	la sugerencia	suggestion

Examples:

No dudo su competencia.	I don't doubt your competence.
Habla con impaciencia.	He speaks impatiently.
No nos gustan sus sugerencias.	We don't like their suggestions.

Nouns That End in *-ante* or *-iente*

Some *-ar*, *-er*, and *-ir* infinitives drop their ending and add *-ante* (for *-ar* verbs) or *-iente* (for *-er* and *-ir* verbs) to form nouns that express "one who," as shown in the following table:

Nouns That End in *-ante* or *-iente*

Infinitive	English	Noun	English
caminar	to walk	caminante	one who walks
corresponder	to correspond	correspondiente	one who corresponds
demandar	to demand	demandante	one who demands (plaintiff)
expedir	to expedite	expediente	one who expedites
gobernar	to govern	gobernante	one who governs
habitar	to live	habitante	one who lives
ignorar	to ignore	ignorante	one who ignores

(continues)

Nouns That End in *-ante or -iente (continued)*

Infinitive	English	Noun	English
participar	to participate	*participante*	one who participates
remitir	to remit	*remitiente*	one who remits
simpatizar	to get along	*simpatizante*	one who sympathizes

Examples:

Escriba a su correspondiente.	He writes to his correspondent (pen pal).
Es un ignorante.	He is an ignorant person.
Somos participantes en el concurso.	We are participants in the contest.

ADJECTIVES DERIVED FROM INFINITIVES

Some *-ar, -er,* and *-ir* infinitives drop their ending and add *-able* (for *-ar* verbs) or *-ible* (for *-er* and *-ir* verbs) to form adjectives, as shown in the following table:

Adjectives That End in *-able or -ible*

Infinitive	English	Adjective	English
convertir	to convert	*convertible*	convertible
creer	to believe	*creíble*	credible
dirigir	to direct	*dirigible*	steerable
imaginar	to imagine	*imaginable*	imaginable
lavar	to wash	*lavable*	washable
notar	to note	*notable*	notable
preferir	to prefer	*preferible*	preferable
razonar	to reason	*razonable*	reasonable
recomendar	to recommend	*recomendable*	advisable
tolerar	to tolerate	*tolerable*	tolerable

Examples:

No es creíble.	It is not believable.
Esta camisa es lavable.	That shirt can be washed (is washable).
No eres razonable.	You aren't reasonable.

The Perfect Infinitive

The *perfect infinitive* is formed by taking the infinitive of the auxiliary verb, *haber* ("to have"), and the past participle of the verb denoting the action [*see* The Past Participle *in Part VI*]:

Recibí una multa por haber conducido muy rápidamente.	I received a ticket for having driven very fast.
Esa mujer fue conocida por haber escrito novelas.	That woman was well known for having written novels.
Ella se cayó por no haber puesto atención.	She fell for not having paid attention.

PART X

PREPOSITIONS AND CONJUNCTIONS

Prepositions

Prepositions are invariable words or phrases that join words or elements in a sentence, thereby creating a relationship between them. Prepositions establish the following links:

- Noun to noun:

    Tiene un dolor de cabeza.   He has a headache.

- Verb to verb:

    Empieza a tocar el piano.   She begins to play the piano.

- Verb to noun:

    Caminamos por el parque.   We walk through the park.

- Verb to pronoun:

    ¿Por qué hablas contra ella?   Why do you speak against her?

COMMON PREPOSITIONS

Some high-frequency Spanish prepositions and prepositional phrases include those in the following table:

Common Prepositions

Spanish	English
a	to, at
a eso de (+ time)	about (time)
a fuerza de	by perservering
a pesar de	in spite of
a tiempo	on time

(continues)

Common Prepositions *(continued)*

Spanish	English
a través de	across, through
acerca de	about
además de	besides
alrededor de	around
ante	before, in the presence of
antes (de)	before
cerca de	near
con	with
contra	against
de	of
de hoy en adelante	from now on
de otro modo	otherwise
debajo de	beneath, under
delante de	in front of
dentro de	inside, within
desde	since
después (de)	after
detrás de	behind
durante	during
en	in, by, on, at
en cambio	on the other hand
en casa de	at the house of
en lugar de	instead of
en vez de	instead of
encima de	above, on top of
enfrente de	opposite, in front of
entre	between
frente a	in front of
fuera de	outside of
hacia	toward

Spanish	English
hasta	until
lejos de	far
por	for, by
para	for
según	according to
sin	without
sobre	over, above, on, upon
tras	after

Examples:

Tu paraguas está debajo de la mesa.	Your umbrella is under the table.
El cine está enfrente del banco.	The movie theater is in front of the bank.
El agente corrió tras el ladrón.	The agent ran after the thief.

Contractions

The prepositions *a* ("to," "at") and *de* ("of," "from," "about") contract with the masculine, singular definite article, *el,* to become *al* ("to the") and *del* ("of the," "from the," "about the"), respectively:

Voy al gimnasio.	I'm going to the gym.
Sale del suprmercado.	He leaves the supermarket.

USES OF CERTAIN PREPOSITIONS

Different prepositions may have similar meanings but different uses. A complete understanding of when to use a preposition helps to distinguish when and why a certain preposition is called for rather than another.

A

The preposition *a* (which contracts with the masculine singular definite article, *el,* to become *al*) shows the following:

- A person that is the direct object of the sentence:

    No busco a Carlos.   I'm not looking for Carlos.

- Challenge:

  A que no sabe cuando he llegado. I bet you don't know when I arrived.

- Condition:

  A ser esto el problema, yo lo If that were the problem, I'd solve it.
  resolveré.

- The imperative:

  ¡A comenzar! Let's begin!

- Location:

  Ella está a la entrada de la oficina. She is at the entrance to the office.

- Means or manner:

  Lave Ud. esta camisa a mano. Wash this shirt by hand.
  Se vistió a la americana. He dressed like an American.

- Movement:

  Vamos a Madrid. We are going to Madrid.

- Quantity, price, or speed:

  Obtuve una hipoteca al seis I got a mortgage at six percent
  por ciento. (interest).
  Compré los huevos a quinientos I bought the eggs at five hundred
  pesetas la docena. pesetas per dozen.
  Condujo a sesenta kilómetros He was driving at sixty kilometers
  por hora. per hour.

- Time:

  Vamos a cenar a las seis. We're going to eat dinner at
  six o'clock.

The Personal *A*

The personal *a*, which has no English equivalent, is used before the direct object of a verb to indicate that the direct object is one of the following:

- A person:

  Yo veo a Jorge. I see George.

- A pronoun referring to a person:

  No busco a nadie. I'm not looking for anyone.

- A pet:

  Ella está mirando a su gato. She is looking at her cat.

- A geographic name that is not preceded by a definite article (although current usage tends to omit the personal *a* in this case):

  Queremos ver (a) Costa Rica. We want to see Costa Rica.
  Queremos ver el Perú. We want to see Peru.

De

The preposition *de* (which contracts with the masculine, singular definite article, *el,* to become *del*) shows the following:

- Possession:

  Es la revista de Gloria. It's Gloria's magazine.

- Relation:

  Nos paseamos por las calles We went for a walk on the streets
  de Madrid. of Madrid.

- A characteristic:

  Compré un anillo de oro. I bought a gold ring.

- Contents:

  Bebí una taza de té. I drank a cup of tea.

- Origin:

  Somos de los Estados Unidos. We're from the United States.

- Cause:

  Me enfermé de no haber llevado I got sick from not wearing a hat.
  un sombrero.

- Subject or theme:

  Necesito un libro de física. I need a book about physics.
  Hablaban de ella. They were speaking about her.

- Use:

  Le falta una hoja de afeitar. He needs a razor blade.

- Measurement or quantity:

  Hacemos un viaje de un mes. We are taking a one month's vacation.
  Ella salió con un hombre She went out with a fifty-year-old
  de cincuenta años. man.

- Times and dates:

  Nos vamos a las seis de la mañana.   We are leaving at six in the morning.
  Es el dos de febrero.   It is February second.

- Time of day:

  Él trabaja de noche.   He works at night.

- Part of a whole:

  Ellos tomaron un trozo de pastel.   They took a piece of cake.

- A comparison:

  Ese libro era más interesante   That book was more interesting
  de lo que pensaba.   than I thought.

- A superlative:

  Nilsa es la más alta de la clase.   Nilsa is the tallest in the class.

- Means:

  Se casó con ella en un latido del   He married her in a heartbeat.
  corazón.

En

The preposition *en* shows the following:

- Location:

  La escuela está en la Avenida Sexta.   The school is on Sixth Avenue.

- Movement:

  Entramos en el banco.   We entered the bank.

- Means or manner:

  Hable Ud. en voz baja.   Speak in a low voice.
  El artículo está escrito   The article is written in Spanish.
  en español.

- Proportion:

  Los impuestos han bajados en un   The taxes have decreased by two
  dos por ciento.   percent.

- Time and dates:

  Estamos en la primavera.   It's (We are in) spring.
  Estamos en dos mil cinco.   It's (We are in) 2005.

- Subject and occupation:

    Ella es experta en español. She is an expert in Spanish.
    Trabajé en la medicina. I worked in the medical field.

- Means of transportation:

    Vamos a España en avión. We are going to Spain by plane.

Hasta

The preposition *hasta* shows the following:

- Place or location:

    Caminamos hasta la primera calle. We walked to the first street.

- Time:

    No voy a regresar hasta la I am not going to return until
    medianoche. midnight.

- Quantities:

    Trabaja hasta doce horas diarias. He works up to twelve hours a day.

- Farewells:

    Hasta mañana. See you tomorrow.

Para

Because *para* and *por* both express "for," it is essential to learn the uses of each. *Para* shows the following:

- Destination (place) or direction:

    Iré para la casa. I will head for home.

- Destination (recipient):

    Este regalo es para ti. This gift is for you.

- A time in the future:

    Te querré para siempre. I will love you forever.

- A purpose or a goal:

    Trabajo para ganar dinero. I work to earn money.

- The use or function of an object:

    Ella toma pastillas para dormir. She takes pills to sleep.

- Comparisons that qualify:

  Para una americana, habla muy bien el español.

  For an American, she speaks Spanish very well.

- Opinion:

  Para mí, este coche cuesta demasiado.

  To me, this car costs too much.

Por

Por shows the following:

- Motion:

  Ellos caminaron por el bosque.

  They walked through the woods.

- Means or manner:

  Voy a enviar este paquete por correo aéreo.

  I am going to send this package by airmail.

- Substitution or "in exchange for":

  Yo fui al supermercado por mi madre.

  I went to the supermarket for my mother.

- The duration of an action:

  Dormí por ocho horas.

  I slept for eight hours.

- An indefinite period of time:

  Estudiaremos por la noche.

  We will study at night.

- Place:

  Iban bailando por las calles.

  They went dancing in the streets.

- Approximation:

  Su libro está por aquí.

  Your book is somewhere around here.

- "On behalf of" or "for the sake of":

  Lo hablaré por Ud.

  I will speak to him on your behalf (for your sake).

- Choice:

  Ella tiene un gusto por el arte.   She has a taste for art.

- Representation:

  Hablo por todos mis amigos.   I speak for all my friends.

- A reason:

  Por no dormir, se pusó enfermo.   Because he didn't sleep, he became ill.

- Multiplication:

  Dos por dos son cuatro.   Two times two is four.

- "By the" or "per":

  Ganará mucho por hora.   He will earn a lot per hour.
  Lo pagaron por hora.   They will pay him by the hour.
  Las rosas cuestan treinta   The roses cost thirty dollars per dozen.
    dólares por docena.

- An incomplete action followed by an infinitive:

  Hay tres camas por hacer.   There are three beds to make.
  Por aburrido que sea,   However boring it may be, read this
    lea ese libro.   book.

- Estimation or opinion (equivalent to "for" or "as"):

  La tomamos por la maestra.   We took her for the teacher.
  Se le conoce por Anita.   She is known as Anita.

- The agent in a passive construction [*see* The Passive Voice with *Ser in Part XV*]:

  El libro fue escrito por su madre.   The book was written by his mother.

- "For" after the verbs *enviar* ("to send"), *ir* ("to go"), *mandar* ("to order," "to send"), *preguntar* ("to ask"), *regresar* ("to return"), *venir* ("to come"), and *volver* ("to return"):

  Fue (envió, preguntó) por un   He went for (sent for, asked for) a
    abogado.   lawyer.
  Vine (regresé, volví) por   She came (returned, came back) for
    su cheque.   her check.

Adverbial Expressions

Por is also used in common adverbial expressions:

Spanish	English
por eso	therefore, so
por lo común	generally
por lo general	generally
por lo visto	apparently
por supuesto	of course

Examples:

Ricardo no estudió y por eso no salió bien en su examen.	Richard didn't study and, therefore, he didn't do well on his test.
¿Te gusta el chocolate? ¡Por supuesto!	Do you like chocolate? Of course!

COMMON EXPRESSIONS WITH PREPOSITIONS

Some common, high-frequency Spanish expressions contain prepositions:

- *A causa de* ("because of"):

No leyó a causa de su dolor de cabeza.	He didn't read because of his headache.

- *A eso de* ("about" + time):

Llegarán a eso de las dos.	They will arrive at about two o'clock.

- *A fines de* ("at the end of"):

Sus cursos empiezan a fines de verano.	His courses start at the end of summer.

- *A fuerza de* ("by dint of [by persevering]"):

A fuerza de trabajar duro, ganó mucho.	By working a lot, she earned a lot.

- *A la derecha (de)* ("on [to] the right [of]"):

La muchacha se sienta a la derecha de su madre.	The girl sits on her mother's right.

- *A la izquierda (de)* ("on [to] the left [of]"):

¿Dónde están los baños? A la izquierda.	Where are the bathrooms? On the left.

- *A principios de* ("at the beginning of"):

  > *Iré en Europa a principios
  > de mayo.*

  I will go to Europe at the beginning
  of May.

- *A tiempo* ("on time"):

  > *Siempre llego a tiempo.*

  I always arrive on time.

- *Al aire libre* ("in the open air"):

  > *Durmieron al aire libre.*

  They slept in the open air.

- *De hoy en adelante* ("from today on"):

  > *De hoy en adelante no
  > comeré dulces.*

  From today on I won't eat sweets.

- *De otro modo* ("otherwise"):

  > *Los alumnos escuchan de otro
  > modo no saldrán bien.*

  The students listen; otherwise, they
  will not do well.

- *De vez en cuando* ("from time to time"):

  > *Voy al cine de vez en cuando.*

  I go to the movies from time to time.

- *En cambio* ("on the other hand"):

  > *Podríamos ir al parque; en cambio,
  > podríamos ir al cine.*

  We could go to the park; on the
  other hand, we could see a movie.

- *En efecto* ("in fact"):

  > *En efecto, me gusta mucho esquíar.*

  In fact, I like to ski a lot.

- *En la esquina de* ("on the corner of"):

  > *La farmacia está en la esquina de
  > la Avenida Quinta y la Calle Cruz.*

  The drug store is on the corner of
  Fifth Avenue and Cruz Street.

- *En vez de* ("instead of"):

  > *Ella duerme en vez de limpiar la casa.*

  She sleeps instead of cleaning
  the house.

Prepositional Pronouns

Prepositions may be followed by prepositional pronouns [*see* Prepositional Pronouns in *Part II*]:

> *Pienso en ti.*

I'm thinking about you.

> *No quieren salir sin mí.*

They don't want to leave without me.

> *¿Quieres ir al cine conmigo?*

Do you want to go to the movies with me?

Conjunctions

A *conjunction* is a word whose function is to connect words, phrases, or clauses. There are two kinds of conjunctions: coordinating conjunctions and subordinating conjunctions.

COORDINATING CONJUNCTIONS

Coordinating conjunctions connect words, phrases, and clauses that are of equal rank: two nouns, two infinitives, or two main clauses. In Spanish these conjunctions are *y* ("and"), *o* ("or"), *ni* ("neither"), *pero* ("but"), *sino* ("but"), and *que* ("that").

Y

The high-frequency conjunction *y* means "and." *Y* changes to *e* when the word that follows begins with *i-* or *hi-*:

Mi amiga y yo vamos a tomar el almuerzo juntas.	My friend and I are going to have lunch together.
Carlota e Inés son mejores amigas.	Carlota and Inés are best friends.
Los López viajan con sus hijos e hijas.	The Lópezes travel with their sons and daughters.

O

O is used to express "or." *O* changes to *u* when the word that follows begins with *o-* or *ho-*:

¿Quién habla, Susana o Julia?	Who is speaking, Susana or Julia?
Uno u otro me ayudará.	One or the other will help me.
No sé si el ladrón fue mujer u hombre.	I don't know if the thief was a man or a woman.

Ni

Ni can express "neither" or "nor":

No habla ni español ni francés.	He speaks neither Spanish nor French.

Pero

Pero expresses "but" in a general sense or "however":

Me gusta la vainilla pero prefiero el chocolate.	I like vanilla, but (however) I prefer chocolate.
Ella tiene mucha suerte pero no es feliz.	She is very lucky, but (however) she isn't happy.

Sino

Sino expresses "but" in a negative statement to show contradiction:

No bebo café sino té.	I don't drink coffee, but I drink tea.

Pero vs. Sino

Both *pero* and *sino* express "but." However, *pero* is used in a more general sense and can also express "however," and *sino* is used only in a negative statement to show contrast, meaning "on the contrary" or "but rather":

Me gustan todas las frutas, pero prefiero las fresas.	I like all fruits, but (however) I prefer strawberries.
No me gustan las naranjas sino las manzanas.	I don't like oranges, but (rather) I like apples.
No hablo ruso sino español.	I don't speak Russian but (rather) Spanish.

Que

The conjunction *que* expresses "that":

Escribió que no podría venir.	He wrote that he couldn't come.

SUBORDINATING CONJUNCTIONS

Subordinating conjunctions connect subordinate clauses with main clauses. In Spanish these conjunctions are *apenas* ("as soon as"); *así pues* and *luego que* ("so"); *así que, de modo que,* and *de manera que* ("so that"); *aunque* ("although"); *como* ("like," "since," "as"); *conque* ("so," "so . . . then"); *cuando* ("when"); *luego* ("therefore"); *mientras* ("while"); *porque* ("because"); *pues* ("then"); *puesto que* ("since," "as"); *si* ("if"); and *ya que* ("since"). Some coordinating conjunctions in Spanish require the subjunctive if doubt, uncertainty, anticipation, or indefiniteness is implied.

Apenas

Apenas means "as soon as" and takes the indicative:

Apenas salí, el teléfono sonó.	As soon as I went out, the telephone rang.

Así Pues, Luego Que

Así pues and *luego que* mean "so." They take the indicative for present and past actions, and they take the subjunctive for future actions:

Tengo que ir al centro, así pues (luego que), decide si quieres acompañarme.	I have to go to the city, so decide if you want to go with me.
Recibieron una herencia, así pues (luego que) hagan un viaje.	They received an inheritance, so they will take a trip.

Así Que, De Modo Que, De Manera Que

Así que, de modo que, and *de manera que* mean "so (that)." They take the indicative for present and past actions, and they take the subjunctive for future actions:

No llevó su abrigo así que ahora está enfermo.	He didn't wear his coat, so now he is sick.
Hablaré despacio de modo que (de manera que) puedas comprenderme.	I will speak slowly so that you can understand me.

Aunque

Aunque means "although." It takes the indicative for present and past actions, and it takes the subjunctive for future actions:

Aunque es español, habla muy bien el inglés.	Although he is Spanish, he speaks English well.
Yo lo haré aunque no me guste.	I will do it although I won't like it.

Como

Como means "like," "as," or "since" and takes the indicative:

Como todavía no han llegado, no podemos comenzar la conferencia.	Since they haven't arrived yet, we can't begin the conference.

Conque

Conque means "so" and takes the indicative:

> *Conque ¿lo harás o no lo harás?*   So, will you do it or not?

Cuando

Cuando means "when." It takes the indicative for present and past actions, and it takes the subjunctive for future actions:

> *Ella preparó la cena cuando*   She prepared dinner when she arrived home.
> *llegó a casa.*
> *Te ayudaré con tus tareas*   I'll help you with your homework when I
> *cuando regrese.*   return.

Luego

Luego means "therefore" and is followed by the indicative:

> *Pienso, luego existo.*   I think, therefore I am.

Mientras

Mientras means "while." It takes the indicative for present and past actions, and it takes the subjunctive for future actions:

> *Él dormía mientras el profesor*   He was sleeping while the teacher was
> *hablaba.*   speaking.
> *Yo trabajaré mientras yo pueda.*   I will work while (for as long as) I can.

Porque

Porque means "because" and takes the indicative:

> *No salí porque estaba cansada.*   I didn't go out because I was tired.

Pues

Pues means "then" and takes the indicative:

> *¿No te gustan películas de ciencia* You don't like science fiction movies?
> *ficción? Pues, mira una comedia.*   Then watch a comedy.

Puesto Que

Puesto que means "since" or "as" and takes the indicative:

> *No te hablaré puesto que*   I won't talk to you since you are busy.
> *estás ocupado.*

Si

Si means "if" and follows the rules for conditional sentences [*see* Conditional Sentences *in Part VII*]:

> *Si hace mal tiempo me quedaré en casa.*   If the weather is bad, I will stay home.

Ya Que

Ya que means "since" and takes the indicative:

> *Ya que está nevando, no tomo el coche.*   Since it's snowing, I'm not taking the car.

CONJUNCTIVE EXPRESSIONS

A *conjunctive expression* is a group of words used together in a sentence to act as a conjunction. The following are some conjunctive expressions in Spanish:

- *A pesar de* ("in spite of"):

  > *A pesar de todo, lo quiero mucho.*   In spite of everything, I love him a lot.

- *Con todo* ("in spite of"):

  > *Con todo (y con eso), me divertí a la fiesta.*   In spite of everything, I had fun at the party.

- *Excepto que* ("except that"):

  > *Acepto todo excepto que me digas mentiras.*   I accept everything except that you lie to me.

- *Fuera de* ("aside from"):

  > *Fuera de eso, yo no tenía ningunos problemas.*   Aside from that, I didn't have any problems.

- *No obstante* ("however," "nonetheless"):

  > *No tenía mucho dinero, no obstante se compró un coche nuevo.*   He didn't have a lot of money; nonetheless, he bought himself a new car.

- *Por consiguiente* ("consequently," "therefore"):

  > *Tenía que estudiar, por consiguiente no miró la televisión.*   He had to study; consequently, he didn't watch television.

- *Por lo tanto* ("so," "therefore"):

  > *No tenía hambre, por lo tanto no comí nada.*   I wasn't hungry, so I didn't eat anything.

- *Sin embargo* ("however," "nevertheless"):

  > *Estoy cansado, sin embargo continuaré a trabajar.*   I'm tired; however, I'll continue working.

PART XI

INTERROGATIVES AND EXCLAMATIONS

Interrogatives

Interrogatives are used to ask questions. There are two types of questions:

- Those that require a *yes* or *no* answer.
- Those that ask for information.

YES/NO QUESTIONS

Yes/no questions can be asked in four ways:

- **By using intonation:** This is accomplished by raising one's voice at the end of a sentence to which an imaginary question mark has been added. When writing a question, Spanish requires an upside-down question mark at the beginning of the sentence and a regular question mark at the end of the sentence:

¿Tú quieres ir al cine conmigo?	Do you want to go to the movies with me?
¿Ud. no va al centro en tren?	Don't you go to the city by train?

- **By using the tag *¿(no es) verdad?*:** The tag *¿(no es) verdad?* is placed at the end of or after a sentence and can have the following meanings:

  Is(n't) that true (so, right)?
  Is(n't) he/she?
  Are(n't) you/we/they?
  Does(n't) he/she?
  Do(n't) you/we/they?

  Examples:

Él sabe hablar español, ¿no es verdad?	He knows how to speak Spanish, right?
Nosotros cantamos bien, ¿no es verdad?	We sing well, isn't that so (don't we)?

- **By using the tag *¿está bien?*:** The tag *¿está bien?* is placed at the end of or after a sentence and can have the following meanings:

  Is that true all right?
  Is that okay?
  Okay?

  Example:

  Me voy. ¿Está bien?   I'm going. Is that all right? (okay)?

- **By using inversion:** *Inversion* refers to switching the word order of the subject noun or pronoun (when used) and the conjugated verb to form a question:

  Ud. es americano. ¿Es Ud.   You are American. Are you
  americano?   American?
  Linda viene tarde. ¿Viene Linda   Linda is coming late. Is Linda
  tarde?   coming late?
  Uds. se levantaron tarde. ¿Se   You got up late. Did you get up
  levantaron Uds. tarde?   late?

  In most cases, the subject pronoun is omitted:

  Necesitas algo. ¿Necesitas algo?   You need something. Do you need
                                                 something?

  When a conjugated verb is followed by an infinitive, the subject noun or pronoun usually follows the infinitive. To negate the question, put *no* before the conjugated verb or before any pronouns that precede the verb:

  Ud. (no) debe trabajar esta noche.   You do(n't) have to work tonight.
  ¿(No) Debe trabajar Ud. esta   Do(n't) you have to work tonight?
  noche?

  Arturo (no) va a patinar ¿(No) Va   Arturo is(n't) going to skate. Is(n't)
  a patinar Arturo?   Arturo going to skate?
  Ella (no) te habla. ¿No te habla ella? She (doesn't) speak(s) to you.
                                                 Does(n't) she speak to you?

INFORMATION QUESTIONS

Interrogative adjectives, interrogative adverbs, and interrogative pronouns are words that allow you to ask questions when you need information.

Using Interrogative Adjectives

An *interrogative adjective* is a word that asks a question and is followed by a noun. The interrogative adjective *¿qué?* means "what?" or "which?" *¿Qué?* is invariable and precedes a noun whose number is not counted:

¿Qué programa estás mirando?	What program are you watching?
¿Qué libro lees?	Which book are you reading?

Qué may be preceded by a preposition:

¿Para qué sirve este cuchillo?	What is this knife used for?
¿De qué hablan?	What are they speaking about?
¿A qué hora vienen?	At what time are they coming?

The interrogative adjective *¿cuánto?* means "how much/many?" *¿Cuánto?* must agree in number and gender with the noun it modifies, and it precedes a noun that is counted or measured. The following table shows the forms of *¿cuánto?*:

¿Cuánto?

	Singular	Plural
Masculine	*¿cuánto?*	*¿cuántos?*
Feminine	*¿cuánta?*	*¿cuántas?*

Examples:

¿Cuánto tiempo necesitas?	How much time do you need?
¿Cuántos países luchan?	How many countries are fighting?
¿Cuánta nieve cayó?	How much snow fell?
¿Cuántas preguntas tienes?	How many questions do you have?

The forms of *¿cuánto?* may also be preceded by prepositions:

¿Para cuántas personas cocina?	For how many people are you cooking?
¿Con cuánto dinero puedes comprar esta compañía?	With how much money can you buy this company?
¿De cuántos restaurantes hablas?	How many restaurants are you speaking about?

Using Interrogative Adverbs

An *interrogative adverb* is a word that asks a question and is followed by a verb. Interrogative adverbs are most often used with inversion to seek information:

- *¿Cómo?* means "how?":

¿Cómo estás?	How are you?
¿Cómo se escribe su nombre?	How is your name written?

- *¿Cuándo?* means "when?":

¿Cuándo va a llegar Papá Noel?	When is Santa Claus going to come?
¿Cuándo piensas regresar?	When do you intend to return?

- *¿Dónde?* means "where?":

¿Dónde nació Ud.?	Where were you born?
¿Dónde trabajas?	Where do you work?

- *¿Por qué?* means "why?":

¿Por qué lloras?	Why are you crying?
¿Por qué no lo saludó?	Why didn't you greet him?

- *¿Para qué* means "why?" in the sense of "for what purpose or reason?":

¿Para qué necesitas este papel?	Why do you need this paper?
¿Para qué empleas esa máquina?	Why do you use that machine?

Interrogative adverbs can be preceded by prepositions, where they make sense:

¿Adónde (A dónde) va Ud.?	Where are you going?
¿De dónde vienen?	Where do they come from?
¿Por dónde caminan?	Where do they walk?
¿Hasta cuándo trabaja?	Until when do you work?
¿Para cuándo necesita ese libro?	For when do you need this book?

¿*Por Qué?* vs. ¿*Para Qué?*

¿Por qué? asks for a reason and requires an answer with *porque* ("because"):

¿Por qué no va Jorge a la escuela?	Why isn't Jorge going to school?
Porque está enfermo.	Because he is sick.

¿Para qué? asks about a purpose or a reason and requires an answer with *para* ("for," "to," "in order to"):

¿Para qué necesitas mi pluma?	Why do you need my pen?
Para escribir una nota a mi amiga.	To write a note to my friend.

Using Interrogative Pronouns

An *interrogative pronoun* is a word that asks a question and takes the place of a noun. Interrogative pronouns ask the following questions:

"Who(m)?"
"What?"
"Which one(s)?"
"How much?"
"How many?"

An interrogative pronoun is generally followed by a verb.

The interrogative pronoun *¿quien(es)?* asks "who?" or "whom?" and refers to people. *¿Quien?* agrees in number (singular or plural) with the noun it replaces:

Carlota se cayó. ¿Quién se cayó?	Carlota fell. Who fell?
Luz y Ana fueron a España.	Luz and Ana went to Spain.
¿Quiénes fueron a España?	Who went to Spain?

The interrogative pronoun *¿qué?* asks "what?" and refers to things. *¿Qué?* is invariable:

¿Qué vas a hacer?	What are you going to do?
¿Qué necesita Ud.?	What do you need.

Prepositions + *¿Quién?* and *¿Qué?*

A preposition may precede *¿quién(es)?* and asks "whom?":

¿A quién telefoneaste?	Whom did you call?
¿Con quiénes contaban?	Whom were they counting on?

A preposition may precede *¿qué?* and asks "what?":

¿A qué hora vienen?	At what time are they coming?
¿Con qué escribes?	What are you writing with?

The interrogative pronoun *¿cuál(es)?* asks "which one(s)?" or "what?" *¿Cuál(es)?* agrees in number (singular or plural) with the noun to which it refers. *¿Cuál(es)?* is usually followed by the third person singular or plural of the verb *ser* or by the preposition *de*:

¿Cuál es la fecha de hoy?	What is today's date?
¿Cuáles son los días de la semana?	What are the days of the week?
¿Cuál de los muchachos ganó?	Which one of the boys won?
¿Cuáles de los muchachos ganaron?	Which ones of the boys won?

¿Qué? vs. ¿Cuál(es)?

When it precedes a verb, *¿Qué?* means "what?" and inquires about a definition, a description, an opinion, or an explanation:

¿Qué piensas de mi idea?	What do you think of my idea?

When it precedes a noun, *¿Qué?* means "which?" or "what?":

¿Qué CD estás escuchando?	What (Which) CD are you listening to?

When it is followed by the verb *ser* or by a preposition, *¿Cuál(es)?* means "what?" or "which one?" and inquires about a choice or a selection or is used to distinguish one person or thing from another:

¿Cuál es su número de teléfono?	What is your phone number?
¿Cuáles son los mejores?	Which ones are the best?
¿Cuál de esas muchachas habla español?	Which one of those girls speaks Spanish?
¿Cuáles de esas camisas son más baratas?	Which (ones) of those shirts is less expensive?

The interrogative pronoun *¿cuánto?* asks "how much?" and is invariable. The verb that follows *¿cuánto?* agrees in number with the noun to which *¿cuánto?* refers:

¿Cuánto cuesta ese coche?	How much does that car cost?
¿Cuánto valen esas joyas?	How much are those jewels worth?

The interrogative pronoun *¿cuántos(as)?* asks "how many?" and agrees in gender (masculine or feminine) with the noun to which it refers:

¿Los muchachos? ¿Cuántos participan al concurso?	The boys? How many are participating in the race?
¿Las tazas? ¿Cuántas quedan?	The cups? How many remain?

USING *HAY*

Hay is a very versatile form of the verb *haber* ("to have") and is used in an impersonal manner to ask "Is (Are) there?" and to answer "There is (are)." *Hay* can be used alone to ask a yes/no question or with a preceding question word to get information. When a question contains *hay*, so does its answer:

¿Hay un restaurante español en esta ciudad? Sí, hay un restaurante español allá.	Is there a Spanish restaurant in this city? Yes, there is a Spanish restaurant over there.
¿Qué hay en su bolsillo? No hay nada.	What is (there) in your pocket? There is nothing.
¿Cuántos miembros hay en el club? Hay más o menos veinte miembros.	How many members are there in the club? There are twenty members, more or less.

How to Answer Questions

It is important to know key words and phrases that enable you to answer yes/no and information questions.

ANSWERING YES/NO QUESTIONS

To answer a question "yes," use the word *sí*:

¿Quieres acompañarme al cine? Sí, con mucho gusto.	Do you want to go with me to the movies? Yes, I'd love to.

To answer a question "no," use the word *no* or any of the negative words or expressions *[see* Negative Words *in Part XII]. No* is generally placed before the conjugated verb. When a pronoun precedes the verb, *no* is placed before the pronoun:

¿Quieres acompañarme al cine? No, lo siento mucho. Tengo que estudiar.	Do you want to go with me to the movies? No, I'm very sorry. I have to study.

ANSWERING INFORMATION QUESTIONS

Understanding exactly what information is being requested allows you to answer information questions correctly:

- To answer a question that contains *¿Cuánto(a/os/as)?* ("how much?" or "how many?"), give a quantity or an amount:

  ¿Cuántos alumnos están ausentes?   How many students are absent?
  Cuatro (Muchos) alumnos están   Four (Many) students are absent.
     ausentes.

- To answer a question that contains *¿Qué?* (interrogative adjective; "what?" or "which?") *or ¿Cuál?* ("which one(s)?" or "what?"), you may use the definite article + an appropriate adjective (there must be agreement of gender and number with the noun in question) to express "the . . . one(s)" when speaking about color, size, or nationality:

  ¿Qué vestido prefieres? El rojo.   Which dress do you prefer?
                               The red one.

  ¿Cuál de las camisas vas a comprar? Which one of the shirts are you
     La grande.   going to buy? The big one.
  ¿Cuáles de las muchachas no   Which ones of the girls don't speak
     hablan inglés? Las francesas.   English? The French ones.

- To answer a question that contains *¿Cómo?* ("how?"), give an explanation:

  ¿Cómo viajas? En avión.   How are you traveling? By plane.
  ¿Cómo está Ud.? Muy bien, gracias.   How are you? Very well, thank you.

- To answer a question that contains *¿Cuándo?* ("when?"), give a time:

  ¿Cuándo puede Ud. venir?   When can you come?
  Mañana por la tarde.   Tomorrow afternoon.

- To answer a question that contains *¿Dónde?* ("where?"), give a place or a location:

  ¿Dónde están mis zapatos?   Where are my shoes?
  Debajo de su cama.   Under your bed.

- To answer a question that contains *¿Quién(es)?* ("who(m)?"), give a person:

  ¿Quiénes trabajan hoy?   Who is working today?
  Clara y Manuel trabajan.   Clara and Manuel are working.

- To answer a question that contains *¿Por qué?* ("why?"), answer with *porque* ("because"):

  ¿Por qué no me ayudas?   Why don't you help me?
  Porque estoy cansado.   Because I am tired.

Questions with Prepositions

When a question contains a preposition, that preposition must also be used in the answer:

¿Para quién esperas? Para mis amigos.	For whom are you waiting? For my friends.
¿Adónde vas? Al teatro.	Where are you going? To the theater.
¿Con qué juegan los niños? Con una pelota.	What are the children playing with? With a ball.

Exclamations

Exclamations express sentiments and feelings. In Spanish, an upside-down exclamation point precedes the exclamation, and a regular exclamation point follows the exclamation. Exclamations are expressed as follows:

- *¡Qué!* ("what a!" "how!") expresses a quality:

¡Qué bonita es!	How beautiful she is!
¡Qué sorpresa!	What a surprise!

Adding Emphasis

To make an exclamation even more emphatic, use *más* or *tan* after the noun and before the adjective:

¡Qué muchacha tan (más) bonita!	What a beautiful girl!
¡Qué sorpresa tan interesante!	What an interesting surprise!

- *¡Cuánto(a)!* ("how [much]!") is used in the singular and expresses a quantity or an amount:

¡Cuánto tiempo han gastado!	How much time they wasted!
¡Cuánto me gusta esa casa!	How I like that house!
¡Cuánta habilidad tiene!	How much skill he has!

¡Qué De!

¡Qué de! ("how many!") can be used to express a quantity or an amount and is the equivalent of ¡cuánto!:

¡Qué de hombres van a la guerra!   How many men go to war!

- *¡Cuántos(as)!* ("how many!") is used in the plural and expresses a quantity or an amount:

    ¡Cuántos amigos tiene!   How many friends you have!
    ¡Cuántas camisas compraste!   How many shirts you bought!

- *¡Cómo!* ("how!") expresses means or manner:

    ¡Cómo cantan esos muchachos!   How those boys sing!

- *¡Cuán!* ("how!") is used with adjectives and adverbs in a literary sense:

    ¡Cuán rápido cambian las estaciones! How fast the seasons change!

PART XII

NEGATIVES, INDEFINITES, AND RELATIVE PRONOUNS

Negatives

There are several words in Spanish, in addition to *no*, that express *negative* actions, thoughts, or feelings.

NEGATIVE WORDS

The most common negative words used in Spanish include

- *No* ("no," "not"):

    No comprendo.   I don't understand.

- *Nada* ("nothing"):

    Nada me enfada.   Nothing makes me angry.

- *Nadie* ("nobody," "no one"):

    Nadie te telefoneó.   Nobody called you.

- *Ni . . . ni* ("neither . . . nor"):

    No como ni manzanas ni peras.   I eat neither apples nor pears.

- *Ningún(a/os/as)* ("not any," "none"):

    Ningunos muchachos sabían hacerlo.   None of the boys knew how to do it.

- *Nunca* or *jamás* ("never," "not ever"):

    Nunca fui a España.   I never went to Spain.
    ¿Fumabas?¡Jamás!   Did you used to smoke? Never

- *Tampoco* ("neither," "not either"):

    No voy a leer ese libro.   I'm not going to read that book.
    Tampoco voy a comprarlo.   I'm not going to buy it either.

USING NEGATIVES

The following rules apply when using negatives:

- The adverb *no* is placed before the conjugated verb:

  No quiero levantarme.   I don't want to get up.

- *No* may be repeated for stress or emphasis:

  No, no quiero hacerlo.   No, I don't want to do it.

- If a pronoun precedes the conjugated verb, the negative is placed before the pronoun:

No se quedarán aquí.	They will not stay here.
Nunca te dije eso.	I never said that to you.
Nadie lo ha visto.	Nobody has seen him.

- Spanish allows for double and triple negatives. If one of the negatives is *no*, it is placed before the conjugated verb. If *no* is not used, then the other negative word precedes the verb:

No come nada. or *Nada come.*	He's not eating anything.
No lo encontré tampoco. or *Tampoco no lo encontré.*	I didn't find it either.
No viene nadie. or *Nadie viene.*	Nobody is coming.
No escribió nunca a nadie. or *Nunca escribió a nadie.*	He never wrote to anyone.

Negatives and Prepositions

A negative that is preceded by a preposition must keep that preposition when it is placed before a verb:

No busco a nadie. or *A nadie busco.*	I'm not looking for anyone.
No hablaban de nada. or *De nada hablaban.*	They weren't speaking about anything.

- When a single subject is followed by two verbs, *no* is placed before the conjugated verb and the other negative is placed after the infinitive or the negative word is placed before the conjugated verb:

  No quería beber nada. or   She didn't want to drink anything.
  Nada quería beber.

- Negative words may stand alone, without *no*:

¿Que quieres hacer? Nada.	What do you want to do? Nothing.
¿Salen por la noche? Nunca.	Do they go out at night? Never.

- Infinitives may be negated:

Es mejor no decirle nada.	It is better not to tell her anything.

- The negatives *nadie, nada, ninguno, nunca,* and *jamás* are used after comparatives, in phrases that begin with *sin* ("without") or *antes* (*de* or *que*) ("before"), or in questions where negative answers are anticipated:

Él quiere hacerse rico más que nada.	He wants to become rich more than anything else.
Ella escribe mejor que nadie.	She writes better than anybody else.
Te quiero más que nunca.	I love you more than ever.
Ella se durmió sin hacer nada.	She fell asleep without doing anything.
Antes de comer nada, tienes que hacer tu cama.	Before eating anything, you have to make your bed.
Salió antes que nadie.	He went out before anyone else.
¿Has entendido jamás una historia más ridícula?	Have you ever heard a more ridiculous story?

- When used as an adjective, *ninguno(a)* may be replaced by *alguno(a)*, which follows the noun and is more emphatic:

No tenemos ninguna solución.	We have no solution.
No tenemos solución alguna.	We don't have any solution.

NEGATIVE EXPRESSIONS

Commonly used negative expressions include the phrases listed in the following table:

Commonly Used Negative Expressions

Spanish	English
ahora no	not now
creo que no	I don't believe so
de nada	you're welcome
de ningún modo	certainly not
de ninguna manera	by no means

(continues)

Commonly Used Negative Expressions *(continued)*

Spanish	English
más que nada	more than anything
más que nunca	more than ever
ni + subject pronoun + *tampoco*	neither do(es) + subject
ni siquiera	not even
no cabe duda	there's no doubt
no es así	it's not so
no es para tanto	it's not such a big deal
no hay remedio	it can't be helped
no importa	it doesn't matter
no obstante	however
no puede ser	it (that) can't be
¿no te parece?	don't you think so?
no . . . más que	no more than
no . . . sino que	no more than
¿por qué no?	why not
sin novedad	nothing new
todavía no	not yet
ya no	no longer

Examples:

No me gusta ese plato. Ni yo tampoco.	I don't like that dish. Me either.
Ella es muy simpática. ¿No te parece?	She is very nice. Don't you think so?
No cabe duda que saldrás bien.	There is no doubt that you will succeed.

NEGATIVE PREFIXES

The following prefixes can be attached to words to give them a negative meaning or connotation:

- *Anti*
- *Contra*
- *Des*
- *Dis*
- *In* (which becomes *im* before the letter *p*)

The following table shows how these prefixes can be added to affirmative words:

Negative Prefixes

Affirmative	English	Negative	English
accesible	accessible	*inaccesible*	inaccessible
armar	to arm	*desarmar*	to disarm
capacidad	ability	*discapacidad*	disability
cargar	to load	*descargar*	to unload
cómodo	comfortable	*incómodo*	uncomfortable
democrático	democratic	*antidemocrático*	undemocratic
el espionaje	espionage	*el contraespionaje*	counterespionage
estético	aesthetic	*antiestético*	ugly, unsightly
gustar	to be pleasing	*disgustar*	to be displeasing
la paciencia	patience	*la impaciencia*	impatience
penetrable	penetrable	*impenetrable*	impenetrable
poner	to put	*contraponer*	to oppose

Examples:

Me disgusta su actitud.	His attitude displeases me.
Esta silla es incómoda.	This chair is uncomfortable.
Los hombres descargan el camión.	The men unload the truck.

Indefinites and Their Negatives

Indefinites refer to no particular person or thing specifically but to people or things in general.

INDEFINITE PRONOUNS

The following are some *indefinite pronouns* and their negative counterparts:

- *Alguien* ("someone") vs. *nadie* ("no one," "anyone," "nobody," "anybody"):

¿Ves a alguien?	Do you see someone?
No veo a nadie.	I don't see anyone.

- *Algo* ("something") vs. *nada* ("nothing"):

¿Quieres algo?	Do you want something?
No quiero nada.	I want nothing. *or* I don't want anything.

- *Alguno(a/os/as)* ("some") vs. *ninguno(a/os/as)* ("not any," "none"):

¿Invitaste a algunos?	Did you invite some of them?
No invité a ningunos.	I didn't invite any of them.

- *Cualquiera* ("anyone," "anybody," "any one," "anything") vs. *nadie* ("no one," "nobody")/*ninguno* ("none," "neither one"):

Cualquiera puede entender ese poema.	Anyone can understand that poem.
Nadie puede hacer la tarea de biología.	No one can do the biology homework.
¿Te gusta el rojo o el verde? Ninguno.	Do you like the red one or the green one? Neither one.

- *Quien(es)quiera* ("whoever") vs. *nadie* ("no one," "nobody")/*ninguno* ("none," "neither one"):

Quienesquiera sean responsables pagarán.	Whoever is guilty will pay.
Nadie es responsable.	Nobody is responsible.
Ninguno de los dos es responsable.	Neither of the two is responsible.

- *Todo* ("all") vs. *nada* ("nothing"):

Todo está bien.	Everything is all right.
Nada está bien.	Nothing is all right.

- *Todo el mundo* ("everyone," "everybody") vs. *nadie* ("no one," "nobody")/*ninguno* ("none," "neither one"):

Todo el mundo se queja.	Everyone complains.
Nadie se queja.	No one complains.

INDEFINITE ADJECTIVES

The following *indefinite adjectives* all have *ninguno (ningún* before a masculine, singular noun) or *ninguna, ningunos,* or *ningunas* as their negative counterparts:

- *Alguno (algún* before a masculine, singular noun) or *alguna, algunos,* or *algunas* ("some," "any"):

Tiene algunos problemas.	He has some problems.
No tiene ningunos problemas.	He doesn't have any problems.

- *Cierto(a/os/as)* ("certain"):

Ciertas cosas son imposibles.	Certain things are impossible.
Ninguna cosa es imposible.	Nothing is impossible.

- *Uno* (*un* before a masculine, singular noun) or *una, unos,* or *unas* ("one," "some"):

Una mujer está hablando.	A woman is speaking.
Ninguna mujer está hablando.	No woman is speaking.

- *Mucho(a/os/as)* ("many," "much"):

Muchos alumnos estudian.	Many students study.
Ningunos alumnos estudian.	No students study.

- *Tal(es)* ("such"):

A tales hombres les gusta la política.	Such men like politics.
A ningunos hombres les gusta la política.	No men like politics.

- *Cada* ("each," "every"):

Cada persona recibe una flor.	Each person receives a flower.
Ninguna persona recibe una flor.	Nobody receives a flower.

- *Cualquier(a)* ("any," "some"):

Cualquier día será médico.	One day he will be a doctor.
Ningún día será médico.	At no time will he be a doctor.

- *Todo(a/os/as)* ("all," "every"):

Todos los empleados reciben un regalo.	All the employees receive a gift.
Ningunos de los empleados reciben un regalo.	None of the employees receives a gift.

- *Otro(a/os/as)* ("other," "another"):

Otra ocasión será mejor.	Another time will be better.
Ninguna ocasión será mejor.	No other time will be better.

INDEFINITE ADVERBS

The following are *indefinite adverbs* and their negative counterparts:

- *Ya* ("already") vs. *todavía no* ("not yet"):

Ya he visto esta película.	I have already seen this film.
Todavía no he visto esta película.	I haven't seen this film yet.

- *Todavía* or its synonym *aún* ("still") vs. *ya no* ("no longer," "anymore"):

¿Todavía estudias el español?	Are you still studying Spanish?
Ya no lo estudio.	I am no longer studying it.
Aún lo está estudiando.	She is still studying it.

- *Siempre* ("always") vs. *nunca/jamás* ("never"):

Siempre trabaja hasta la medianoche.	He always works until midnight.
Nunca trabaja hasta la medianoche.	He never works until midnight.

- *También* ("also," "too") vs. *tampoco* or *ni . . . tampoco* ("not either," "neither . . . nor"):

Bebo café y también té.	I drink coffee and tea, too.
No bebo ni café ni té tampoco.	I drink neither coffee nor tea.

- *Más de* (+ quantity) ("more than") vs. *no . . . más de* (+ quantity) ("not more than"):

Esta composición tiene más de diez errores.	This composition has more than ten mistakes.
Esta composición no tiene más de diez errores.	This composition doesn't have more than ten mistakes.

NEGATIVE CONJUNCTIONS

The following are *conjunctions* and their negative counterparts:

- *O . . . o* ("either . . . or") vs. *ni . . . ni* ("neither . . . nor"):

¿Tiene (o) limón o azúcar?	Do you take (either) lemon or sugar?
No tomo(ni) limón ni azúcar.	I take neither lemon nor sugar.

Using *O . . . o* and *Ni . . . ni*

Each part of *o . . . o* and *ni . . . ni* precedes the stressed word or words. The use of the first *o* and the first *ni* is optional:

¿Quieres (o) mirar la televisión o escuchar la radio?	Do you want to watch television or listen to the radio?
No quiero (ni) mirar la televisión ni escuchar la radio.	I don't want to watch television or listen to the radio.

- *Pero* ("but") vs. *sino* ("but"):

Él quiere ganar mucho dinero pero no quiere trabajar duro.	He wants to earn a lot of money, but he doesn't want to work hard.
No llevo una falda verde sino negra.	I'm not wearing a green skirt but (rather) a black one.

Pero is used in a general sense and can also mean "however." *Sino* is used only in a negative statement to show contrasting ideas or to show "on the contrary."

Comparisons

When using *sino,* comparisons are made with parallel parts of speech—nouns are compared to other nouns, adjectives to other adjectives, and infinitives to other infinitives:

No como carne sino pollo.	I don't eat meat but rather chicken.
No compré los pequeños sino los grandes.	I didn't buy the little ones but rather the big ones.
No me gusta patinar sino esquiar.	I don't like to skate but rather to ski.

Relative Pronouns

A *relative pronoun* (for example, "who," "which," "that") joins a main clause to a dependent clause. A relative pronoun introduces the dependent clause, which refers to someone or something mentioned in the main clause. The person or thing to which the relative pronoun refers is called the *antecedent*. The clause introduced by the relative pronoun is called the *relative clause*. Consider this example:

Here is the book that you need.

In this example, *the book* is the antecedent, *that* is the relative pronoun, and *you need* is the relative clause.

A relative clause may serve as a subject, a direct object, or an object of a preposition. The following table lists the relative pronouns that are used in Spanish:

Relative Pronouns

When the Antecedent Is:	Use This:	Which Means:
a person (subject) a thing (object) the object of the preposition *a, en, con,* or *de* (when referring only to things)	*que*	who(m) that which
a person (subject or direct/indirect object) an object of the prepositions *a, en, con,* or *de*	*quien/quienes*	who(m)
a person or a thing	*el (la, los, las) cual(es)* *el (la, los, las) que*	who which
used after a preposition (except *a, en, con,* and *de*)	*el (la, los, las) cual(es)* *el (la, los, las) que*	which
implied but not mentioned	*el (la, los, las) que* *quien/quienes*	those
neuter (an object or an idea)	*lo que*	that which, what
neuter (and previously mentioned)	*lo cual*	which

Examples:

El Señor Rueda es un profesor que enseña bien.	Mr. Rueda is a teacher who teaches well.
Elena es la muchacha con quien Miguel sale.	Elena is the girl with whom Michael goes out.
Los que estudian reciben buenas notas.	Those who study get good grades.
No entiendo lo que él dijo.	I don't understand what he said.
La muchcha la cual llora es mi hermana.	The girl who is crying is my sister.

QUE

Que ("who," "whom," "which," "that"), which is the most commonly used relative pronoun in Spanish, refers to both people and things. Although *que* must be expressed in Spanish, it is frequently omitted in English. *Que* can serve as the subject or object of a relative clause or as the object of the prepositions *a, en, con,* or *de* when they refer to things (these prepositions precede the relative pronoun):

- *Que* as a subject:

¿Dónde está el hombre que me ayudaba?	Where is the man who was helping me?

- *Que* as an object:

El Prado es un museo que visito a menudo.	El Prado is a museum (that) I visit often.

- *Que* as the object of a preposition that refers to a thing(s):

Es la pintura de que hablaba la profesora.	That's the picture (that) the teacher was speaking about.

De + Que

Que can be used after the preposition *de* to refer to people:

El ingeniero de que le hablé es muy inteligente.	The engineer about whom I spoke to you is very intelligent.

QUIEN/QUIENES

Quien/quienes ("who," "whom") can refer to the subject or to the direct or indirect object of the main clause. *Quien/quienes* can also serve as the object of the prepositions *a, en, con,* or *de* when they refer to people. Note that when used as relative pronouns, *quien* and *quienes* do not have accents:

- *Quien* as a subject:

La mujer quien ríe es mi madre.	The woman who is laughing is my mother.

- *Quien* as an object:

Es la niña a quien él busca.	That's the child he is looking for.

- *Quien* as the object of a preposition that refers to people:

Son los muchachos de quienes ella hablaba.	Those are the boys she was talking about.

Other Applications of *Quien/Quienes*

Quien/quienes is used as a subject (when no antecedent exists in the sentence) to express "he (she, those, the one, the ones) who":

Quien trabaja duro gana mucho.	He who works hard earns a lot.

Quien/quienes can replace *que* to introduce a clause that is not necessary to the meaning of the sentence:

> *El muchacho, quien me escribió cartas de amor, está en mi clase de español.* — The boy, who writes love letters to me, is in my Spanish class.

Quien/quienes, when used as a direct object referring to people, requires the personal *a* and may replace *que* in more formal sentences:

> *Es la muchacha (que) a quien el miraba.* — That's the girl he was looking at.

EL (LOS, LA, LAS) CUAL(ES)/QUE

El (los, la, las) cual and *el (los, la, las) que* ("who," "which") refer to people or things and are used primarily after prepositions that are longer than one syllable to refer to things. They are also used to avoid confusion when there is more than one antecedent or for emphasis. *De* and *el* combine to become *del* before *que* and *cual*:

> *Subimos al techo del edificio, desde lo cual (el cual) vimos toda la ciudad.* — We went up to the roof of the building, from which we saw all of the city.

> *El padre de María, el cual (el que) es profesor, es muy simpático.* — Maria's father, who is a teacher, is very nice.

Antecedents and No Antecedents

When there are two antecedents, *el (los, la, las) cual(es)* or *el (los, la, las) que* refers to "the former," and *quien(es)* or *que* refers to "the latter":

> *La hermana de María, la cual (la que) es profesora, es muy simpática.* — The sister of María, who is a teacher, is very nice. (The sister is the teacher.)

> *La hermana de María, quien (que) es profesora, es muy simpática.* — The sister of María, a teacher, is very nice. (María is the teacher.)

When there is no antecedent, *el (los, la, las) que* may be used to replace *quien* as a subject:

> *El que trabaja duro gana mucho.* — He who works hard earns a lot.

> *Los que viajan aprenden mucho de la cultura de un país.* — Those who travel learn a lot about the culture of a country.

LO QUE

Lo que ("that which," "what") is the neuter form of *el que* and is used when there is no antecedent mentioned. *Lo que* can be used as follows:

- As the subject of a verb to express "what" or "that which":

¿Sabe Ud. lo que pasó?	Do you know what happened?
Lo que me aburro es un día en casa.	What bores me is a day at home.

- As the object of a verb to express "what" or "that which":

No comprendí lo que me explicó.	I didn't understand what (that which) you explained to me.
Dígame lo que piensa de mi traje nuevo.	Tell me what you think of my new suit.

- After *todo* to express "everything that" or "all that":

No oí todo lo que ella dijo.	I didn't hear everything (all) that she said.

Lo Que with Ideas and Concepts

Lo que can refer to a previously mentioned idea or concept:

Ella siempre llega a tiempo, lo que no me sorprende.	She always arrives on time, which doesn't surprise me.

Lo que (not *lo cual*) can also refer to an understood or implicit idea or concept that was not mentioned:

Lo que me gusta es comer en un restaurante.	What I like is to eat in a restaurant.

LO CUAL

Lo cual ("that," "which"), which is not used as frequently as *lo que,* is usually found in a dependent clause after a prepositional phrase:

Este coche cuesta demasiado, en vista de lo cual, no puedo comprarlo.	This car costs too much; in view of that, I can't buy it.

Popular Usage of Relative Pronouns

Popular usage allows for the substitution of the adverbs *como* ("how"), *donde* ("where"), *cuanto* ("how much"), and sometimes *cuando* ("when") for the relative pronouns *que*, *lo que*, and *el cual*:

Esta es la escuela en que (donde) estudié.	That is the school where I studied.
No me gusta la manera en que (como) cocina.	I don't like the way she cooks.
Todo lo que (cuanto) escribía nos parecía bien.	All that he wrote seemed good to us.
Ella lo conoció en el momento en el cual (el que, cuando) era profesora.	She met him at the time when she was a teacher.

THE RELATIVE ADJECTIVE *CUYO*

Cuyo(a/os/as) means "whose" and is possessive in nature. *Cuyo(a/os/as)* is used as an adjective and agrees in number and gender with the object that is possessed and not with the possessor. *Cuyo(a/os/as)* may refer to objects or people:

Ese muchacho, cuya novia habla, es mi primo.	That boy, whose girlfriend is speaking, is my cousin.
La casa, cuyos dormitorios son grandes, es la nuestra.	The house, whose bedrooms are big, is ours.

PART XIII

REFLEXIVE VERBS

Reflexive and Non-reflexive Verbs

A *reflexive verb* is different from a non-reflexive verb in that it needs a reflexive pronoun to show that the action of the verb is performed upon the subject. The subject and the reflexive pronoun refer to the same person or thing. In English, the words "myself," "yourself," "himself," "herself," "ourselves," "yourselves," and "themselves" show reflexive action. All verbs in Spanish end in -*ar*, -*er*, or -*ir*. Reflexive verbs have these endings but also have -*se* attached to that ending (for example, *lavarse* ["to wash oneself"]).

Some Spanish verbs have reflexive and non-reflexive forms, depending on whether the subject is the recipient of the action. When the action is performed for or upon someone or something else, the verb is no longer reflexive:

Me lavo.	I wash myself. (reflexive)
Lavo mi coche.	I wash my car. (non-reflexive)

Some verbs that are usually not reflexive may be made reflexive by adding the appropriate reflexive pronoun:

Hablo a mi amiga.	I talk to my friend. (non-reflexive)
Me hablo.	I talk to myself. (reflexive)

Common Reflexive Verbs

Common high-frequency reflexive verbs are listed in the following table:

Common Reflexive Verbs

Verb	English
abonarse	to subscribe
abrazarse	to hug each other
abrocharse	to fasten
aburrirse	to become bored
acordarse (de)	to remember
acostarse	to go to bed, to lie down
afeitarse	to shave
aficionarse (a)	to become fond (of)
ahogarse	to drown, to suffocate
alegrarse (de)	to be glad
alejarse (de)	to get away from
aplicarse	to apply oneself
apoderarse (de)	to take possession (of)
apresurarse (a)	to hurry
aprovecharse (de)	to avail oneself (of), to profit (by)
apurarse	to get upset, to worry, to hurry (Latin American countries)
arrepentirse (de)	to repent
asegurarse (de)	to make sure
asustarse	to become frightened
atreverse (a)	to dare
ausentarse	to absent oneself
bañarse	to bathe oneself
besarse	to kiss each other
burlarse (de)	to make fun of
callarse	to be silent

Verb	English
cambiarse	to change (clothing)
cansarse	to become tired
casarse	to get married
cepillarse	to brush one's hair or teeth
colocarse	to place oneself
concentrarse	to concentrate, to be focused
conducirse (comportarse)	to behave
contentarse	to be contented
convencerse (de)	to convince oneself (of)
cuidarse (de)	to take care of (to worry about)
darse	to give in
decidirse (a)	to make up one's mind
desanimarse	to get discouraged
desayunarse	to have breakfast
desmayarse	to faint
despedirse	to say goodbye, to take leave of
despertarse	to wake up
detenerse (a)	to stop
dirigirse (a)	to address
divertirse	to have fun
dormirse	to fall asleep
ducharse	to take a shower
ejercitarse (en)	to train (in)
empeñarse (en)	to insist (on)
encontrarse	to be located, to meet
enfadarse (con)	to get angry (with)
engañarse	to be mistaken; to kid, to delude, to deceive oneself
enojarse	to become angry
enterarse (de)	to find out about

(continues)

Common Reflexive Verbs *(continued)*

Verb	English
equivocarse	to be mistaken
escaparse	to escape
esconderse (de)	to hide (from)
esforzarse	to force oneself, to try hard
familiarse	to familiarize oneself
fiarse (de)	to trust
figurarse	to imagine
fijarse (en)	to notice
hacerse (a) (con)	to become
impacientarse	to lose patience
irse	to go away, to leave
lavarse	to wash oneself
levantarse	to get up (when the entire body is involved)
llamarse	to be called, to be named
llevarse	to take away
maquillarse	to apply makeup
marcharse	to go away
mojarse	to get wet
moverse	to move
negarse (de)	to refuse (to)
olvidarse (de)	to forget
pararse (a)	to stop
parecerse (a)	to resemble
pasearse	to go for a walk
peinarse	to comb one's hair
pelearse (con)	to fight (with)
ponerse	to put on, to become, to place oneself, to become
preocuparse	to worry
probarse	to try on

Verb	English
protegerse	to protect oneself
quedarse	to remain
quejarse (de)	to complain (about)
quitarse	to remove, to take off (one's clothes)
reírse (de)	to laugh at
relajarse	to relax
reprocharse	to reproach oneself
resfriarse	to catch a cold
romperse	to break (a part of one's body)
secarse	to dry oneself
sentarse	to sit down
sentirse	to feel
tratarse (de)	to concern
vestirse	to get dressed
volverse	to become, to turn around

Reflexive Pronouns

A reflexive verb or a verb conjugated reflexively requires a specific *reflexive pronoun* that refers the action of the verb back to the subject noun or pronoun. The reflexive pronoun is generally, but not always, placed before the conjugated form of the verb and serves as a direct or indirect object, indicating that the subject and object of the verb are one and the same. The verb that follows the reflexive pronoun is then conjugated accordingly, as shown in the following table:

Reflexive Pronouns

Reflexive Verb	English	Subject	Reflexive Pronoun	Conjugation
levantarse	to get up	*yo*	*me*	*me levanto*
vestirse	to get dressed	*tú*	*te*	*te vistes*
divertirse	to have fun	*él, ella, Ud.*	*se*	*se divierte*
irse	to go away	*nosotros*	*nos*	*nos vamos*
dormirse	to fall asleep	*vosotros*	*os*	*os dormís*
sentarse	to sit	*ellos, ellas, Uds.*	*se*	*se sientan*

Examples:

Generalmente, me levanto temprano.	I generally wake up early.
Ella se divierte a la fiesta.	She has fun at the party.
Ellos no se sientan.	They don't sit down.

POSITIONING OF REFLEXIVE PRONOUNS

Reflexive pronouns have different positions, depending on the tense and the mood of the sentence in which they are used. The rules for the placement of reflexive pronouns are as follows:

- In simple tenses and moods (except for the imperative and the indicative), the reflexive pronoun is placed before the conjugated verb:

Tense or Mood	Spanish	English
Present	*Me divierto.*	I have fun.
Preterit	*Me divertí.*	I had fun.
Imperfect	*Me divertía.*	I was having fun.
Future	*Me divertiré.*	I will have fun.
Conditional	*Me divertiría.*	I would have fun.
Present subjunctive	*Él espera que me divierta.*	He hopes I have fun.
Imperfect subjunctive	*Él esperaba que me divirtiera (divirtiese).*	He hoped I had fun.

Expressing Possession

Because the reflexive pronoun clearly identifies who is performing the action, possession is understood. A definite article, rather than a possessive adjective, is used to show possession:

Se lava las manos a menudo.	He washes his hands often.
Nos cepillamos los dientes.	We brush our teeth.

- In compound tenses and moods, the reflexive pronoun precedes the conjugated form of the helping verb, *haber* ("to have"):

Tense or Mood	Spanish	English
Present perfect	*Me he divertido.*	I had fun.
Preterit perfect	*Me hube divertido.*	I had had fun.
Pluperfect	*Me había divertido.*	I had had fun.
Future perfect	*Me haré divertido.*	I will have had fun.
Conditional perfect	*Me haría divertido.*	I would have had fun.
Present perfect subjunctive	*Él espera que me haya divertido.*	He hopes that I had fun.
Pluperfect subjunctive	*Él esperaba que me hubiera (hubiese) divertido.*	He hoped that I had had fun.

- With an infinitive, the reflexive pronoun may follow the infinitive and be attached to it or may precede the conjugated verb:

Quiero divertirme.	I want to have fun.
Me quiero divertir.	I want to have fun.

- With a gerund, the reflexive pronoun may follow the gerund and be attached to it or may precede the conjugated verb. When it is attached to the gerund, it is necessary to count back three vowels and add an accent to maintain proper stress:

Estoy divirtiéndome.	I'm having a good time.
Me estoy divirtiendo.	I'm having a good time.

- In negative commands, the reflexive pronoun precedes the conjugated verb:

¡No te levantes!	Don't get up!

- In affirmative commands, the reflexive pronoun follows the verb and is attached to it. It is necessary to count back three vowels and add an accent to maintain proper stress:

¡Diviértase!	Have fun!
¡Levántate!	Get up!

Subject Pronouns

Subject pronouns are generally not used in reflexive constructions (except when clarification is needed) because the reflexive pronoun identifies the subject:

Me acuesto temprano.	I go to bed early.
Ella se peina.	She is combing her hair.

Uses of Reflexive Verbs

Reflexive verbs may have different meanings from their non-reflexive counterparts, they may be reflexive in Spanish but non-reflexive in English, they may be used to express reciprocal actions, or they may be used to express passive actions.

VERBS WITH DIFFERENT REFLEXIVE AND NON-REFLEXIVE MEANINGS

A verb may have different meanings, depending on whether it is used reflexively or non-reflexively, as shown in the following table:

Verbs with Different Reflexive and Non-reflexive Meanings

Infinitive	English	Reflexive Verb	English
aburrir	to bore	*aburrirse*	to become bored
acordar	to agree	*acordarse de*	to remember
acostar	to put to bed	*acostarse*	to go to bed, to lie down
alegrar	to cheer up	*alegrarse*	to be glad, to rejoice
asustar	to frighten	*asustarse*	to become frightened
bañar	to bathe (someone)	*bañarse*	to bathe oneself
burlar	to mock, to deceive	*burlarse*	to make fun of
cansar	to tire	*cansarse*	to become tired
casar	to marry	*casarse*	to get married
colocar	to place (something)	*colocarse*	to place oneself, to get a job
conducir	to drive	*conducirse*	to behave
dirigir	to direct	*dirigirse a*	to address
dormir	to sleep	*dormirse*	to fall asleep
encontrar	to meet, to find	*encontrarse*	to be located
enfadar	to anger, to irritate	*enfadarse (con)*	to get angry, to get annoyed
engañar	to deceive	*engañarse*	to be mistaken; to kid, to delude, or to deceive oneself
esconder	to hide (something)	*esconderse*	to hide oneself
hacer	to make, to do	*hacerse*	to become

Infinitive	English	Reflexive Verb	English
ir	to go	*irse*	to go away
levantar	to raise (something)	*levantarse*	to get up
llamar	to call	*llamarse*	to be called, to call oneself
marchar	to walk, to march	*marcharse*	to leave
negar	to deny	*negarse*	to refuse
parar	to stop (something)	*pararse*	to stop oneself, to get up
parecer	to seem, to appear	*parecerse*	to look like
poner	to put (something)	*ponerse*	to put (something on), to become, to place oneself
probar	to prove	*probarse*	to try on
quitar	to remove	*quitarse*	to take off
sentar	to seat	*sentarse*	to sit down
volver	to return	*volverse*	to become, to turn around

Examples:

El profesor sienta los alumnos por orden alfabético.
The teacher seats the students in alphabetical order.

El profesor se sienta.
The teacher sits.

Este producto quita el polvo.
This product removes dust.

Me quito el sombrero.
I take off my hat.

VERBS USED REFLEXIVELY IN SPANISH AND NON-REFLEXIVELY IN ENGLISH

Some verbs are used reflexively in Spanish but are non-reflexive in English, as shown in the following table:

Verbs That Are Reflexive in Spanish and Non-reflexive in English

Verb	English
abalanzarse	to rush forward
abstenterse (de)	to abstain (from)
acercarse (a)	to approach
acordarse (de)	to remember

(continues)

Verbs That Are Reflexive in Spanish and Non-reflexive in English *(continued)*

Verb	English
adueñarse (de)	to take possession (of)
apoderarse de	to take possession (of)
apresurarse (a)	to hurry
aprovecharse (de)	to take advantage of
arrepentirse (de)	to repent, to regret
asustarse	to get frightened
atreverse (a)	to dare (to)
burlarse de	to make fun of
desayunarse	to eat breakfast
desmayarse	to faint
empeñarse en	to insist (on)
enterarse de	to find out about
escaparse (de)	to escape (from)
fiarse de	to trust
figurarse	to imagine
fijarse (en)	to notice
irse	to go away
negarse (a)	to refuse (to)
olvidarse (de)	to forget
parecerse (a)	to resemble
pasearse	to stroll
quejarse (de)	to complain (about)
reírse de	to laugh at
sincerarse (con)	to be honest (with)
suicidarse	to commit suicide
tratarse (de)	to be a matter of

RECIPROCAL ACTIONS

Plural reflexive constructions can be used to express reciprocal actions that correspond to the English "each other" or "one another":

Se escriben todas las noches por correo electrónico.	They e-mail each other (one another) every night.
Ellos se abrazaron.	They hugged each other (one another).

For purposes of clarification, or to stress the meaning of the reflexive pronoun, *uno a otro (una a otra)* or *el uno al otro (la una a la otra),* meaning "each other," may be used:

Se miraban una a otra (la una a la otra).	They were looking at each other.
Se aman uno a otro (el uno al otro).	They love each other.

PASSIVE ACTIONS

Reflexive verbs are often used in the third person singular or plural to express a passive action when the subject is a thing (not a person) and when the agent (the person performing the action) is not mentioned:

Aquí se habla español.	Spanish is spoken here.
Los vestidos se venderán en esa tienda.	Clothing will be sold in that store.

Idioms with Reflexive Verbs

Reflexive verbs are used to form some idiomatic expressions, as shown in the following table:

Idiomatic Expressions That Use Reflexive Verbs

Spanish	English
aburrirse como una ostra	to be bored stiff
acostarse con las gallinas	to go to bed early
ahogarse en un vaso de agua	to make a mountain out of a molehill
andarse con chiquitas	to beat around the bush
andarse por las ramas	to go off on tangents
calentarse la cabeza por	to agonize about something

(continues)

Idiomatic Expressions That Use Reflexive Verbs *(continued)*

Spanish	English
darse cuenta de	to realize something
darse la mano	to shake hands
darse por vencido	to throw in the towel
darse prisa	to hurry
dársela (con queso) a alguien	to fool someone
desahogarse	to let off steam
enamorarse perdidamente de alguien	to fall head over heels in love with someone
encogerse de hombros	to shrug one's shoulders
encontrarse con la horma de su zapato	to meet one's match
estrujarse el cerebro (la mollera)	to rack one's brain
guardarse un as en la manga	to have an ace up one's sleeve
hacerse amigos	to become friends
hacerse tarde	to become late
hacerse una idea de algo	to imagine what something is like
hacérsele agua la boca a (alguien)	to make someone's mouth water
meterse en belenes	to get into trouble
quedarse tan ancho	to feel pleased with oneself
partirse de risa	to laugh one's head off
ponerse de mil colores	to become bright red
romperse la cabeza	to rack one's brain
soltarse la melena	to let one's hair down
tenerse por muy listo	to think oneself very clever
traerse algún manejo sucio	to be up to something shady
venderse como rosquilla	to sell like hotcakes

PART XIV

ADJECTIVES, ADVERBS, AND COMPARISONS

Adjectives

An *adjective* is a descriptive word that modifies a noun. Spanish adjectives differ from those in English in that they must agree in gender (masculine or feminine) and number (singular or plural) with the nouns they modify. They also generally, but not always, follow the noun they describe.

GENDER OF ADJECTIVES

Some adjectives in Spanish require a change in letter to show that the adjective is masculine or feminine, while other adjectives are the same for both genders.

Adjectives That Require a Change in Letter

Most masculine adjectives end in -*o*, and their feminine counterparts end in -*a*, as shown in the following table:

Adjectives That End in -*o*

Masculine	Feminine	English
aburrido	*aburrida*	boring
afortunado	*afortunada*	fortunate
alto	*alta*	tall
ambicioso	*ambiciosa*	ambitious
amplio	*amplia*	wide
antiguo	*antigua*	old

(continues)

Adjectives That End in *-o (continued)*

Masculine	Feminine	English
atractivo	atractiva	attractive
bajo	baja	short
barato	barata	cheap
bonito	bonita	pretty
bueno	buena	good
caro	cara	expensive
cómico	cómica	funny
cómodo	cómoda	comfortable
contento	contenta	happy
dedicado	dedicada	dedicated
delgado	delgada	thin
delicioso	deliciosa	delicious
deprimado	deprimada	depressed
divertido	divertida	fun
enfermo	enferma	sick
enojado	enojada	angry
estrecho	estrecha	narrow
famoso	famosa	famous
feo	fea	ugly
flaco	flaca	thin
furioso	furiosa	furious
generoso	generosa	generous
gordo	gorda	fat
guapo	guapa	pretty, good-looking
limpio	limpia	clean
listo	lista	ready
magnífico	magnífica	magnificent

Masculine	Feminine	English
malo	*mala*	bad
moderno	*moderna*	modern
moreno	*morena*	dark-haired
necesario	*necesaria*	necessary
negro	*negra*	black
nervioso	*nerviosa*	nervous
nuevo	*nueva*	new
ordinario	*ordinaria*	ordinary
orgulloso	*orgullosa*	proud
pardo	*parda*	brown
pequeño	*pequeña*	small
perezoso	*perezosa*	lazy
perfecto	*perfecta*	perfect
preocupado	*preocupada*	worried
rico	*rica*	rich
romántico	*romántica*	romantic
rubio	*rubia*	blond
serio	*seria*	serious
simpático	*simpática*	nice
sincero	*sincera*	sincere
sucio	*sucia*	dirty
tímido	*tímida*	shy
todo	*toda*	all
tonto	*tonta*	foolish
viejo	*vieja*	old

Examples:

La alumna tímida es muy ambiciosa. The shy student is very ambitious.

Mi coche nuevo es muy moderno. My new car is very modern.

Adjectives that end in -*dor* also add -*a* to form the feminine. Adjectives that end in *án*, -*ón*, or -*ín* drop their accent if one is present and add -*a* to form the feminine, as shown in the following table:

Adjectives That End in -*dor*, -*án*, -*ón*, or -*ín*

Masculine	Feminine	English
amenazador	*amenazadora*	threatening
conservador	*conservadora*	conservative
encantador	*encantadora*	enchanting
hablador	*habladora*	talkative
trabajador	*trabajadora*	hardworking
haragán	*haragana*	lazy
holgazán	*holgazana*	lazy
picarón	*picarona*	naughty (roguish)
chiquitín	*chiquitina*	tiny

Examples:

El hombre conservador es trabajador. The conservative man is hardworking.

La muchacha habladora es chiquitina. The talkative girl is tiny.

Adjectives of Nationality

Some adjectives of nationality that end in a consonant drop their accent if one is present and add -*a* to form the feminine:

Juan es portugués (alemán, francés, inglés, japonés). Juan is Portuguese (German, French, English, Japanese).

María es portuguesa (alemana, francesa, inglesa, japonesa). María is Portuguese (German, French, English, Japanese).

Adjectives That Do Not Require Changes

Masculine adjectives that end in *-e, -a,* or a consonant remain invariable in their feminine forms, as shown in the following table:

Adjectives That Do Not Require Changes

Adjective	English
agradable	pleasant
alegre	happy
amable	nice
arrogante	arrogant
azul	blue
brillante	brillant, bright
caliente	hot
cortés	courteous
débil	weak
diferente	different
diligente	diligent
egoísta	selfish
elegante	elegant
excelente	excellent
fácil	easy
feliz	happy
feroz	ferocious
fiel	faithful
fuerte	strong
genial	brilliant, great
grande	big
horrible	horrible
importante	important
impresionante	impressive

(continues)

Adjectives That Do Not Require Changes *(continued)*

Adjective	English
independiente	independent
insoportable	unbearable
inteligente	intelligent
interesante	interesting
joven	young
leal	loyal
materialista	materialistic
optimista	optimistic
pesimista	pessimistic
pobre	poor
popular	popular
puntual	punctual
realista	realistic
responsable	responsible
sagaz	wise
sociable	sociable
triste	sad
tropical	tropical
valiente	brave

Examples:

> *La casa azul es elegante.*   The blue house is elegant.
> *Esta isla tropical es popular.*   That tropical island is popular.

Invariable Adjectives

Some adjectives, despite their endings, are used for both genders, as shown in the following table:

Invariable Adjectives

Adjective	English
alerta	alert

Adjective	English
azteca	Aztec
belga	Belgian
hipócrita	hypocritical
iraní	Irani
marrón	brown
marroquí	Moroccan
maya	Mayan
rosa	pink
sefardita	Sephardic

Examples:

Compré el vestido rosa y la falda marrón.
I bought the pink dress and the brown skirt.

Hablé con el hombre sefardita y la mujer iraní.
I spoke with the Sephardic man and the Irani woman.

PLURALS OF ADJECTIVES

Spanish adjectives agree in number with the nouns they modify. A noun that ends in a vowel is made plural by adding an *-s* to the singular form, as shown in the following table:

Plurals of Nouns That End in Vowels

Singular	Plural	English
divertido	*divertidos*	fun
famosa	*famosas*	famous
interesante	*interesantes*	interesting

Examples:

Esos deportes son muy divertidos.
Those sports are a lot of fun.

Esas mujeres bonitas son famosas.
Those beautiful women are famous.

Yo vi muchas películas interesantes.
I saw many interesting films.

Modifying Nouns of Different Genders

When two or more nouns of different genders are modified by an adjective, the masculine, plural form is always used:

Su hijo y su hija son rubios.   Her son and her daughter are blond.

El golf y la natación son divertidos. Golf and swimming are fun.

A noun that ends in a consonant is made plural by adding -es to the singular form, as shown in the following table:

Plurals of Nouns That End in Consonants

Singular	Plural	English
fácil	fáciles	easy
hablador	habladores	talkative
popular	populares	popular

Examples:

Los exámenes eran fáciles.   The tests were easy.
Esos niños son habladores.   Those children are talkative.
Leí muchos libros populares.   I read many popular books.

Exceptions to Plural Adjective Rules

For an adjective whose singular form ends in -z, change -z to -c before adding the -es plural ending:

Ana es feliz.   Ana is happy.

Ana y Luisa son felices.   Ana and Luisa are happy.

In order to maintain the original stress, some adjectives gain or lose an accent in their plural form:

Él es jóven.	He is young.		
Ellos son jóvenes.	They are young.		
Él es francés.	He is French.		
Ellos son franceses.	They are French.		
Él es alemán.	He is German.		
Ellos son alemanes.	They are German.		
Él es cortés.	He is polite.		
Ellos son corteses.	They are courteous.		

POSITIONING OF ADJECTIVES

Spanish adjectives may either precede or follow the nouns they modify, depending on the type of adjective used, the meaning and intent of the speaker, and the amount of emphasis being used.

Adjectives That Follow the Noun

In Spanish, unlike in English, descriptive adjectives normally follow the nouns they modify:

Tengo una casa grande.	I have a big house.
Fui a un restaurante romántico.	I went to a romantic restaurant.

Adjectives That Precede the Noun

A descriptive adjective that emphasizes an inherent characteristic or the quality of a noun precedes that noun:

La blanca nieve cubrió las montañas.	The white snow covered the mountains. (Whiteness is an inherent characteristic of snow.)
Nadé en el mar a pesar de sus fuertes olas.	I swam in the sea despite its strong waves. (Emphasis is on the strength of the waves.)

An adjective that imposes a limit (for example, numbers, possessive and demonstrative adjectives, adjectives of quantity) generally precedes the noun it modifies. Common adjectives of quantity are shown in the following table:

Common Adjectives of Quantity

Adjective	English
alguno(as)	some
cada	each, every
uanto(a/-os/as)	as much
más	more
menos	less
ningunos(as)	no, not any
numerosos(as)	numerous
otro(a/os/as)	other, another
poco(a/os/as)	few, little
tanto(a/os/as)	so many, much
todo(a/os/as)	all, every
unos(as)	some
varios(as)	several

The following examples show the placement of limiting adjectives before the nouns they modify:

Leí dos artículos interesantes.	I read two interesting articles.
¿Dónde está mi sombrero?	Where is my hat?
Esa muchacha es bonita.	That girl is pretty.
Varios alumnos están ausentes.	Several students are absent.
No tengo otra pluma.	I don't have another pen.
Hay muchos problemas.	There are a lot of problems.
Nunca entendí tales cosas.	I never understood such things.

Two Adjectives Modifying One Noun

In certain cases, a noun may be modified by more than one adjective. Each adjective is put in its proper position based on the rules of placement described previously. When two adjectives follow the noun, they are joined by *y* ("and"):

Necesito otro coche nuevo.	I need another new car.
Tres otras personas vienen.	Three other people are coming.
Tu hermana es sincera y generosa.	Your sister is sincere and generous.

ADJECTIVES WHOSE MEANING CHANGES

Some adjectives change meaning depending on whether they precede or follow the noun they modify. Adjectives that precede the noun generally have a more literal meaning, while those that follow the noun are more figurative:

una costumbre antigua	an old (ancient) custom
una antigua costumbre	an old (former) custom
un amor cierto	a true love
un cierto amor	a certain (indefinite) love
una persona grande	a tall (large, big in size) person
una gran persona	a great person (in moral character)
el problema mismo	the problem itself
el mismo problema	the same problem
un barco nuevo	a new boat (brand new)
un nuevo barco	a new boat (new to the owner, different)
la mujer pobre	the poor woman (without money)
la pobre mujer	the unfortunate woman
una solución simple	a silly solution
una simple solución	a simple solution
un perro triste	a sad (unhappy) dog
un triste perro	a sad (sorry, wretched) dog
un conocido viejo	an old acquaintance (elderly)
un viejo conocido	an old acquaintance (dear, long-time)

The adjective *bueno* has the same meaning whether it is used before or after the noun it modifies; the same is true of *malo*:

unas ideas buenas or *unas buenas ideas*	some good ideas
unos años malos or *unos malos años*	some bad years

SHORTENED FORMS OF ADJECTIVES

Certain Spanish adjectives have shortened forms in the following instances:

- Some masculine, singular adjectives drop their final *-o* when used directly before a masculine, singular noun. An accent is placed on the *u* of *algún* ("some," "any," "not any") and *ningún* ("no," "not any") when there is no *-o*:

Adjective	Shortened Form	English
uno	*un muchacho*	a boy
bueno	*un buen libro*	a good book
malo	*un mal ejemplo*	a bad example

Adjective	Shortened Form	English
primero	*el primer piso*	the first floor
tercero	*el tercer mes*	the third month
alguno	*algún día*	some day
ninguno	*ningún problema*	no problem

An exception to this rule is that when an adjective is separated from the noun it modifies by a preposition, the original form of the adjective is used:

Uno de mis amigas me espera.	One of my friends is waiting for me.
Es el primero de enero.	It's January first.

- *Grande* ("great," "important," "famous") becomes *gran* when used before (but not after) a noun of either gender:

Una gran señora viene a hablarnos.	A great woman is coming to speak to us.
Esa señora es grande.	That woman is big.

- *Ciento* ("one hundred") becomes *cien* when used before a noun of either gender and before the numbers *mil* and *millones*. This shortened form is not used when any other number follows it or with numbers that are multiples of one hundred:

Cien hombres y cien mujeres participaron al concurso.	One hundred men and one hundred women participated in the race.
Necesito ciento cincuenta dólares.	I need one hundred fifty dollars.
Hay cien mil doscientos habitantes en ese país.	There are one hundred thousand, two hundred inhabitants in that country.

- *Santo* becomes *San* before the name of a masculine saint, except for those beginning with *To-* or *Do-*:

San José está en California.	San José is in California.
Vamos a Santo Domingo.	We are going to Santo Domingo.

Lo + Adjective

The neuter article, *lo,* can be used before a masculine, singular noun to create an abstract subject:

Lo importante es aprender una lengua extranjera.	The important thing is to learn a foreign language.
Lo necesario es estudiar mucho.	What is necessary is to study a lot.

Adverbs

An *adverb* is a word that modifies a verb, an adjective, or another adverb and expresses "how" or "in what manner" the subject performs the action. English adverbs often end in -ly, and their Spanish counterparts often end in *-mente*. Adverbs do not require any changes for agreement according to gender and number because they do not modify nouns.

FORMATION OF ADVERBS

Spanish adverbs are formed by adding *-mente* to the feminine form of an adjective. When there is no distinct feminine form, as in the case where an adjective ends in *-e* or a consonant, *-mente* is added to the singular form of the adjective, as shown in the following table:

Formation of Adverbs

Masculine Adjective	Feminine Adjective	Adverb	English
claro	*clara*	*claramente*	clearly
cortés	*cortés*	*cortésmente*	politely
diligente	*diligente*	*diligentemente*	diligently
especial	*especial*	*especialmente*	especially
feroz	*feroz*	*ferozmente*	ferociously
final	*final*	*finalmente*	finally
frecuente	*frecuente*	*frecuentemente*	frequently
rápido	*rápida*	*rapidamente*	rapidly
recién	*recién*	*recientemente (recién* before a past participle)	recently

Examples:

Voy a la piscina frecuentemente.	I go to the pool frequently.
Ellos trabajaron diligentemente.	They worked diligently.
Ella siempre habla cortésmente.	She always speaks politely.
El recién nacido lloró recientemente.	The newborn cried recently.

More Than One Adverb

When a verb is modified by more than one adverb, only the last adverb uses the -*mente* ending, and the other adverbs use the feminine, singular form of the adjective:

El profesor enseña clara, paciente,   The teacher teaches clearly,
   y lentamente.   patiently, and slowly.

ADVERBIAL PHRASES

An *adverbial phrase* is composed of a group of words that work together as an adverb. Adverbial phrases are formed as follows:

- By using the preposition *con* ("with"), *en* ("in"), or *por* ("by") + noun
- By using the expressions *de manera* ("in a . . . way") or *de modo* ("in a . . . way") + adjective

The following table illustrates how this is done:

Adverbial Phrases

Phrase	Adverb	English
con claridad	*claramente*	clearly
de manera profunda	*profundamente*	profoundly
de modo cuidado	*cuidadosamente*	carefully
en silencio	*silenciosamente*	silently
por instinto	*instintivamente*	instinctively

Examples:

Ella habla claramente.   She speaks clearly.
Ella habla con claridad.   She speaks clearly.
Ella habla de manera clara.   She speaks clearly
Ella habla de modo claro.   She speaks clearly.

ADVERBS NOT FORMED FROM ADJECTIVES

Some Spanish adverbs and adverbial expressions are not formed from adjectives. These adverbs generally express time, order, location, and quantity and answer the questions "How?" "Where?" "When?" and "How much?" The following adverbs are distinct and totally unrelated to any Spanish adjective:

Adverb	English
a fondo	thoroughly
a menudo, muchas veces	often
a veces	sometimes
abajo	downstairs
acá	here
ahí	there
ahora	now
ahora mismo	right now
al fin	finally
algo	something
allá	there
allí	there
anoche	last night
anteayer	day before yesterday
antes	before
apenas	hardly
aquí	here
arriba	upstairs
aún	still
ayer	yesterday
bastante	quite, enough, rather
bien	well
casi	almost
cerca	near
cuando	when
cuanto antes	as soon as possible
de buena gana	willingly
de mala gana	unwillingly
de nuevo	again

(continues)

(continued)

Adverb	English
de pronto	suddenly
de repente	suddenly
de vez en cuando	from time to time
demasiado, excesivamente	too, excessively
dentro de poco	shortly
derecho	straight ahead
despacio	slowly
después	afterward
enfrente	in front of, opposite
enseguida	immediately
entonces	then
esta noche	tonight
hoy	today
hoy (en) día	nowadays
jamás	never
lejos	far
luego	then
mal	badly
mañana	tomorrow
más	more
más tarde	later
mejor	better
menos	less
mientras	meanwhile
muchas veces	often
mucho	a lot
muy	very
nada	nothing
nunca	never

Adverb	English
peor	worse
pocas veces	seldom
poco	little
por consiguiente	consequently
por supuesto	of course
primero	first
pronto	soon
rara vez	seldom
siempre	always
sin duda	undoubtedly
sin embargo	however, nevertheless
tal vez	perhaps
también	also, too
tan	as, to
tanto	so much
tarde	late
temprano	soon, early
todavía	still, yet
todos los días	every day
ya	already
ya no	no longer

Examples:

¿Tiene Ud. bastante dinero?	Do you have enough money?
Te adoro tanto.	I adore you so much.
Ya no fumo.	I no longer smoke.

Lo + Adverb

The neuter article, *lo,* can be used before an adverb of quantity to form a noun:

Lo poco que me dieron no es suficiente.   The little that they gave me isn't enough.

Lo más que haces, lo más aprendes.   The more you do, the more you learn.

ADJECTIVES VS. ADVERBS

The Spanish words in the following table serve as both adjectives and adverbs. As adverbs, the words remain invariable. As adjectives, however, the following should be noted:

- *Mucho, poco,* and *demasiado* agree in number and gender with the nouns they modify.
- *Mejor* and *peor* agree in number only with *-es* added to form the plural.
- *Más* and *menos* are invariable.

Words Used as Both Adjectives and Adverbs

Word		Used As Adjective		Used as Adverb	
Spanish	English	Spanish	English	Spanish	English
más	more	*Tengo más oportunidades.*	I have more opportunities.	*Hablo más rápidamente.*	I speak more.
menos	less, fewer	*Tengo menos oportunidades.*	I have fewer opportunities.	*Hablo menos rápidamente.*	I speak less quickly.
poco	few, little	*Tengo pocas oportunidades.*	I have few opportunities.	*Hablo poco.*	I speak a little.
mucho	much, many	*Tengo muchas oportunidades.*	I have many opportunities.	*Hablo mucho.*	I speak a lot.
mejor	better	*Tengo mejores oportunidades.*	I have better opportunities.	*Hablo mejor.*	I speak better.
peor	worse	*Tengo peores oportunidades.*	I have worse opportunities.	*Hablo peor.*	I speak worse.
demasiado	too much, too many	*Tengo demasiadas oportunidades.*	I have too many opportunities.	*Hablo demasiado.*	I speak too much.

Distinct Forms

The following distinctions are important:

- *Bueno* ("good") and *malo* ("bad") are adjectives and agree in number and gender with the nouns they modify:

Tengo buenas notas.	I have good grades.
Ella tuvo malos sueños.	She had bad dreams.

- *Bien* ("well") and *mal* ("badly") are adverbs and show no agreement:

Ud. baila bien.	You dance well.
Cantamos mal.	We sing badly.

POSITIONING OF ADVERBS

An adverb is generally placed after the verb it modifies. Sometimes, however, the position of an adverb in a sentence is variable, and the adverb may be placed where it would logically be placed in English:

Ella trabaja pacientemente.	She works patiently.
Claramente, Ud. no comprende bien.	Clearly, you don't understand well.

Two adverbs that have the *-mente* ending cannot appear in the same sentence. To avoid this problem, use *con* + noun, *de manera* + noun, or *de modo* + noun for one of the adverbs. In a series of adverbs, add *-mente* only to the last adverb:

Generalmente, los alumnos contestan con cortesía (de manera cortés, de modo cortés).	Generally, the students answer politely.
Ella piensa profunda e intensamente.	She thinks profoundly and intensely.

Comparisons

Two types of *comparisons* can be made: a comparison showing inequality, where two things are deemed to be of greater or lesser superiority, and a comparison of equality, where things are deemed to be equal. Comparisons are most often made using adjectives and adverbs, but they may also be made using nouns or verbs.

COMPARISONS OF EQUALITY

Comparisons of equality show that two things are equal. Comparisons of equality are made in the following manner:

- Adjectives and adverbs are compared by using *tan* + adjective or adverb + *como* ("as . . . as"):

Ella es tan inteligente como yo.	She is as smart as I am.
Él habla tan fluentemente como tú.	He speaks as fluently as you.

- Nouns are compared by using *tanto(a/os/as)* + noun + *como* ("as much/many . . . as"):

Hice tantas faltas como Ud.	I made as many mistakes as you.

- Verbs are compared by using *tanto como* ("as much as"):

Ella estudia tanto como su hermana.	She studies as much as her sister.

COMPARISONS OF INEQUALITY

Comparisons of inequality show that two things are unequal. Comparisons of inequality are made in the following manner:

- Adjectives, adverbs, and nouns are compared to show superiority by using *más* + (adjective, adverb, or noun) + *que* + (name, noun, or subject pronoun):

Mi hermana es más alta que yo.	My sister is taller than I am.
Julio trabaja más hábilmente que Juan.	Julio works more skillfully than Juan.
Hay más calorías en chocolate que en pan.	There are more calories in chocolate than in bread.

- Adjectives, adverbs, and nouns are compared to show inferiority by using *menos* + adverb + *que* + (name, noun, or subject pronoun):

Soy menos optimista que él.	I am less optimistic than he.
Llora menos amargamente que Ana.	She cries less bitterly than Ana.
Mi composición tiene menos faltas que la tuya.	My composition has fewer mistakes than yours.

EXPRESSING "THAN" IN COMPARATIVE SENTENCES

"Than" is usually expressed with *que* in a comparison:

Él es más fuerte que yo.	He is stronger than I am.

If a number is used in a negative comparative sentence, *que* expresses "than." If, however, the sentence is affirmative, *de* is used to express "than":

No recibí más (menos) que cien dólares.	I didn't receive more (less) than one hundred dollars.
Recibí más (menos) de cincuenta dólares.	I received more than fifty dollars.

If the comparison uses one verb for both clauses, *que* expresses "than." If, however, the sentence contains two different verbs, and the noun in question is the object of both verbs, *de* + definite article *(el, la, los, las)* + *que* is used to express "than":

Ahorro más (menos) dinero que mi hermano.	I save more (less) money than my brother.
Ahorro más dinero del que gana mi hermano.	I save more money than my brother earns. ("Money" is the object of the verb "save" and the verb "earns.")

If the noun in question is not the object of both verbs, or if an adjective or an adverb is being compared, *de lo que,* which is invariable, is used to express "than":

Ahorro más dinero de lo que se imaginan mis padres.	I save more money than my parents imagine. ("Money" is the object of the verb "save," but "money" is not the object of the verb "imagine.")
Ella es más inteligente de lo que piensa Ud.	She is more intelligent than you think.
Naturalmente, él corre más rápido de lo que camina.	Naturally, he runs more quickly than he walks.

The Superlative

Unlike the comparative, which compares things, the *superlative* shows that something is the best of its kind. Whereas the English comparative generally ends in -er, the superlative ends in -est.

THE RELATIVE SUPERLATIVE

The *relative superlative* shows the superiority of someone or something with relation to some other people or things. It is formed in one of the following ways:

- Subject + verb + *el (la, los, las)* + *más (menos)* + adjective + *de*:

Ella es la más inteligente de la clase.	She is the smartest in the class.

- Subject + verb + *el (la, los, las)* + noun + *más (menos)* + adjective + *de*:

  Ella es la alumna más inteligente de la clase.　　　She is the smartest student in the class.

THE ABSOLUTE SUPERLATIVE

The *absolute superlative* expresses the best of its kind. It is formed in one of the following ways:

- Add *-ísimo, -ísima, -ísimos,* or *-ísimas* to the adjective, according to the gender and number of the noun it is modifying. An adjective or adverb that ends in a vowel drops the final vowel before adding the absolute superlative ending. The meaning of the absolute superlative is the same as *muy* + adjective ("very" + adjective):

  Tus perros son gordísimos.　　　Your dogs are very fat.
  Ella es bellísima.　　　She is very beautiful.
  Te quiero muchísimo.　　　I love you a lot.

Irregularities in Superlatives

Adjectives that end in *-co(a)*, *-go(a)*, *-ble*, or *-z* change *c* to *qu*, *g* to *gu*, *ble* to *bil*, and *z* to *c*, respectively, before adding the absolute superlative ending:

  Uds. son comiquísimos.　　　You are very funny.

  La piscina es grandísima.　　　The pool is very large.

  La profesora es amabilísima.　　　The teacher is very friendly.

  Ellas son felicísimas.　　　They are very happy.

- For adverbs, add *-mente* to the feminine, singular absolute superlative of the adjective (*-ísima* ending):

  Él conduce lentísimamente.　　　He drives very slowly.
  Ella piensa profundísimamente.　　　She thinks very profoundly.

- For adverbs in a phrase that expresses possibility, use the neuter article, *lo,* in the formula subject + verb + *lo* + *más (menos)* + adverb (+ *de* + noun):

  Él corre lo más rápido.　　　He runs the fastest.
  Esa muchacha habla lo menos cortésmente de todas.　　　That girl speaks the least courteously of all.

IRREGULAR COMPARATIVES AND SUPERLATIVES

Some Spanish adjectives and adverbs have irregular forms in the comparative and the superlative, as shown in the following table:

Comparison of Adjectives

Adjective		Comparative		Superlative	
Spanish	English	Spanish	English	Spanish	English
bueno(a/os/as)	good	*mejor(es)*	better	*el (la) mejor, los (las) mejores*	the best
malo(a/os/as)	bad	*peor(es)*	worse	*el (la) peor, los (las) peores*	the worst
viejo(a/os/as)	old	*mayor(es)*	greater, older	*el (la) mayor,*	the greatest, the oldest
grande(s)	great, big	*más grande(s)*	larger	*los (las) mayores, el (la) más grande, los (las) más grandes*	the largest
		menos grande(s)	less large	*el (la) menos grande, los (las) menos grandes*	the least large
joven (jóvenes)	young	*menor(es)*	younger, minor, lesser	*el (la) menor, los (las) menores*	the least, the youngest
pequeño (a/os/as)	small	*más pequeño (a/os/as)*	smaller	*el (la) más pequeño(a), los (las) más pequeños(as)*	the smallest
		menos pequeño (a/os/as)	less small	*el (la) menos pequeño(a), los (las) menos pequeños(as)*	the least small

Examples:

Mis ideas son buenas pero las tuyas son las mejores.	My ideas are good, but yours are the best.
Sus notas son malas pero las mías son peores.	Your grades are bad, but mine are worse.
Mi abuelo es el mayor de la familia.	My grandfather is the oldest in the family.
Tu primo es más pequeño que tú.	Your cousin is smaller than you.

Mejor and *Peor/Mayor* and *Menor*

The adjectives *mejor* ("better") and *peor* ("worse") generally precede the noun they modify, whereas *mayor* ("older") and *menor* ("younger") generally follow the noun:

Eres mi mejor amiga.	You are my best friend.
Mi hermana menor es artista.	My younger sister is an artist.

The irregular adverbs *bien* ("well") and *mal* ("badly") compare as follows:

Comparison of Adverbs

Adverb		Comparative		Superlative	
Spanish	English	Spanish	English	Spanish	English
bien	well	*mejor*	better	*el mejor*	the best
mal	badly	*peor*	worse	*el peor*	the worst

Examples:

Tú bailas bien pero yo bailo mejor.	You dance well, but I dance better.
Él nada el peor de todos.	He swims the worst of everyone.

Grande and *Pequeño* vs. *Mayor* and *Menor*

The adjectives *grande* ("big") and *pequeño* ("little") have comparative forms with different meanings. *Más grande* and *más pequeño* compare differences in physical height and size, whereas *mayor* ("older") and *menor* ("younger") compare differences in age or status:

Soy más pequeña que mi hermana.	I'm smaller than my sister.
Mi hermana mayor no viene a la fiesta.	My older sister isn't coming to the party.
Es un problema de menor importancia.	It's a minor problem.

PART XV

THE PASSIVE VOICE

The Passive Voice Defined

The *active voice* is the voice that is normally used in conversation and writing. In the active voice, the subject noun or pronoun performs the action. In contrast, in the *passive voice*, the subject or subject pronoun is acted upon by another agent, either a person or a thing. The passive voice is not generally used and is, in fact, avoided in conversation. It is, however, seen in writing:

Voice	Spanish	English
Active	*La muchacha lavó el coche.*	The girl washed the car.
Passive	*El coche fue lavado por la muchacha.*	The car was washed by the girl.

Active vs. Passive

The subject and object in a sentence in the active voice become the object (the agent) and the subject, respectively, in a passive sentence:

Voice	Spanish	English
Active	*La muchacha leyó el poema.*	The girl (subject) read the poem (object).
Passive	*El poema fue leído por la muchacha.*	The poem (subject) was read by the girl (object/agent).

The Passive Voice with *Ser*

The passive construction in Spanish is similar to the English passive construction if the agent (the one performing the action) is mentioned or implied, and it follows this formula: subject + *ser* ("to be," in the appropriate tense) + past participle + *por* ("by") + agent:

Este libro fue escrito por Gail Stein.   This book was written by Gail Stein.

In the passive voice, the past participle acts as an adjective and, therefore, must agree in number and gender with the subject of the sentence:

> *Estas tortas fueron preparadas*   These pies were prepared by my father.
> *por mi padre.*

THE PASSIVE VOICE IN SIMPLE TENSES AND MOODS

The passive voice in simple tenses and moods is formed by using the simple forms of *ser* as shown in the following table:

The Passive Voice in Simple Tenses and Moods

Tense or Mood	Example	English
Present	*La profesora **es** respetada por sus colegas.*	The teacher is respected by her colleagues.
Preterit	*El regalo no **fue** recibido por Julio.*	The gift was not received by Julio.
Imperfect	*Las reglas **eran** repetidas por los alumnos.*	The rules were repeated by the students.
Future	*Los obradores **serán** pagados por su jefe.*	The workers will be paid by their boss.
Conditional	*La música **sería** apreciado por todo el mundo.*	The music would be appreciated by everyone.

Pronouns After *Por*

The following prepositional pronouns are used after *por*: *mí, ti, él, ella, Ud., nosotros, vosotros, ellos, ellas,* and *Uds.*:

La carta fue escrita por mí.	The letter was written by me.
El coche será comprado por ti.	The car will be bought by you.
¿Es celebrada esa fiesta por Uds.?	Is that holiday celebrated by you?

THE PASSIVE VOICE IN COMPOUND TENSES AND MOODS

The passive voice in compound tenses and moods is formed by using the compound forms of *ser* (which remain invariable) followed by the past participle of the action (which agrees in number and gender with the subject), as shown in the following table:

The Passive Voice in Compound Tenses and Moods

Tense or Mood	Example	English
Present perfect	*Ese trabajo **ha sido** terminado por esas mujeres.*	That work has been finished by those women.
Pluperfect	*Las camas **habían sido** hechos por mis hijos.*	The beds had been made by my children.
Future perfect	*Los edificios **habrán sido** construidos por esa compañía.*	The buildings will have been built by that company.
Conditional perfect	*La mesa **habría sido** puesto por ellos.*	The table would have been set by them.

Using *De* Before an Agent

The preposition *por* ("by") generally precedes the agent in a sentence in the passive voice. *De* (which also means "by" when used in the passive voice) may be used, however, if the past participle expresses feeling or emotion, as opposed to action:

La obra fue apreciada del público.	The play was appreciated by the public.
El presidente era temido de todo el mundo.	The president was feared by everyone.

Substitute Constructions for the Passive

Substitute constructions for the passive include the following:

- A reflexive construction with *se* is preferred when the agent isn't mentioned or implied and when the subject is a thing. When *se* is used, the verb agrees with the noun subject, which generally follows the verb:

Se vende este coche.	This car is for sale.
Aquí se venden periódicos.	Newspapers are sold here.

- The pronoun *se* may also be used as an indefinite subject, meaning "one," "people," "they," or "you." In this construction, *se* is not reflexive in nature, and it is used only in the third person singular form (*él*):

  - *se dice* ("it is said," "one says," "people say," "they say," "you say"):

Se dice que saber es poder.	It is said that knowledge is power.

  - *se cree* ("it is believed," "one believes," "people believe," "they believe," "you believe"):

Se cree que la vida no existe en la luna.	People believe that life doesn't exist on the moon.

  - *se sabe* ("it is known," "one knows," "people know," "they know," "you know"):

Se sabe que la tierra es redonda.	One knows that the earth is round.

- Without *se*, the third person plural forms of the verbs are used:

Dicen que saber es poder.	It is said that knowledge is power.
Creen que la vida no existe en la luna.	People believe that life doesn't exist on the moon.
Saben que la tierra es redonda.	One knows that the earth is round.

- The pronoun *se* is also used when the agent isn't mentioned or implied and a person is acted upon. Although the person acted upon is a direct object, the forms *le* and *les* (instead of *lo* and *los*) are used for masculine, singular and masculine, plural subjects, respectively. *La* and *las* are used for feminine, singular and feminine, plural subjects:

Se ayudará al hombre.	The man will be helped. (Someone will help the man.)

Se le ayudará.	He will be helped. (Someone will help him.)
Se sorprendió a los niños.	The children were surprised. (Someone surprised the children.)
Se les sorprendió.	They were surprised. (Someone surprised them.)
Se obedece a la profesora.	The teacher is obeyed. (Someone will obey the teacher.)
Se la obedece.	She is obeyed. (Someone will obey her.)
Se acusarán a las mujeres.	The women will be accused. (Someone will accuse them.)
Se las acusarán.	They will be accused. (Someone will accuse them.)

Using an Active Construction

The active third person plural form (*ellos*) is often preferred to the indefinite *se* construction:

Ayudarán al hombre.	They will help the man.
Sorprendieron a los niños.	They surprised the children.
Obedecen a la profesora.	They obey the teacher.
Acusarán a las mujeres.	They will accuse the women.

GLOSSARY

A

absolute superlative A construction that expresses the best in a category. [*See Part XIV for more information.*]

active voice A voice in which the subject acts. [*See Part XV for more information.*]

adjective A word that modifies a noun or a pronoun. [*See Part XIV for more information.*]

adverb A word that modifies a verb, an adjective, or another adverb. [*See Part XIV for more information.*]

antecedent A word or group of words to which a relative pronoun refers. [*See Part XII for more information.*]

articles Small words that are generally classified as adjectives. They indicate that a noun or noun substitute will follow. [*See Part II for more information.*]

auxiliary verb *See* helping verb. [*See Parts VI and VII for more information.*]

C

cardinal number A number used for counting (for example, one, two, three). [*See Part I for more information.*]

cognate A word that is the same or similar in both Spanish and English (for example, *el hospital* is a hospital and *un automóvil* is an automobile). [*See Part II for more information.*]

comparative A construction that compares two things and ranks one as better or worse than the other. [*See Part XIV for more information.*]

compound mood A mood that requires a helping verb. [*See Part VII for more information.*]

compound tense A past, present, or future tense that requires a helping verb plus a past participle. [*See Part VI for more information.*]

conditional A mood that expresses what the subject *would* do under certain circumstances or conditions. [*See Part IV for more information.*]

conditional perfect A mood that expresses what the subject *would have done* under certain circumstances or conditions. [*See Part VII for more information.*]

conjugation The action of changing the ending of a verb (in the correct tense or mood) so that it agrees with the subject noun or pronoun performing the task. [*See Part III for more information.*]

conjunction A word that is used to connect words, phrases, or clauses. [*See Part X for more information.*]

contraction The combination of two words into one. [*See Part II for more information.*]

coordinating conjunction A conjunction that connects words, phrases, and clauses that are of equal rank. [*See Part X for more information.*]

D

definite article An article—in Spanish, *el* or *la* ("the")—or *los* and *las* ("the")—that indicates a specific person or thing (for example, the car). [*See Part II for more information.*]

demonstrative adjective An adjective that precedes a noun in order to indicate or point out the person, place, or thing referred to. In Spanish *este, estos, esta, estas* ("this/these") and *ese, esos, esa, esas* and *aquel, aquellos, aquella, aquellas* ("that/those") are demonstrative adjectives. [*See Part II for more information.*]

demonstrative pronoun A pronoun that stands alone to indicate or point out the person or thing referred to. In Spanish *éste, éstos, ésta, éstas* ("this/these") and *ése, ésos, ésa, ésas* and *aquél, aquéllos, aquélla, aquéllas* ("that/those") are demonstrative pronouns. [*See Part II for more information.*]

direct object A noun or pronoun that answers the question "whom" or "what" the subject is acting upon. A direct object may refer to a person, a place, a thing, or an idea. [*See Part II for more information.*]

E

exclamation A word or phrase used to show surprise, delight, incredulity, emphasis, or other strong emotion. [*See Part XI for more information.*]

F

first person The *yo* singular form of a verb or the *nosotros* plural form of a verb. [*See Part III for more information.*]

formal command The *Ud.* singular command form or the *Uds.* plural command form of a verb. [*See Part VIII for more information.*]

future A tense that expresses what the subject will do or is going to do or what action will or is going to take place in a future time. [*See Part III for more information.*]

future perfect A tense that expresses what the subject will have done by a future time. [*See Part VI for more information.*]

G

gender A classification that indicates whether a word is masculine or feminine. [*See Part II for more information.*]

gerund A verb form that expresses an action that is taking place. In English, a gerund ends in *-ing.* [*See Part V for more information.*]

H

helping verb Also called an *auxiliary verb*, one of two elements needed to form a compound tense or mood. In Spanish, the auxiliary verb is *haber* ("to have"). [*See Parts VI and VII for more information.*]

I

idiom A word or an expression whose meaning cannot be readily understood by either its grammar or the words used (for example, *Llueve a cántaros.* ["It's raining cats and dogs."]). [*See Part II for more information.*]

imperative A verb form used to give commands or make requests. [*See Part VIII for more information.*]

imperfect A past tense that expresses a continuous, repeated, habitual, or incomplete action, situation, or event in the past that *was* going on at an indefinite time or that used to happen in the past. [*See Part III for more information.*]

imperfect subjunctive A mood that has the same applications as the present subjunctive but refers to an action that has already occurred or that would or would not occur under certain circumstances. [*See Part IV for more information.*]

indefinite adjective An adjective that expresses "any" *(alguno [algún]-a, -os, -as);* "any, some" *(cualquier[-a]);* no *(ninguno [ningún], ninguna, ningunos, ningunas);* "other, another" *(otro[-a, -os, -as]);* "certain" *(cierto[-a, -os, -as]);* "one" *(uno [un]),* "some" *(unos, unas);* "each, every" *(cada);* "every, all" *(todo[-a, -os, -as] "many, much" (mucho[-a, -os, -as]);* "such" *(tal[-es);* and so on. [*See Part XII for more information.*]

indefinite adverb An adverb that expresses "already" *(ya);* "not yet" *(todavía no);* "still" *(todavía);* "no longer" *(ya no);* "always" *(siempre);* "never" *(nunca, jamás);* "also" *(también);* "neither" *(tampoco, ni . . . [tampoco]);* "more than" *(más de);* "not more than" *(no más de).* [*See Part XII for more information.*]

indefinite article An article—in Spanish, *un* or *una* ("a," "an") or *unos* and *unas* ("some")—that refers to persons and objects not specifically identified (for example, a city). [*See Part II for more information.*]

indefinite pronoun A pronoun that expresses "any," "no one" *(nadie);* "none" *(ninguno [-a, -os, -as]);* "some" *(alguno[-a, -os, -as]);* "everyone" *(todo el mundo);* "someone" *(alguien);* "anyone" *(nadie* or *cualquiera);* "something" *(algo);* "anything" *(cualquiera);* "nothing" *(nada);* "whoever" *(quien[es]quiera);* "all" *(todo);* and so on. [*See Part XII for more information.*]

indicative A verb tense (past, present, or future) that states a fact. [*See Part III for more information.*]

indirect command A command form that expresses "let" or "let's." [*See Part VIII for more information.*]

indirect object A noun or pronoun that refers only to people and that tells "to whom" or "for whom" the subject is doing something. [*See Part II for more information.*]

infinitive The basic "to" form of a verb (for example, *hablar* ["to speak"]). [*See Part IX for more information.*]

informal command The *tú* singular command form or the *vosotros* plural command form. [*See Part VIII for more information.*]

interrogative A word that asks a question (for example, *¿qué?* ["what"], *¿cómo?* ["how"]). [*See Part XI for more information.*]

intonation The action of asking a question by inserting a rising inflection at the end of the statement. [*See Part XI for more information.*]

invariable A word that does not change. [*See Part XIV for more information.*]

inversion The reversal of the word order of the subject pronoun and the conjugated verb in order to form a question. [*See Part XI for more information.*]

irregular verb A verb that doesn't follow the regular rules of conjugation. [*See Part III for more information.*]

M

marker An article or adjective that indicates the gender (masculine or feminine) and the number (singular or plural) of a noun. [*See Part II for more information.*]

mood The manner in which the action or state of a verb is perceived or how the speaker envisions the action or state being expressed. In Spanish there are five moods: the indicative, the conditional, the subjunctive, the imperative, and the infinitive. [*See Part IV for more information.*]

N

neuter A word that has no gender (that is, no masculine or feminine form). [*See Part II for more information.*]

noun A word used to name a person, a place, a thing, an idea, or a quality. [*See Part II for more information.*]

number A classification that indicates whether a word is singular or plural. [*See Part II for more information.*]

O

object pronoun A word that takes the place of a direct or indirect object noun. [*See Part II for more information.*]

ordinal number A number that is used to express rank order (for example, first, second, third). [*See Part I for more information.*]

P

passive A voice in which the subject is acted upon. [*See Part XV for more information.*]

past conditional A tense that expresses what the subject *would have done* under certain conditions. [*See Part VII for more information.*]

past participle A verb form that expresses an action that *has occurred* in the past. [*See Part VI for more information.*]

perfect infinitive A verb form that uses the infinitive of the helping verb *haber* and the past participle. [*See Part X for more information.*]

personal pronoun A subject, prepositional, or object pronoun. [*See Part II for more information.*]

pluperfect A tense that expresses what the subject had done. [*See Part VI for more information.*]

pluperfect subjunctive A mood that expresses an action or event that occurred and was completed in the past. [*See Part VII for more information.*]

plural A word that expresses more than one. [*See Part II for more information.*]

possessive adjective An adjective that shows that something belongs to someone (for example, *mi* ["my"], *tu* ["your"]). Spanish possessive adjectives have short and long forms. [*See Part II for more information.*]

possessive pronoun A pronoun that replaces a possessive adjective and its accompanying noun (for example, *el mío, los míos, la mía, las mías* ["mine"]). [*See Part II for more information.*]

preposition A word used to relate elements in a sentence: noun to noun, verb to verb, or verb to noun/pronoun (for example, *a* ["to"], *de* ["of"], *por* ["for"]). [*See Part X for more information.*]

prepositional pronoun A pronoun used after a preposition. [*See Part II for more information.*]

present A tense that expresses what is happening now. [*See Part III for more information.*]

present perfect A tense that expresses an action that began in the past and continues up to the present or an action that was completed at an unspecified time in the past but is somehow connected to the present. [*See Part VI for more information.*]

present perfect subjunctive A mood that expresses an action or event that occurred and was completed in the past in the dependent clause before the action of the main clause took place. [*See Part VII for more information.*]

present subjunctive A mood that expresses unreal, hypothetical, theoretical, imaginary, uncorroborated, or unconfirmed conditions or situations that result from doubts, emotions, wishes, wants, needs, desires, feelings, speculations, and suppositions. [*See Part IV for more information.*]

preterit A tense that expresses a *completed* past action or event. [*See Part XIV for more information.*]

preterit perfect A tense that expresses an action or event that had ended in the past. [*See Part III for more information.*]

progressive tense A past, present, or future form of a verb that shows what the subject is in the act of doing at the time mentioned. [*See Part V for more information.*]

pronoun A word that is used to replace a noun (a person, a place, a thing, an idea, or a quality). [*See Part II for more information.*]

R

reflexive pronoun A pronoun that is used with a reflexive verb. [*See Part XIII for more information.*]

reflexive verb A verb that shows that the subject is performing the action upon itself. [*See Part XIII for more information.*]

regular verb A verb that follows the regular rules for conjugation. [*See Part III for more information.*]

relative pronoun A pronoun that joins a main clause (that is, a clause that can stand alone) to a dependent clause (for example, *que* ["who," "whom," "that," "which"] *quien/quienes* ["who," "whom"]). [*See Part XII for more information.*]

S

second person The *tú* singular form of a verb or the *vosotros* plural form of a verb. [*See Part III for more information.*]

simple tense A tense in which only one verb form is needed to express when the action occurs. [*See Part III for more information.*]

spelling-change verb A verb that has a spelling change before certain letters to preserve the original sound of the verb, in accordance with the rules for Spanish pronunciation. [*See Part III for more information.*]

stem-changing verb A verb that has a change in the stem vowel when it is conjugated. [*See Part III for more information.*]

subject A noun or pronoun that performs the action of the verb. [*See Part II for more information.*]

subject pronoun A pronoun that replaces a noun subject, whether it is a person or a thing (for example, *él* ["he," "it"]). [*See Part II for more information.*]

subjunctive A mood that expresses wishing, emotion, doubt, or denial. [*See Parts IV and VII for more information.*]

subordinating conjunction A conjunction that connects subordinate clauses with main clauses (for example, *aunque* ["although"], *apenas* ["as soon as"]). [*See Part X for more information.*]

superlative A construction that indicates that something is the best or worst in its category. [*See Part XIV for more information.*]

T

tense The time in which the action of a verb takes place. [*See Parts III and VI for more information.*]

third person The *él, ella,* or *Ud.* singular form of a verb or the *ellos, ellas,* or *Uds.* plural forms of a verb. [*See Part III for more information.*]

V

verb A word that shows an action or a state of being. [*See Part III for more information.*]

verbal A word that is derived from a verb but used as a noun or as an adjective (or sometimes as an adverb). The three verbals are gerunds, participles, and infinitives. [*See Parts V, VI, and IX for more information.*]

VERB CHARTS

Use the charts that follow as a quick reference tool for verb conjugation in all tenses and moods. Verbs are separated as regular (*-ar*, *-er*, *-ir*), stem-changing, spelling-change, those with both stem and spelling changes, and irregular.

Regular Verbs

-AR VERBS

amar ("to love")

Gerund

amando

Past Participle

amado

Commands

Pronoun	Affirmative	Negative
Ud.	ame	no ame
Uds.	amen	no amen
tú	ama	no ames
vosotros	amad	no améis
nosotros	amemos	no amemos

Mood	Simple Tenses		Compound Tenses	
	Singular	*Plural*	*Singular*	*Plural*
	Present		**Present Perfect**	
	amo	amamos	he amado	hemos amado
	amas	amáis	has amado	habéis amado
	ama	aman	ha amado	han amado
	Preterit		**Preterit Perfect**	
	amé	amamos	hube amado	hubimos amado
	amaste	amasteis	hubiste amado	hubisteis amado
	amó	amaron	hubo amado	hubieron amado
	Imperfect		**Pluperfect**	
Indicative	amaba	amábamos	había amado	habíamos amado
	amabas	amabais	habías amado	habíais amado
	amaba	amaban	había amado	habían amado
	Future		**Future Perfect**	
	amaré	amaremos	habré amado	habremos amado
	amarás	amaréis	habrás amado	habréis amado
	amará	amarán	habrá amado	habrán amado
	Conditional		**Conditional Perfect**	
	amaría	amaríamos	habría amado	habríamos amado
	amarías	amaríais	habrías amado	habríais amado
	amaría	amarían	habría amado	habrían amado
	Present		**Present Perfect**	
	ame	amemos	haya amado	hayamos amado
	ames	améis	hayas amado	hayáis amado
Subjunctive	ame	amen	haya amado	hayan amado
	Imperfect		**Pluperfect**	
	amara	amáramos	hubiera amado	hubiéramos amado
	amaras	amarais	hubieras amado	hubierais amado
	amara	amaran	hubiera amado	hubieran amado

-*ER* VERBS
correr ("to run")
Gerund
corriendo

Past Participle
corrido

Commands

Pronoun	Affirmative	Negative
Ud.	corra	no corra
Uds.	corran	no corran
tú	corre	no corras
vosotros	corred	no corráis
nosotros	corramos	no corramos

Mood	Simple Tenses		Compound Tenses	
	Singular	*Plural*	*Singular*	*Plural*
Indicative	**Present**		**Present Perfect**	
	corro	corremos	he corrido	hemos corrido
	corres	corréis	has corrido	habéis corrido
	corre	corren	ha corrido	han corrido
	Preterit		**Preterit Perfect**	
	corrí	corrimos	hube corrido	hubimos corrido
	corriste	corristeis	hubiste corrido	hubisteis corrido
	corrió	corrieron	hubo corrido	hubieron corrido
	Imperfect		**Pluperfect**	
	corría	corríamos	había corrido	habíamos corrido
	corrías	corríais	habías corrido	habíais corrido
	corría	corrían	había corrido	habían corrido
	Future		**Future Perfect**	
	correré	correremos	habré corrido	habremos corrido
	correrás	correréis	habrás corrido	habréis corrido
	correrá	correrán	habrá corrido	habrán corrido
	Conditional		**Conditional Perfect**	
	correría	correríamos	habría corrido	habríamos corrido
	correrías	correríais	habrías corrido	habríais corrido
	correría	correrían	habría corrido	habrían corrido
Subjunctive	**Present**		**Present Perfect**	
	corra	corramos	haya corrido	hayamos corrido
	corras	corráis	hayas corrido	hayáis corrido
	corra	corran	haya corrido	hayan corrido
	Imperfect		**Pluperfect**	
	corriera	corriéramos	hubiera corrido	hubiéramos corrido
	corrieras	corrierais	hubieras corrido	hubierais corrido
	corriera	corrieran	hubiera corrido	hubieran corrido

-IR VERBS

decidir ("to decide")

Gerund
decidiendo

Past Participle
decidido

Commands

Pronoun	Affirmative	Negative
Ud.	decida	no decida
Uds.	decidan	no decidan
tú	decide	no decidas
vosotros	decidid	no decidáis
nosotros	decidamos	no decidamos

Mood	Simple Tenses		Compound Tenses	
	Singular	*Plural*	*Singular*	*Plural*
Indicative	**Present**		**Present Perfect**	
	decido	decidimos	he decidido	hemos decidido
	decides	decidís	has decidido	habéis decidido
	decide	deciden	ha decidido	han decidido
	Preterit		**Preterit Perfect**	
	decidí	decidimos	hube decidido	hubimos decidido
	decidiste	decidisteis	hubiste decidido	hubisteis decidido
	decidió	decidieron	hubo decidido	hubieron decidido
	Imperfect		**Pluperfect**	
	decidía	decidíamos	había decidido	habíamos decidido
	decidías	decidíais	habías decidido	habíais decidido
	decidía	decidían	había decidido	habían decidido
	Future		**Future Perfect**	
	decidiré	decidiremos	habré decidido	habremos decidido
	decidirás	decidiréis	habrás decidido	habréis decidido
	decidirá	decidirán	habrá decidido	habrán decidido
	Conditional		**Conditional Perfect**	
	decidiría	decidiríamos	habría decidido	habríamos decidido
	decidirías	decidiríais	habrías decidido	habríais decidido
	decidiría	decidirían	habría decidido	habrían decidido
Subjunctive	**Present**		**Present Perfect**	
	decida	decidamos	haya decidido	hayamos decidido
	decidas	decidáis	hayas decidido	hayáis decidido
	decida	decidan	haya decidido	hayan decidido
	Imperfect		**Pluperfect**	
	decidiera	decidiéramos	hubiera decidido	hubiéramos decidido
	decidieras	decidierais	hubieras decidido	hubierais decidido
	decidiera	decidieran	hubiera decidido	hubieran decidido

Spelling-Change Verbs

-*CAR* VERBS

secar ("to dry")

Gerund
secando

Past Participle
secado

Commands

Pronoun	Affirmative	Negative
Ud.	seque	no seque
Uds.	sequen	no sequen
tú	seca	no seques
vosotros	secad	no sequéis
nosotros	sequemos	no sequemos

Mood	Simple Tenses		Compound Tenses	
	Singular	*Plural*	*Singular*	*Plural*
Indicative	**Present**		**Present Perfect**	
	seco	secamos	he secado	hemos secado
	secas	secáis	has secado	habéis secado
	seca	secan	ha secado	han secado
	Preterit		**Preterit Perfect**	
	sequé	secamos	hube secado	hubimos secado
	secaste	secasteis	hubiste secado	hubisteis secado
	secó	secaron	hubo secado	hubieron secado
	Imperfect		**Pluperfect**	
	secaba	secábamos	había secado	habíamos secado
	secabas	secabais	habías secado	habíais secado
	secaba	secaban	había secado	habían secado
	Future		**Future Perfect**	
	secaré	secaremos	habré secado	habremos secado
	secarás	secaréis	habrás secado	habréis secado
	secará	secarán	habrá secado	habrán secado
	Conditional		**Conditional Perfect**	
	secaría	secaríamos	habría secado	habríamos secado
	secarías	secaríais	habrías secado	habríais secado
	secaría	secarían	habría secado	habrían secado
Subjunctive	**Present**		**Present Perfect**	
	seque	sequemos	haya secado	hayamos secado
	seques	sequéis	hayas secado	hayáis secado
	seque	sequen	haya secado	hayan secado
	Imperfect		**Pluperfect**	
	secara	secáramos	hubiera secado	hubiéramos secado
	secaras	secarais	hubieras secado	hubierais secado
	secara	secaran	hubiera secado	hubieran secado

Other High-Frequency -car Verbs

Verb	English
acercar	to bring near
aplicar	to apply
arrancar	to pull out
buscar	to look for
chocar	to collide
colocar	to put, to place
comunicar	to communicate
criticar	to criticize
educar	to educate
equivocar	to be wrong
explicar	to explain
identificar	to identify
indicar	to indicate
marcar	to note
modificar	to modify
notificar	to notify
pescar	to fish
picar	to prick, to pierce
platicar	to chat
practicar	to practice
rectificar	to rectify
revocar	to revoke
significar	to mean
tocar	to touch
verificar	to verify

-GAR VERBS

apagar ("to extinguish")

Gerund
apagando

Past Participle
apagado

Commands

Pronoun	Affirmative	Negative
Ud.	apague	no apague
Uds.	apaguen	no apaguen
tú	apaga	no apagues
vosotros	apagad	no apaguéis
nosotros	apaguemos	no apaguemos

Mood	Simple Tenses		Compound Tenses	
	Singular	*Plural*	*Singular*	*Plural*
Indicative	**Present**		**Present Perfect**	
	apago	apagamos	he apagado	hemos apagado
	apagas	apagáis	has apagado	habéis apagado
	apaga	apagan	ha apagado	han apagado
	Preterit		**Preterit Perfect**	
	apagué	apagamos	hube apagado	hubimos apagado
	apagaste	apagasteis	hubiste apagado	hubisteis apagado
	apagó	apagaron	hubo apagado	hubieron apagado
	Imperfect		**Pluperfect**	
	apagaba	apagábamos	había apagado	habíamos apagado
	apagabas	apagabais	habías apagado	habíais apagado
	apagaba	apagaban	había apagado	habían apagado
	Future		**Future Perfect**	
	apagaré	apagaremos	habré apagado	habremos apagado
	apagarás	apagaréis	habrás apagado	habréis apagado
	apagará	apagarán	habrá apagado	habrán apagado
	Conditional		**Conditional Perfect**	
	apagaría	apagaríamos	habría apagado	habríamos apagado
	apagarías	apagaríais	habrías apagado	habríais apagado
	apagaría	apagarían	habría apagado	habrían apagado
Subjunctive	**Present**		**Present Perfect**	
	apague	apaguemos	haya apagado	hayamos apagado
	apagues	apaguéis	hayas apagado	hayáis apagado
	apague	apaguen	haya apagado	hayan apagado
	Imperfect		**Pluperfect**	
	apagara	apagáramos	hubiera apagado	hubiéramos apagado
	apagaras	apagarais	hubieras apagado	hubierais apagado
	apagara	apagaran	hubiera apagado	hubieran apagado

Other High-Frequency -gar *Verbs*

Verb	English
abrigar	to shelter
cargar	to load
encargar	to order
llegar	to arrive
pagar	to pay

-GUAR VERBS

atestiguar ("to testify")

Gerund
atestiguando

Past Participle
atestiguado

Commands

Pronoun	Affirmative	Negative
Ud.	atestigüe	no atestigüe
Uds.	atestigüen	no atestigüen
tú	atestigua	no atestigües
vosotros	atestiguad	no atestigüéis
nosotros	atestigüemos	no atestigüemos

Mood	Simple Tenses		Compound Tenses	
	Singular	*Plural*	*Singular*	*Plural*
Indicative	**Present**		**Present Perfect**	
	atestiguo	atestiguamos	he atestiguado	hemos atestiguado
	atestiguas	atestiguáis	has atestiguado	habéis atestiguado
	atestigua	atestiguan	ha atestiguado	han atestiguado
	Preterit		**Preterit Perfect**	
	atestigüé	atestiguamos	hube atestiguado	hubimos atestiguado
	atestiguaste	atestiguasteis	hubiste atestiguado	hubisteis atestiguado
	atestiguó	atestiguaron	hubo atestiguado	hubieron atestiguado
	Imperfect		**Pluperfect**	
	atestiguaba	atestiguábamos	había atestiguado	habíamos atestiguado
	atestiguabas	atestiguabais	habías atestiguado	habíais atestiguado
	atestiguaba	atestiguaban	había atestiguado	habían atestiguado
	Future		**Future Perfect**	
	atestiguaré	atestiguaremos	habré atestiguado	habremos atestiguado
	atestiguarás	atestiguaréis	habrás atestiguado	habréis atestiguado
	atestiguará	atestiguarán	habrá atestiguado	habrán atestiguado
	Conditional		**Conditional Perfect**	
	atestiguaría	atestiguaríamos	habría atestiguado	habríamos atestiguado
	atestiguarías	atestiguaríais	habrías atestiguado	habríais atestiguado
	atestiguaría	atestiguarían	habría atestiguado	habrían atestiguado
Subjunctive	**Present**		**Present Perfect**	
	atestigüe	atestigüemos	haya atestiguado	hayamos atestiguado
	atestigües	atestigüéis	hayas atestiguado	hayáis atestiguado
	atestigüe	atestigüen	haya atestiguado	hayan atestiguado
	Imperfect		**Pluperfect**	
	atestiguara	atestiguáramos	hubiera atestiguado	hubiéramos atestiguado
	atestiguaras	atestiguarais	hubieras atestiguado	hubierais atestiguado
	atestiguara	atestiguaran	hubiera atestiguado	hubieran atestiguado

-ZAR VERBS

avanzar ("to advance")

Gerund
avanzando

Past Participle
avanzado

Commands

Pronoun	Affirmative	Negative
Ud.	avance	no avance
Uds.	avancen	no avancen
tú	avanza	no avances
vosotros	avancad	no avancéis
nosotros	avancemos	no avancemos

Mood	Simple Tenses		Compound Tenses	
	Singular	*Plural*	*Singular*	*Plural*
Indicative	**Present**		**Present Perfect**	
	avanzo	avanzamos	he avanzado	hemos avanzado
	avanzas	avanzáis	has avanzado	habéis avanzado
	avanza	avanzan	ha avanzado	han avanzado
	Preterit		**Preterit Perfect**	
	avancé	avanzamos	hube avanzado	hubimos avanzado
	avanzaste	avanzasteis	hubiste avanzado	hubisteis avanzado
	avanzó	avanzaron	hubo avanzado	hubieron avanzado
	Imperfect		**Pluperfect**	
	avanzaba	avanzábamos	había avanzado	habíamos avanzado
	avanzabas	avanzabais	habías avanzado	habíais avanzado
	avanzaba	avanzaban	había avanzado	habían avanzado
	Future		**Future Perfect**	
	avanzaré	avanzaremos	habré avanzado	habremos avanzado
	avanzarás	avanzaréis	habrás avanzado	habréis avanzado
	avanzará	avanzarán	habrá avanzado	habrán avanzado
	Conditional		**Conditional Perfect**	
	avanzaría	avanzaríamos	habría avanzado	habríamos avanzado
	avanzarías	avanzaríais	habrías avanzado	habríais avanzado
	avanzaría	avanzarían	habría avanzado	habrían avanzado
Subjunctive	**Present**		**Present Perfect**	
	avance	avancemos	haya avanzado	hayamos avanzado
	avances	avancéis	hayas avanzado	hayáis avanzado
	avance	avancen	haya avanzado	hayan avanzado
	Imperfect		**Pluperfect**	
	avanzara	avanzáramos	hubiera avanzado	hubiéramos avanzado
	avanzaras	avanzarais	hubieras avanzado	hubierais avanzado
	avanzara	avanzaran	hubiera avanzado	hubieran avanzado

Other High-Frequency -zar Verbs

Verb	English
alcanzar	to reach
aterrizar	to land
autorizar	to authorize
cruzar	to cross
enlazar	to tie up
especializar	to specialize
gozar	to enjoy
lanzar	to throw
memorizar	to memorize
organizar	to organize
realizar	to fulfill
rizar	to curl
utilizar	to utilize

-*IAR* VERBS

guiar ("to guide")

Gerund
guiando

Past Participle
guiado

Commands

Pronoun	Affirmative	Negative
Ud.	guíe	no guíe
Uds.	guíen	no guíen
tú	guía	no guíes
vosotros	guiad	no guiéis
nosotros	guíemos	no guíemos

Mood	Simple Tenses		Compound Tenses	
	Singular	*Plural*	*Singular*	*Plural*
Indicative	**Present**		**Present Perfect**	
	guío	guiamos	he guiado	hemos guiado
	guías	guiáis	has guiado	habéis guiado
	guía	guían	ha guiado	han guiado
	Preterit		**Preterit Perfect**	
	guié	guiamos	hube guiado	hubimos guiado
	guiaste	guiasteis	hubiste guiado	hubisteis guiado
	guió	guiaron	hubo guiado	hubieron guiado
	Imperfect		**Pluperfect**	
	guiaba	guiábamos	había guiado	habíamos guiado
	guiabas	guiabais	habías guiado	habíais guiado
	guiaba	guiaban	había guiado	habían guiado
	Future		**Future Perfect**	
	guiaré	guiaremos	habré guiado	habremos guiado
	guiarás	guiaréis	habrás guiado	habréis guiado
	guiará	guiarán	habrá guiad	habrán guiado
	Conditional		**Conditional Perfect**	
	guiaría	guiaríamos	habría guiado	habríamos guiado
	guiarías	guiaríais	habrías guiado	habríais guiado
	guiaría	guiarían	habría guiado	habrían guiado
Subjunctive	**Present**		**Present Perfect**	
	guíe	guiemos	haya guiado	hayamos guiado
	guíes	guiéis	hayas guiado	hayáis guiado
	guíe	guíen	haya guiado	hayan guiado
	Imperfect		**Pluperfect**	
	guiara	guiáramos	hubiera guiado	hubiéramos guiado
	guiaras	guiarais	hubieras guiado	hubierais guiado
	guiara	guiaran	hubiera guiado	hubieran guiado

Other High-Frequency -iar Verbs

Verb	English
criar	to raise
desviar	to divert
enviar	to send
espiar	to spy
esquiar	to ski
fiar	to trust
fotografiar	to photograph
liar	to tie up
rociar	to spray
vaciar	to empty
variar	to vary

-UAR VERBS

actuar ("to act")

Gerund
actuando

Past Participle
actuado

Commands

Pronoun	Affirmative	Negative
Ud.	actúe	no actúe
Uds.	actúen	no actúen
tú	actúa	no actúes
vosotros	actuad	no actuéis
nosotros	actuemos	no actuemos

Mood	Simple Tenses		Compound Tenses	
	Singular	*Plural*	*Singular*	*Plural*
	Present		**Present Perfect**	
Indicative	actúo	actuamos	he actuado	hemos actuado
	actúas	actuáis	has actuado	habéis actuado
	actúa	actúan	ha actuado	han actuado
	Preterit		**Preterit Perfect**	
	actué	actuamos	hube actuado	hubimos actuado
	actuaste	actuasteis	hubiste actuado	hubisteis actuado
	actuó	actuaron	hubo actuado	hubieron actuado
	Imperfect		**Pluperfect**	
	actuaba	actuábamos	había actuado	habíamos actuado
	actuabas	actuabais	habías actuado	habíais actuado
	actuaba	actuaban	había actuado	habían actuado
	Future		**Future Perfect**	
	actuaré	actuaremos	habré actuado	habremos actuado
	actuarás	actuaréis	habrás actuado	habréis actuado
	actuará	actuarán	habrá actuado	habrán actuado
	Conditional		**Conditional Perfect**	
	actuaría	actuaríamos	habría actuado	habríamos actuado
	actuarías	actuaríais	habrías actuado	habríais actuado
	actuaría	actuarían	habría actuado	habrían actuado
Subjunctive	**Present**		**Present Perfect**	
	actúe	actuemos	haya actuado	hayamos actuado
	actúes	actuéis	hayas actuado	hayáis actuado
	actúe	actúen	haya actuado	hayan actuado
	Imperfect		**Pluperfect**	
	actuara	actuáramos	hubiera actuado	hubiéramos actuado
	actuaras	actuarais	hubieras actuado	hubierais actuado
	actuara	actuaran	hubiera actuado	hubieran actuado

Other High-Frequency -uar *Verbs*

Verb	English
acentuar	to accentuate
continuar	to continue
evaluar	to evaluate
habituar	to accustom someone to
perpetuar	to perpetuate
situar	to situate

VOWEL + -CER VERBS

parecer ("to seem")

Gerund
pareciendo

Past Participle
parecido

Commands

Pronoun	Affirmative	Negative
Ud.	parezca	no parezca
Uds.	parezcan	no parezcan
tú	parece	no parezcas
vosotros	pareced	no parezcáis
nosotros	parezcamos	no parezcamos

Mood	Simple Tenses		Compound Tenses	
	Singular	*Plural*	*Singular*	*Plural*
Indicative	**Present**		**Present Perfect**	
	parezco	parecemos	he parecido	hemos parecido
	pareces	parecéis	has parecido	habéis parecido
	parece	parecen	ha parecido	han parecido
	Preterit		**Preterit Perfect**	
	parecí	parecimos	hube parecido	hubimos parecido
	pareciste	parecisteis	hubiste parecido	hubisteis parecido
	pareció	parecieron	hubo parecido	hubieron parecido
	Imperfect		**Pluperfect**	
	parecía	parecíamos	había parecido	habíamos parecido
	parecías	parecíais	habías parecido	habíais parecido
	parecía	parecían	había parecido	habían parecido
	Future		**Future Perfect**	
	pareceré	pareceremos	habré parecido	habremos parecido
	parecerás	pareceréis	habrás parecido	habréis parecido
	parecerá	parecerán	habrá parecido	habrán parecido
	Conditional		**Conditional Perfect**	
	parecería	pareceríamos	habría parecido	habríamos parecido
	parecerías	pareceríais	habrías parecido	habríais parecido
	parecería	parecerían	habría parecido	habrían parecido
Subjunctive	**Present**		**Present Perfect**	
	parezca	parezcamos	haya parecido	hayamos parecido
	parezcas	parezcáis	hayas parecido	hayáis parecido
	parezca	parezcan	haya parecido	hayan parecido
	Imperfect		**Pluperfect**	
	pareciera	pareciéramos	hubiera parecido	hubiéramos parecido
	parecieras	parecierais	hubieras parecido	hubierais parecido
	pareciera	parecieran	hubiera parecido	hubieran parecido

Other High-Frequency Vowel + -cer *Verbs*

Verb	English
agradecer	to thank
aparecer	to appear
conocer	to know
crecer	to grow
desobedecer	to disobey
desaparecer	to disappear
establecer	to establish
merecer	to merit, to deserve
nacer	to be born
obedecer	to obey
obscurecer	to darken
ofrecer	to offer
padecer	to suffer
permanecer	to remain
reconocer	to recognize

CONSONANT + -CER VERBS

convencer ("to convince")

Gerund
convenciendo

Past Participle
convencido

Commands

Pronoun	Affirmative	Negative
Ud.	convenza	no convenza
Uds.	convenzan	no convenzan
tú	convence	no convenzas
vosotros	convenced	no convenzáis
nosotros	convenzamos	no convenzamos

Mood	Simple Tenses		Compound Tenses	
	Singular	*Plural*	*Singular*	*Plural*
Indicative	**Present**		**Present Perfect**	
	convenzo	convencemos	he convencido	hemos convencido
	convences	convencéis	has convencido	habéis convencido
	convence	convencen	ha convencido	han convencido
	Preterit		**Preterit Perfect**	
	convencí	convencimos	hube convencido	hubimos convencido
	convenciste	convencisteis	hubiste convencido	hubisteis convencido
	convenció	convencieron	hubo convencido	hubieron convencido
	Imperfect		**Pluperfect**	
	convencía	convencíamos	había convencido	habíamos convencido
	convencías	convencíais	habías convencido	habíais convencido
	convencía	convencían	había convencido	habían convencido
	Future		**Future Perfect**	
	convenceré	convenceremos	habré convencido	habremos convencido
	convencerás	convenceréis	habrás convencido	habréis convencido
	convencerá	convencerán	habrá convencido	habrán convencido
	Conditional		**Conditional Perfect**	
	convencería	convenceríamos	habría convencido	habríamos convencido
	convencerías	convenceríais	habrías convencido	habríais convencido
	convencería	convencerían	habría convencido	habrían convencido
Subjunctive	**Present**		**Present Perfect**	
	convenza	convenzamos	haya convencido	hayamos convencido
	convenzas	convenzáis	hayas convencido	hayáis convencido
	convenza	convenzan	haya convencido	hayan convencido
	Imperfect		**Pluperfect**	
	convenciera	convenciéramos	hubiera convencido	hubiéramos convencido
	convencieras	convencierais	hubieras convencido	hubierais convencido
	convenciera	convencieran	hubiera convencido	hubieran convencido

Other High-Frequency Consonant + -cer Verbs

Verb	English
ejercer	to exercise
vencer	to conquer

-GER VERBS

proteger ("to protect")

Gerund
protegiendo

Past Participle
protegido

Commands

Pronoun	Affirmative	Negative
Ud.	proteja	no proteja
Uds.	protejan	no protejan
tú	protege	no protejas
vosotros	proteged	no protejáis
nosotros	protejamos	no protejamos

Mood	Simple Tenses		Compound Tenses	
	Singular	*Plural*	*Singular*	*Plural*
Indicative	**Present**		**Present Perfect**	
	protejo	protegemos	he protegido	hemos protegido
	proteges	protegéis	has protegido	habéis protegido
	protege	protegen	ha protegido	han protegido
	Preterit		**Preterit Perfect**	
	protegí	protegimos	hube protegido	hubimos protegido
	protegiste	protegisteis	hubiste protegido	hubisteis protegido
	protegió	protegieron	hubo protegido	hubieron protegido
	Imperfect		**Pluperfect**	
	protegía	protegíamos	había protegido	habíamos protegido
	protegías	protegíais	habías protegido	habíais protegido
	protegía	protegían	había protegido	habían protegido
	Future		**Future Perfect**	
	protegeré	protegeremos	habré protegido	habremos protegido
	protegerás	protegeréis	habrás protegido	habréis protegido
	protegerá	protegerán	habrá protegido	habrán protegido
	Conditional		**Conditional Perfect**	
	protegería	protegeríamos	habría protegido	habríamos protegido
	protegerías	protegeríais	habrías protegido	habríais protegido
	protegería	protegerían	habría protegido	habrían protegido
Subjunctive	**Present**		**Present Perfect**	
	proteja	protejamos	haya protegido	hayamos protegido
	protejas	protejáis	hayas protegido	hayáis protegido
	proteja	protejan	haya protegido	hayan protegido
	Imperfect		**Pluperfect**	
	protegiera	protegiéramos	hubiera protegido	hubiéramos protegido
	protegieras	protegierais	hubieras protegido	hubierais protegido
	protegiera	protegieran	hubiera protegido	hubieran protegido

Other High-Frequency -ger Verbs

Verb	English
coger	to seize
emerger	to emerge
escoger	to choose
recoger	to gather, to pick up

VOWEL + -*CIR* VERBS

traducir ("to translate")

Gerund
traduciendo

Past Participle
traducido

Commands

Pronoun	Affirmative	Negative
Ud.	traduzca	no traduzca
Uds.	traduzcan	no traduzcan
tú	traduce	no traduzcas
vosotros	traducid	no traduzcáis
nosotros	traduzcamos	no traduzcamos

Mood	Simple Tenses		Compound Tenses	
	Singular	*Plural*	*Singular*	*Plural*
Indicative	**Present**		**Present Perfect**	
	traduzco	traducimos	he traducido	hemos traducido
	traduces	traducís	has traducido	habéis traducido
	traduce	traducen	ha traducido	han traducido
	Preterit		**Preterit Perfect**	
	traduje	tradujimos	hube traducido	hubimos traducido
	tradujiste	tradujisteis	hubiste traducido	hubisteis traducido
	tradujo	tradujeron	hubo traducido	hubieron traducido
	Imperfect		**Pluperfect**	
	traducía	traducíamos	había traducido	habíamos traducido
	traducías	traducíais	habías traducido	habíais traducido
	traducía	traducían	había traducido	habían traducido
	Future		**Future Perfect**	
	traduciré	traduciremos	habré traducido	habremos traducido
	traducirás	traduciréis	habrás traducido	habréis traducido
	traducirá	traducirán	habrá traducido	habrán traducido
	Conditional		**Conditional Perfect**	
	traduciría	traduciríamos	habría traducido	habríamos traducido
	traducirías	traduciríais	habrías traducido	habríais traducido
	traduciría	traducirían	habría traducido	habrían traducido
Subjunctive	**Present**		**Present Perfect**	
	traduzca	traduzcamos	haya traducido	hayamos traducido
	traduzcas	traduzcáis	hayas traducido	hayáis traducido
	traduzca	traduzcan	haya traducido	hayan traducido
	Imperfect		**Pluperfect**	
	tradujera	tradujéramos	hubiera traducido	hubiéramos traducido
	tradujeras	tradujerais	hubieras traducido	hubierais traducido
	tradujera	tradujeran	hubiera traducido	hubieran traducido

Other High-Frequency Vowel + -cir Verbs

Verb	English
conducir	to drive
producir	to produce
reproducir	to reproduce
reducir	to reduce

Consonant + -*cir* Verbs

esparcir ("to spread")

Gerund
esparciendo

Past Participle
esparcido

Commands

Pronoun	Affirmative	Negative
Ud.	esparza	no esparza
Uds.	esparzan	no esparzan
tú	esparce	no esparzas
vosotros	esparcid	no esparzáis
nosotros	esparzamos	no esparzamos

Mood	Simple Tenses		Compound Tenses	
	Singular	*Plural*	*Singular*	*Plural*
Indicative	**Present**		**Present Perfect**	
	esparzo	esparcimos	he esparcido	hemos esparcido
	esparces	esparcís	has esparcido	habéis esparcido
	esparce	esparcen	ha esparcido	han esparcido
	Preterit		**Preterit Perfect**	
	esparcí	esparcimos	hube esparcido	hubimos esparcido
	esparciste	esparcisteis	hubiste esparcido	hubisteis esparcido
	esparció	esparcieron	hubo esparcido	hubieron esparcido
	Imperfect		**Pluperfect**	
	esparcía	esparcíamos	había esparcido	habíamos esparcido
	esparcías	esparcíais	habías esparcido	habíais esparcido
	esparcía	esparcían	había esparcido	habían esparcido
	Future		**Future Perfect**	
	esparciré	esparciremos	habré esparcido	habremos esparcido
	esparcirás	esparciréis	habrás esparcido	habréis esparcido
	esparcirá	esparcirán	habrá esparcido	habrán esparcido
	Conditional		**Conditional Perfect**	
	esparciría	esparciríamos	habría esparcido	habríamos esparcido
	esparcirías	esparciríais	habrías esparcido	habríais esparcido
	esparciría	esparcirían	habría esparcido	habrían esparcido
Subjunctive	**Present**		**Present Perfect**	
	esparza	esparzamos	haya esparcido	hayamos esparcido
	esparzas	esparzáis	hayas esparcido	hayáis esparcido
	esparza	esparzan	haya esparcido	hayan esparcido
	Imperfect		**Pluperfect**	
	esparciera	esparciéramos	hubiera esparcido	hubiéramos esparcido
	esparcieras	esparcierais	hubieras esparcido	hubierais esparcido
	esparciera	esparcieran	hubiera esparcido	hubieran esparcido

Another high-frequency consonant + -*cir* verb is *fruncir* ("to frown").

-*GIR* VERBS

exigir ("to demand")

Gerund
exigiendo

Past Participle
exigido

Commands

Pronoun	Affirmative	Negative
Ud.	exija	no exija
Uds.	exijan	no exijan
tú	exige	no exijas
vosotros	exigid	no exijáis
nosotros	exijamos	no exijamos

Mood	Simple Tenses		Compound Tenses	
	Singular	*Plural*	*Singular*	*Plural*
Indicative	**Present**		**Present Perfect**	
	exijo	exigimos	he exigido	hemos exigido
	exiges	exigís	has exigido	habéis exigido
	exige	exigen	ha exigido	han exigido
	Preterit		**Preterit Perfect**	
	exigí	exigimos	hube exigido	hubimos exigido
	exigiste	exigisteis	hubiste exigido	hubisteis exigido
	exigió	exigieron	hubo exigido	hubieron exigido
	Imperfect		**Pluperfect**	
	exigía	exigíamos	había exigido	habíamos exigido
	exigías	exigíais	habías exigido	habíais exigido
	exigía	exigían	había exigido	habían exigido
	Future		**Future Perfect**	
	exigiré	exigiremos	habré exigido	habremos exigido
	exigirás	exigiréis	habrás exigido	habréis exigido
	exigirá	exigirán	habrá exigido	habrán exigido
	Conditional		**Conditional Perfect**	
	exigiría	exigiríamos	habría exigido	habríamos exigido
	exigirías	exigiríais	habrías exigido	habríais exigido
	exigiría	exigirían	habría exigido	habrían exigido
Subjunctive	**Present**		**Present Perfect**	
	exija	exijamos	haya exigido	hayamos exigido
	exijas	exijáis	hayas exigido	hayáis exigido
	exija	exijan	haya exigido	hayan exigido
	Imperfect		**Pluperfect**	
	exigiera	exigiéramos	hubiera exigido	hubiéramos exigido
	exigieras	exigierais	hubieras exigido	hubierais exigido
	exigiera	exigieran	hubiera exigido	hubieran exigido

Other High-Frequency -gir *Verbs*

Verb	English
dirigir	to direct
fingir	to pretend
surgir	to appear

-*UIR* VERBS (BUT NOT -*GUIR* VERBS)

destruir ("to destroy")

Gerund
destruyendo

Past Participle
destruído

Commands

Pronoun	Affirmative	Negative
Ud.	destruya	no destruya
Uds.	destruyan	no destruyan
tú	destruye	no destruyas
vosotros	destruid	no destruyáis
nosotros	destruyamos	no destruyamos

Mood	Simple Tenses		Compound Tenses	
	Singular	*Plural*	*Singular*	*Plural*
Indicative	**Present**		**Present Perfect**	
	destruyo	destruimos	he destruído	hemos destruído
	destruyes	destruís	has destruído	habéis destruído
	destruye	destruyen	ha destruído	han destruído
	Preterit		**Preterit Perfect**	
	destruí	destruimos	hube destruído	hubimos destruído
	destruiste	destruisteis	hubiste destruído	hubisteis destruído
	destruyó	destruyeron	hubo destruído	hubieron destruído
	Imperfect		**Pluperfect**	
	destruía	destruíamos	había destruído	habíamos destruído
	destruías	destruíais	habías destruído	habíais destruído
	destruía	destruían	había destruído	habían destruído
	Future		**Future Perfect**	
	destruiré	destruiremos	habré destruído	habremos destruído
	destruirás	destruiréis	habrás destruído	habréis destruído
	destruirá	destruirán	habrá destruído	habrán destruído
	Conditional		**Conditional Perfect**	
	destruiría	destruiríamos	habría destruído	habríamos destruído
	destruirías	destruiríais	habrías destruído	habríais destruído
	destruiría	destruirían	habría destruído	habrían destruído
Subjunctive	**Present**		**Present Perfect**	
	destruya	destruyamos	haya destruído	hayamos destruído
	destruyas	destruyáis	hayas destruído	hayáis destruído
	destruya	destruyan	haya destruído	hayan destruído
	Imperfect		**Pluperfect**	
	destruyera	destruyéramos	hubiera destruído	hubiéramos destruído
	destruyeras	destruyerais	hubieras destruído	hubierais destruído
	destruyera	destruyeran	hubiera destruído	hubieran destruído

Other High-Frequency -uir *Verbs*

Verb	English
concluir	to conclude
construir	to construct
diminuir	to diminish
distribuir	to distribute
excluir	to exclude
fluir	to flow
huir	to flee
incluir	to include
instruir	to instruct
sustituir	to substitute

-*GUIR* VERBS

extinguir ("to extinguish")

Gerund
extinguiendo

Past Participle
extinguido

Commands

Pronoun	Affirmative	Negative
Ud.	extinga	no extinga
Uds.	extingan	no extingan
tú	extingue	no extingas
vosotros	extinguid	no extingáis
nosotros	extingamos	no extingamos

Mood	Simple Tenses		Compound Tenses	
	Singular	*Plural*	*Singular*	*Plural*
Indicative	**Present**		**Present Perfect**	
	extingo	extinguimos	he extinguido	hemos extinguido
	extingues	extinguís	has extinguido	habéis extinguido
	extingue	extinguen	ha extinguido	han extinguido
	Preterit		**Preterit Perfect**	
	extinguí	extinguimos	hube extinguido	hubimos extinguido
	extinguiste	extinguisteis	hubiste extinguido	hubisteis extinguido
	extinguió	extinguieron	hubo extinguido	hubieron extinguido
	Imperfect		**Pluperfect**	
	extinguía	extinguíamos	había extinguido	habíamos extinguido
	extinguías	extinguíais	habías extinguido	habíais extinguido
	extinguía	extinguían	había extinguido	habían extinguido
	Future		**Future Perfect**	
	extinguiré	extinguiremos	habré extinguido	habremos extinguido
	extinguirás	extinguiréis	habrás extinguido	habréis extinguido
	extinguirá	extinguirán	habrá extinguido	habrán extinguido
	Conditional		**Conditional Perfect**	
	extinguiría	extinguiríamos	habría extinguido	habríamos extinguido
	extinguirías	extinguiríais	habrías extinguido	habríais extinguido
	extinguiría	extinguirían	habría extinguido	habrían extinguido
Subjunctive	**Present**		**Present Perfect**	
	extinga	extingamos	haya extinguido	hayamos extinguido
	extingas	extingáis	hayas extinguido	hayáis extinguido
	extinga	extingan	haya extinguido	hayan extinguido
	Imperfect		**Pluperfect**	
	extinguiera	extinguiéramos	hubiera extinguido	hubiéramos extinguido
	extinguieras	extinguierais	hubieras extinguido	hubierais extinguido
	extinguiera	extinguieran	hubiera extinguido	hubieran extinguido

Another high-frequency -*guir* verb is *distinguir* ("to distinquish").

-EER VERBS

leer ("to read")

Gerund
leyendo

Past Participle
leído

Commands

Pronoun	Affirmative	Negative
Ud.	lea	no lea
Uds.	lean	no lean
tú	lee	no leas
vosotros	leed	no leáis
nosotros	leamos	no leamos

Mood	Simple Tenses		Compound Tenses	
	Singular	**Plural**	**Singular**	**Plural**
Indicative	**Present**		**Present Perfect**	
	leo	leemos	he leído	hemos leído
	lees	leéis	has leído	habéis leído
	lee	leen	ha leído	han leído
	Preterit		**Preterit Perfect**	
	leí	leímos	hube leído	hubimos leído
	leíste	leísteis	hubiste leído	hubisteis leído
	leyó	leyeron	hubo leído	hubieron leído
	Imperfect		**Pluperfect**	
	leía	leíamos	había leído	habíamos leído
	leías	leíais	habías leído	habíais leído
	leía	leían	había leído	habían leído
	Future		**Future Perfect**	
	leeré	leeremos	habré leído	habremos leído
	leerás	leeréis	habrás leído	habréis leído
	leerá	leerán	habrá leído	habrán leído
	Conditional		**Conditional Perfect**	
	leería	leeríamos	habría leído	habríamos leído
	leerías	leeríais	habrías leído	habríais leído
	leería	leerían	habría leído	habrían leído
Subjunctive	**Present**		**Present Perfect**	
	lea	leamos	haya leído	hayamos leído
	leas	leáis	hayas leído	hayáis leído
	lea	lean	haya leído	hayan leído
	Imperfect		**Pluperfect**	
	leyera	leyéramos	hubiera leído	hubiéramos leído
	leyeras	leyerais	hubieras leído	hubierais leído
	leyera	leyeran	hubiera leído	hubieran leído

Another high-frequency -eer verb is creer ("to believe").

Stem-Changing Verbs

-AR VERBS WITH *E*→*IE* STEM CHANGES

recomendar ("to recommend")

Gerund

recomendando

Past Participle

recomendado

Commands

Pronoun	Affirmative	Negative
Ud.	recomiende	no recomiende
Uds.	recomienden	no recomienden
tú	recomienda	no recomiendes
vosotros	recomendad	no recomendéis
nosotros	recomendemos	no recomendemos

Mood	Simple Tenses		Compound Tenses	
	Singular	*Plural*	*Singular*	*Plural*
Indicative	**Present**		**Present Perfect**	
	recomiendo	recomendamos	he recomendado	hemos recomendado
	recomiendas	recomendáis	has recomendado	habéis recomendado
	recomienda	recomiendan	ha recomendado	han recomendado
	Preterit		**Preterit Perfect**	
	recomendé	recomendamos	hube recomendado	hubimos recomendado
	recomendaste	recomendasteis	hubiste recomendado	hubisteis recomendado
	recomendó	recomendaron	hubo recomendado	hubieron recomendado
	Imperfect		**Pluperfect**	
	recomendaba	recomendábamos	había recomendado	habíamos recomendado
	recomendabas	recomendabais	habías recomendado	habíais recomendado
	recomendaba	recomendaban	había recomendado	habían recomendado
	Future		**Future Perfect**	
	recomendaré	recomendaremos	habré recomendado	habremos recomendado
	recomendarás	recomendaréis	habrás recomendado	habréis recomendado
	recomendará	recomendarán	habrá recomendado	habrán recomendado
	Conditional		**Conditional Perfect**	
	recomendaría	recomendaríamos	habría recomendado	habríamos recomendado
	recomendarías	recomendaríais	habrías recomendado	habríais recomendado
	recomendaría	recomendarían	habría recomendado	habrían recomendado
Subjunctive	**Present**		**Present Perfect**	
	recomiende	recomendemos	haya recomendado	hayamos recomendado
	recomiendes	recomendéis	hayas recomendado	hayáis recomendado
	recomiende	recomienden	haya recomendado	hayan recomendado
	Imperfect		**Pluperfect**	
	recomendara	recomendáramos	hubiera recomendado	hubiéramos recomendado
	recomendaras	recomendarais	hubieras recomendado	hubierais recomendado
	recomendara	recomendaran	hubiera recomendado	hubieran recomendado

Other High-Frequency -ar Verbs with e→ie Stem Changes

Verb	English
asentar	to seat
atravesar	to go through
calentar	to heat
cerrar	to close
despertar	to wake up
encerrar	to lock up
encomendar	to trust
enterrar	to bury
helar	to freeze
nevar	to snow
quebrar	to break
remendar	to mend
sentar	to seat
temblar	to tremble
tentar	to touch, to try

-AR VERBS WITH *O→UE* STEM CHANGES

encontrar ("to meet")

Gerund
encontrando

Past Participle
encontrado

Commands

Pronoun	Affirmative	Negative
Ud.	encuentre	no encuentre
Uds.	encuentren	no encuentren
tú	encuentra	no encuentres
vosotros	encontrad	no encontréis
nosotros	encontremos	no encontremos

Mood	Simple Tenses		Compound Tenses	
	Singular	*Plural*	*Singular*	*Plural*
Indicative	**Present**		**Present Perfect**	
	encuentro	encontramos	he encontrado	hemos encontrado
	encuentras	encontráis	has encontrado	habéis encontrado
	encuentra	encuentran	ha encontrado	han encontrado
	Preterit		**Preterit Perfect**	
	encontré	encontramos	hube encontrado	hubimos encontrado
	encontraste	encontrastéis	hubiste encontrado	hubisteis encontrado
	encontró	encontraron	hubo encontrado	hubieron encontrado
	Imperfect		**Pluperfect**	
	encontraba	encontrábamos	había encontrado	habíamos encontrado
	encontrabas	encontrabais	habías encontrado	habíais encontrado
	encontraba	encontraban	había encontrado	habían encontrado
	Future		**Future Perfect**	
	encontraré	encontraremos	habré encontrado	habremos encontrado
	encontrarás	encontraréis	habrás encontrado	habréis encontrado
	encontrará	encontrarán	habrá encontrado	habrán encontrado
	Conditional		**Conditional Perfect**	
	encontraría	encontraríamos	habría encontrado	habríamos encontrado
	encontrarías	encontrarías	habrías encontrado	habríais encontrado
	encontraría	encontrarían	habría encontrado	habrían encontrado
Subjunctive	**Present**		**Present Perfect**	
	encuentre	encontremos	haya encontrado	hayamos encontrado
	encuentres	encontréis	hayas encontrado	hayáis encontrado
	encuentre	encuentren	haya encontrado	hayan encontrado
	Imperfect		**Pluperfect**	
	encontrara	encontráramos	hubiera encontrado	hubiéramos encontrado
	encontraras	encontrarais	hubieras encontrado	hubierais encontrado
	encontrara	encontraran	hubiera encontrado	hubieran encontrado

Other High-Frequency -ar *Verbs with* o→ue *Stem Changes*

Verb	English
acordar	to agree
acostar	to put to bed
aprobar	to approve
consolar	to console
contar	to tell
costar	to cost
demostrar	to demonstrate
mostrar	to show
probar	to try (on)
sonar	to ring
soñar	to dream
tostar	to toast
tronar	to thunder
volar	to fly

-CAR VERBS WITH O→UE STEM CHANGES

revolcar ("to knock down")

Gerund
revolcando

Past Participle
revolcado

Commands

Pronoun	Affirmative	Negative
Ud.	revuelque	no revuelque
Uds.	revuelquen	no revuelquen
tú	revuelca	no revuelques
vosotros	revolcad	no revolquéis
nosotros	revolquemos	no revolquemos

Mood	Simple Tenses		Compound Tenses	
	Singular	*Plural*	*Singular*	*Plural*
Indicative	**Present**		**Present Perfect**	
	revuelco	revolcamos	he revolcado	hemos revolcado
	revuelcas	revolcáis	has revolcado	habéis revolcado
	revuelca	revuelcan	ha revolcado	han revolcado
	Preterit		**Preterit Perfect**	
	revolqué	revolcamos	hube revolcado	hubimos revolcado
	revolcaste	revolcasteis	hubiste revolcado	hubisteis revolcado
	revolcó	revolcaron	hubo revolcado	hubieron revolcado
	Imperfect		**Pluperfect**	
	revolcaba	revolcábamos	había revolcado	habíamos revolcado
	revolcabas	revolcabais	habías revolcado	habíais revolcado
	revolcaba	revolcaban	había revolcado	habían revolcado
	Future		**Future Perfect**	
	revolcaré	revolcaremos	habré revolcado	habremos revolcado
	revolcarás	revolcaréis	habrás revolcado	habréis revolcado
	revolcará	revolcarán	habrá revolcado	habrán revolcado
	Conditional		**Conditional Perfect**	
	revolcaría	revolcaríamos	habría revolcado	habríamos revolcado
	revolcarías	revolcaríais	habrías revolcado	habríais revolcado
	revolcaría	revolcarían	habría revolcado	habrían revolcado
Subjunctive	**Present**		**Present Perfect**	
	revuelque	revolquemos	haya revolcado	hayamos revolcado
	revuelques	revolquéis	hayas revolcado	hayáis revolcado
	revuelque	revuelquen	haya revolcado	hayan revolcado
	Imperfect		**Pluperfect**	
	revolcara	revolcáramos	hubiera revolcado	hubiéramos revolcado
	revolcaras	revolcarais	hubieras revolcado	hubierais revolcado
	revolcara	revolcaran	hubiera revolcado	hubieran revolcado

Another high-frequency *-car* verb with an *o→ue* stem change is *volcar* ("to overturn," "to empty").

-GAR VERBS WITH I→IE STEM CHANGES

plegar ("to fold")

Gerund
plegando

Past Participle
plegado

Commands

Pronoun	Affirmative	Negative
Ud.	pliegue	no pliegue
Uds.	plieguen	no plieguen
tú	pliega	no pliegues
vosotros	plegad	no pleguéis
nosotros	pleguemos	no pleguemos

Mood	Simple Tenses		Compound Tenses	
	Singular	*Plural*	*Singular*	*Plural*
Indicative	**Present**		**Present Perfect**	
	pliego	plegamos	he plegado	hemos plegado
	pliegas	plegáis	has plegado	habéis plegado
	pliega	pliegan	ha plegado	han plegado
	Preterit		**Preterit Perfect**	
	plegué	plegamos	hube plegado	hubimos plegado
	plegaste	plegasteis	hubiste plegado	hubisteis plegado
	plegó	plegaron	hubo plegado	hubieron plegado
	Imperfect		**Pluperfect**	
	plegaba	plegábamos	había plegado	habíamos plegado
	plegabas	plegabais	habías plegado	habíais plegado
	plegaba	plegaban	había plegado	habían plegado
	Future		**Future Perfect**	
	plegaré	plegaremos	habré plegado	habremos plegado
	plegarás	plegaréis	habrás plegado	habréis plegado
	plegará	plegarán	habrá plegado	habrán plegado
	Conditional		**Conditional Perfect**	
	plegaría	plegaríamos	habría plegado	habríamos plegado
	plegarías	plegaríais	habrías plegado	habríais plegado
	plegaría	plegarían	habría plegado	habrían plegado
Subjunctive	**Present**		**Present Perfect**	
	pliegue	pleguemos	haya plegado	hayamos plegado
	pliegues	pleguéis	hayas plegado	hayáis plegado
	pliegue	plieguen	haya plegado	hayan plegado
	Imperfect		**Pluperfect**	
	plegara	plegáramos	hubiera plegado	hubiéramos plegado
	plegaras	plegarais	hubieras plegado	hubierais plegado
	plegara	plegaran	hubiera plegado	hubieran plegado

Other High-Frequency -gar *Verbs with* i→ie *Stem Changes*

Verb	English
fregar	to rub
negar	to deny
sosegar	to calm

-GAR VERBS WITH O→UE STEM CHANGES

colgar ("to hang up")

Gerund
colgando

Past Participle
colgado

Commands

Pronoun	Affirmative	Negative
Ud.	cuelgue	no cuelgue
Uds.	cuelguen	no cuelguen
tú	cuelga	no cuelgues
vosotros	colgad	no colguéis
nosotros	colguemos	no colguemos

Mood	Simple Tenses		Compound Tenses	
	Singular	*Plural*	*Singular*	*Plural*
Indicative	**Present**		**Present Perfect**	
	cuelgo	colgamos	he colgado	hemos colgado
	cuelgas	colgáis	has colgado	habéis colgado
	cuelga	cuelgan	ha colgado	han colgado
	Preterit		**Preterit Perfect**	
	colgué	colgamos	hube colgado	hubimos colgado
	colgaste	colgasteis	hubiste colgado	hubisteis colgado
	colgó	colgaron	hubo colgado	hubieron colgado
	Imperfect		**Pluperfect**	
	colgaba	colgábamos	había colgado	habíamos colgado
	colgabas	colgabais	habías colgado	habíais colgado
	colgaba	colgaban	había colgado	habían colgado
	Future		**Future Perfect**	
	colgaré	colgaremos	habré colgado	habremos colgado
	colgarás	colgaréis	habrás colgado	habréis colgado
	colgará	colgarán	habrá colgado	habrán colgado
	Conditional		**Conditional Perfect**	
	colgaría	colgaríamos	habría colgado	habríamos colgado
	colgarías	colgaríais	habrías colgado	habríais colgado
	colgaría	colgarían	habría colgado	habrían colgado
Subjunctive	**Present**		**Present Perfect**	
	cuelgue	colguemos	haya colgado	hayamos colgado
	cuelgues	colguéis	hayas colgado	hayáis colgado
	cuelgue	cuelguen	haya colgado	hayan colgado
	Imperfect		**Pluperfect**	
	colgara	colgáramos	hubiera colgado	hubiéramos colgado
	colgaras	colgarais	hubieras colgado	hubierais colgado
	colgara	colgaran	hubiera colgado	hubieran colgado

Other High-Frequency -gar *Verbs with* o→ue *Stem Changes*

Verb	English
descolgar	to unhook
rogar	to beg

-GAR VERBS WITH U→UE STEM CHANGES

jugar ("to play")

Gerund
jugando

Past Participle
jugado

Commands

Pronoun	Affirmative	Negative
Ud.	juegue	no juegue
Uds.	jueguen	no jueguen
tú	juega	no juegues
vosotros	jugad	no juguéis
nosotros	juguemos	no juguemos

Mood	Simple Tenses		Compound Tenses	
	Singular	*Plural*	*Singular*	*Plural*
Indicative	**Present**		**Present Perfect**	
	juego	jugamos	he jugado	hemos jugado
	juegas	jugáis	has jugado	habéis jugado
	juega	juegan	ha jugado	han jugado
	Preterit		**Preterit Perfect**	
	jugué	jugamos	hube jugado	hubimos jugado
	jugaste	jugasteis	hubiste jugado	hubisteis jugado
	jugó	jugaron	hubo jugado	hubieron jugado
	Imperfect		**Pluperfect**	
	jugaba	jugábamos	había jugado	habíamos jugado
	jugabas	jugabais	habías jugado	habíais jugado
	jugaba	jugaban	había jugado	habían jugado
	Future		**Future Perfect**	
	jugaré	jugaremos	habré jugado	habremos jugado
	jugarás	jugaréis	habrás jugado	habréis jugado
	jugará	jugarán	habrá jugado	habrán jugado
	Conditional		**Conditional Perfect**	
	jugaría	jugaríamos	habría jugado	habríamos jugado
	jugarías	jugaríais	habrías jugado	habríais jugado
	jugaría	jugarían	habría jugado	habrían jugado
Subjunctive	**Present**		**Present Perfect**	
	juegue	juguemos	haya jugado	hayamos jugado
	juegues	juguéis	hayas jugado	hayáis jugado
	juegue	jueguen	haya jugado	hayan jugado
	Imperfect		**Pluperfect**	
	jugara	jugáramos	hubiera jugado	hubiéramos jugado
	jugaras	jugarais	hubieras jugado	hubierais jugado
	jugara	jugaran	hubiera jugado	hubieran jugado

-ZAR VERBS WITH I→IE STEM CHANGES

empezar ("to begin")

Gerund
empezando

Past Participle
empezado

Commands

Pronoun	Affirmative	Negative
Ud.	empiece	no empiece
Uds.	empiecen	no empiecen
tú	empieza	no empieces
vosotros	empezad	no empecéis
nosotros	empecemos	no empecemos

Mood	Simple Tenses		Compound Tenses	
	Singular	*Plural*	*Singular*	*Plural*
Indicative	**Present**		**Present Perfect**	
	empiezo	empezamos	he empezado	hemos empezado
	empiezas	empezáis	has empezado	habéis empezado
	empieza	empiezan	ha empezado	han empezado
	Preterit		**Preterit Perfect**	
	empecé	empezamos	hube empezado	hubimos empezado
	empezaste	empezasteis	hubiste empezado	hubisteis empezado
	empezó	empezaron	hubo empezado	hubieron empezado
	Imperfect		**Pluperfect**	
	empezaba	empezábamos	había empezado	habíamos empezado
	empezabas	empezabais	habías empezado	habíais empezado
	empezaba	empezaban	había empezado	habían empezado
	Future		**Future Perfect**	
	empezaré	empezaremos	habré empezado	habremos empezado
	empezarás	empezaréis	habrás empezado	habréis empezado
	empezará	empezarán	habrá empezado	habrán empezado
	Conditional		**Conditional Perfect**	
	empezaría	empezaríamos	habría empezado	habríamos empezado
	empezarías	empezaríais	habrías empezado	habríais empezado
	empezaría	empezarían	habría empezado	habrían empezado
Subjunctive	**Present**		**Present Perfect**	
	empiece	empecemos	haya empezado	hayamos empezado
	empieces	empecéis	hayas empezado	hayáis empezado
	empiece	empiecen	haya empezado	hayan empezado
	Imperfect		**Pluperfect**	
	empezara	empezáramos	hubiera empezado	hubiéramos empezado
	empezaras	empezarais	hubieras empezado	hubierais empezado
	empezara	empezaran	hubiera empezado	hubieran empezado

Other High-Frequency -zar *Verbs with* i→ie *Stem Changes*

Verb	English
comenzar	to begin
tropezar	to hit, to stumble

-ZAR VERBS WITH *o→ue* STEM CHANGES

almorzar ("to eat lunch")

Gerund
almorzando

Past Participle
almorzado

Commands

Pronoun	Affirmative	Negative
Ud.	almuerce	no almuerce
Uds.	almuercen	no almuercen
tú	almuerza	no almuerces
vosotros	almorzad	no almorcéis
nosotros	almorcemos	no almorcemos

Mood	Simple Tenses		Compound Tenses	
	Singular	*Plural*	*Singular*	*Plural*
Indicative	**Present**		**Present Perfect**	
	almuerzo	almorzamos	he almorzado	hemos almorzado
	almuerzas	almorzáis	has almorzado	habéis almorzado
	almuerza	almuerzan	ha almorzado	han almorzado
	Preterit		**Preterit Perfect**	
	almorcé	almorzamos	hube almorzado	hubimos almorzado
	almorzaste	almorzasteis	hubiste almorzado	hubisteis almorzado
	almorzó	almorzaron	hubo almorzado	hubieron almorzado
	Imperfect		**Pluperfect**	
	almorzaba	almorzábamos	había almorzado	habíamos almorzado
	almorzabas	almorzabais	habías almorzado	habíais almorzado
	almorzaba	almorzaban	había almorzado	habían almorzado
	Future		**Future Perfect**	
	almorzaré	almorzaremos	habré almorzado	habremos almorzado
	almorzarás	almorzaréis	habrás almorzado	habréis almorzado
	almorzará	almorzarán	habrá almorzado	habrán almorzado
	Conditional		**Conditional Perfect**	
	almorzaría	almorzaríamos	habría almorzado	habríamos almorzado
	almorzarías	almorzaríais	habrías almorzado	habríais almorzado
	almorzaría	almorzarían	habría almorzado	habrían almorzado
Subjunctive	**Present**		**Present Perfect**	
	almuerce	almorcemos	haya almorzado	hayamos almorzado
	almuerces	almorcéis	hayas almorzado	hayáis almorzado
	almuerce	almuercen	haya almorzado	hayan almorzado
	Imperfect		**Pluperfect**	
	almorzara	almorzáramos	hubiera almorzado	hubiéramos almorzado
	almorzaras	almorzarais	hubieras almorzado	hubierais almorzado
	almorzara	almorzaran	hubiera almorzado	hubieran almorzado

Other High-Frequency -zar *Verbs with* o→ue *Stem Changes*

Verb	English
esforzar	to strengthen
forzar	to force
reforzar	to reinforce

-ZAR VERBS WITH O→ÜE STEM CHANGES

avergonzar ("to shame")

Gerund
avergonzando

Past Participle
avergonzado

Commands

Pronoun	Affirmative	Negative
Ud.	avergüence	no avergüence
Uds.	avergüencen	no avergüencen
tú	avergüenza	no avergüences
vosotros	avergonzad	no avergoncéis
nosotros	avergoncemos	no avergoncemos

Mood	Simple Tenses		Compound Tenses	
	Singular	*Plural*	*Singular*	*Plural*
Indicative	**Present**		**Present Perfect**	
	avergüenzo	avergonzamos	he avergonzado	hemos avergonzado
	avergüenzas	avergonzáis	has avergonzado	habéis avergonzado
	avergüenza	avergüerzan	ha avergonzado	han avergonzado
	Preterit		**Preterit Perfect**	
	avergoncé	avergonzamos	hube avergonzado	hubimos avergonzado
	avergonzaste	avergonzasteis	hubiste avergonzado	hubisteis avergonzado
	avergonzó	avergonzaron	hubo avergonzado	hubieron avergonzado
	Imperfect		**Pluperfect**	
	avergonzaba	avergonzábamos	había avergonzado	habíamos avergonzado
	avergonzabas	avergonzabais	habías avergonzado	habíais avergonzado
	avergonzaba	avergonzaban	había avergonzado	habían avergonzado
	Future		**Future Perfect**	
	avergonzaré	avergonzaremos	habré avergonzado	habremos avergonzado
	avergonzarás	avergonzaréis	habrás avergonzado	habréis avergonzado
	avergonzará	avergonzarán	habrá avergonzado	habrán avergonzado
	Conditional		**Conditional Perfect**	
	avergonzaría	avergonzaríamos	habría avergonzado	habríamos avergonzado
	avergonzarías	avergonzaríais	habrías avergonzado	habríais avergonzado
	avergonzaría	avergonzarían	habría avergonzado	habrían avergonzado
Subjunctive	**Present**		**Present Perfect**	
	avergüence	avergoncemos	haya avergonzado	hayamos avergonzado
	avergüences	avergoncéis	hayas avergonzado	hayáis avergonzado
	avergüence	avergüencen	haya avergonzado	hayan avergonzado
	Imperfect		**Pluperfect**	
	avergonzara	avergonzáramos	hubiera avergonzado	hubiéramos avergonzado
	avergonzaras	avergonzarais	hubieras avergonzado	hubierais avergonzado
	avergonzara	avergonzaran	hubiera avergonzado	hubieran avergonzado

-ER VERBS WITH E→IE STEM CHANGES

entender ("to understand")

Gerund
entendiendo

Past Participle
entendido

Commands

Pronoun	Affirmative	Negative
Ud.	entienda	no entienda
Uds.	entiendan	no entiendan
tú	entiende	no entiendas
vosotros	entended	no entendáis
nosotros	entendamos	no entendamos

Mood	Simple Tenses		Compound Tenses	
	Singular	*Plural*	*Singular*	*Plural*
Indicative	**Present**		**Present Perfect**	
	entiendo	entendemos	he entendido	hemos entendido
	entiendes	entendéis	has entendido	habéis entendido
	entiende	entienden	ha entendido	han entendido
	Preterit		**Preterit Perfect**	
	entendí	entendimos	hube entendido	hubimos entendido
	entendiste	entendisteis	hubiste entendido	hubisteis entendido
	entendió	entendieron	hubo entendido	hubieron entendido
	Imperfect		**Pluperfect**	
	entendía	entendíamos	había entendido	habíamos entendido
	entendías	entendíais	habías entendido	habíais entendido
	entendía	entendían	había entendido	habían entendido
	Future		**Future Perfect**	
	entenderé	entenderemos	habré entendido	habremos entendido
	entenderás	entenderéis	habrás entendido	habréis entendido
	entenderá	entenderán	habrá entendido	habrán entendido
	Conditional		**Conditional Perfect**	
	entendería	entenderíamos	habría entendido	habríamos entendido
	entenderías	entenderíais	habrías entendido	habríais entendido
	entendería	entenderían	habría entendido	habrían entendido
Subjunctive	**Present**		**Present Perfect**	
	entienda	entendamos	haya entendido	hayamos entendido
	entiendas	entendáis	hayas entendido	hayáis entendido
	entienda	entiendan	haya entendido	hayan entendido
	Imperfect		**Pluperfect**	
	entendiera	entendiéramos	hubiera entendido	hubiéramos entendido
	entendieras	entendierais	hubieras entendido	hubierais entendido
	entendiera	entendieran	hubiera entendido	hubieran entendido

Other High-Frequency -er *Verbs with* e→ie *Stem Changes*

Verb	English
defender	to defend
encender	to incite, to light
perder	to lose
querer	to wish, to want

-ER VERBS WITH E→UE STEM CHANGES

morder ("to bite")

Gerund
mordiendo

Past Participle
mordido

Commands

Pronoun	Affirmative	Negative
Ud.	muerda	no muerda
Uds.	muerdan	no muerdan
tú	muerde	no muerdas
vosotros	morded	no mordáis
nosotros	mordamos	no mordamos

Mood	Simple Tenses		Compound Tenses	
	Singular	*Plural*	*Singular*	*Plural*
Indicative	**Present**		**Present Perfect**	
	muerdo	mordemos	he mordido	hemos mordido
	muerdes	mordéis	has mordido	habéis mordido
	muerde	muerden	ha mordido	han mordido
	Preterit		**Preterit Perfect**	
	mordí	mordimos	hube mordido	hubimos mordido
	mordiste	mordisteis	hubiste mordido	hubisteis mordido
	mordió	mordieron	hubo mordido	hubieron mordido
	Imperfect		**Pluperfect**	
	mordía	mordíamos	había mordido	habíamos mordido
	mordías	mordíais	habías mordido	habíais mordido
	mordía	mordían	había mordido	habían mordido
	Future		**Future Perfect**	
	morderé	morderemos	habré mordido	habremos mordido
	morderás	morderéis	habrás mordido	habréis mordido
	morderá	morderán	habrá mordido	habrán mordido
	Conditional		**Conditional Perfect**	
	mordería	morderíamos	habría mordido	habríamos mordido
	morderías	morderíais	habrías mordido	habríais mordido
	mordería	morderían	habría mordido	habrían mordido
Subjunctive	**Present**		**Present Perfect**	
	muerda	mordamos	haya mordido	hayamos mordido
	muerdas	mordáis	hayas mordido	hayáis mordido
	muerda	muerdan	haya mordido	hayan mordido
	Imperfect		**Pluperfect**	
	mordiera	mordiéramos	hubiera mordido	hubiéramos mordido
	mordieras	mordierais	hubieras mordido	hubierais mordido
	mordiera	mordieran	hubiera mordido	hubieran mordido

Other High-Frequency -er Verbs with o→ue *Stem Changes*

Verb	English
doler	to hurt
envolver (p.p. *envuelto*)	to wrap up
llover	to rain
resolver (p.p. *resuelto*)	to resolve
soler	to usually do something
volver (p.p. *vuelto*)	to return

-IR VERBS WITH I→IE STEM CHANGES

sentir ("to feel")

Gerund
sintiendo

Past Participle
sentido

Commands

Pronoun	Affirmative	Negative
Ud.	sienta	no sienta
Uds.	sientan	no sientan
tú	siente	no sientas
vosotros	sentid	no sintáis
nosotros	sintamos	no sintamos

Mood	Simple Tenses		Compound Tenses	
	Singular	*Plural*	*Singular*	*Plural*
Indicative	**Present**		**Present Perfect**	
	siento	sentimos	he sentido	hemos sentido
	sientes	sentís	has sentido	habéis sentido
	siente	sienten	ha sentido	han sentido
	Preterit		**Preterit Perfect**	
	sentí	sentimos	hube sentido	hubimos sentido
	sentiste	sentisteis	hubiste sentido	hubisteis sentido
	sintió	sintieron	hubo sentido	hubieron sentido
	Imperfect		**Pluperfect**	
	sentía	sentíamos	había sentido	habíamos sentido
	sentías	sentíais	habías sentido	habíais sentido
	sentía	sentían	había sentido	habían sentido
	Future		**Future Perfect**	
	sentiré	sentiremos	habré sentido	habremos sentido
	sentirás	sentiréis	habrás sentido	habréis sentido
	sentirá	sentirán	habrá sentido	habrán sentido
	Conditional		**Conditional Perfect**	
	sentiría	sentiríamos	habría sentido	habríamos sentido
	sentirías	sentiríais	habrías sentido	habríais sentido
	sentiría	sentirían	habría sentido	habrían sentido
Subjunctive	**Present**		**Present Perfect**	
	sienta	sintamos	haya sentido	hayamos sentido
	sientas	sintáis	hayas sentido	hayáis sentido
	sienta	sientan	haya sentido	hayan sentido
	Imperfect		**Pluperfect**	
	sintiera	sintiéramos	hubiera sentido	hubiéramos sentido
	sintieras	sintierais	hubieras sentido	hubierais sentido
	sintiera	sintieran	hubiera sentido	hubieran sentido

Other High-Frequency -ir *Verbs with* e→ie *Stem Changes*

Verb	English
advertir	to warn, to advise
arrepentir	to repent
consentir	to allow
convertir	to convert
digerir	to digest
divertir	to amuse
herir	to wound
hervir	to boil
inferir	to infer
invertir	to invest
mentir	to lie
preferir	to prefer
referir	to refer
sugerir	to suggest

-IR VERBS WITH I→IE STEM CHANGES

adquirir ("to acquire")

Gerund
adquiriendo

Past Participle
adquirido

Commands

Pronoun	Affirmative	Negative
Ud.	adquiera	no adquiera
Uds.	adquieran	no adquieran
tú	adquiere	no adquieras
vosotros	adquirid	no adquiráis
nosotros	adquiramos	no adquiramos

Mood	Simple Tenses		Compound Tenses	
	Singular	*Plural*	*Singular*	*Plural*
Indicative	**Present**		**Present Perfect**	
	adquiero	adquirimos	he adquirido	hemos adquirido
	adquieres	adquirís	has adquirido	habéis adquirido
	adquiere	adquieren	ha adquirido	han adquirido
	Preterit		**Preterit Perfect**	
	adquirí	adquirimos	hube adquirido	hubimos adquirido
	adquiriste	adquiristeis	hubiste adquirido	hubisteis adquirido
	adquirió	adquirieron	hubo adquirido	hubieron adquirido
	Imperfect		**Pluperfect**	
	adquiría	adquiríamos	había adquirido	habíamos adquirido
	adquirías	adquiríais	habías adquirido	habíais adquirido
	adquiría	adquirían	había adquirido	habían adquirido
	Future		**Future Perfect**	
	adquiriré	adquiriremos	habré adquirido	habremos adquirido
	adquirirás	adquiriréis	habrás adquirido	habréis adquirido
	adquirirá	adquirirán	habrá adquirido	habrán adquirido
	Conditional		**Conditional Perfect**	
	adquiriría	adquiriríamos	habría adquirido	habríamos adquirido
	adquirirías	adquiriríais	habrías adquirido	habríais adquirido
	adquiriría	adquirirían	habría adquirido	habrían adquirido
Subjunctive	**Present**		**Present Perfect**	
	adquiera	adquiramos	haya adquirido	hayamos adquirido
	adquiera	adquiráis	hayas adquirido	hayáis adquirido
	adquiera	adquieran	haya adquirido	hayan adquirido
	Imperfect		**Pluperfect**	
	adquiriera	adquiriéramos	hubiera adquirido	hubiéramos adquirido
	adquirieras	adquirierais	hubieras adquirido	hubierais adquirido
	adquiriera	adquirieran	hubiera adquirido	hubieran adquirido

Another high-frequency -ir verb with an i→ie stem change is *inquirir* ("to inquire").

-IR VERBS WITH O→UE STEM CHANGES

dormir ("to sleep")

Gerund
durmiendo

Past Participle
dormido

Commands

Pronoun	Affirmative	Negative
Ud.	duerma	no duerma
Uds.	duerman	no duerman
tú	duerme	no duermas
vosotros	dormid	no durmáis
nosotros	durmamos	no durmamos

Mood	Simple Tenses		Compound Tenses	
	Singular	*Plural*	*Singular*	*Plural*
Indicative	**Present**		**Present Perfect**	
	duermo	dormimos	he dormido	hemos dormido
	duermes	dormís	has dormido	habéis dormido
	duerme	duermen	ha dormido	han dormido
	Preterit		**Preterit Perfect**	
	dormí	dormimos	hube dormido	hubimos dormido
	dormiste	dormisteis	hubiste dormido	hubisteis dormido
	durmió	durmieron	hubo dormido	hubieron dormido
	Imperfect		**Pluperfect**	
	dormía	dormíamos	había dormido	habíamos dormido
	dormías	dormíais	habías dormido	habíais dormido
	dormía	dormían	había dormido	habían dormido
	Future		**Future Perfect**	
	dormiré	dormiremos	habré dormido	habremos dormido
	dormirás	dormiréis	habrás dormido	habréis dormido
	dormirá	dormirán	habrá dormido	habrán dormido
	Conditional		**Conditional Perfect**	
	dormiría	dormiríamos	habría dormido	habríamos dormido
	dormirías	dormiríais	habrías dormido	habríais dormido
	dormiría	dormirían	habría dormido	habrían dormido
Subjunctive	**Present**		**Present Perfect**	
	duerma	durmamos	haya dormido	hayamos dormido
	duermas	durmáis	hayas dormido	hayáis dormido
	duerma	duerman	haya dormido	hayan dormido
	Imperfect		**Pluperfect**	
	durmiera	durmiéramos	hubiera dormido	hubiéramos dormido
	durmieras	durmierais	hubieras dormido	hubierais dormido
	durmiera	durmieran	hubiera dormido	hubieran dormido

Another high-frequency *-ir* verb with an *o→ue* stem change is *morir* ("to die").

-*IR* VERBS WITH *E→I* STEM CHANGES

servir ("to serve")

Gerund
sirviendo

Past Participle
servido

Commands

Pronoun	Affirmative	Negative
Ud.	sirva	no sirva
Uds.	sirvan	no sirvan
tú	sirve	no sirvas
vosotros	servid	no sirváis
nosotros	sirvamos	no sirvamos

Mood	Simple Tenses		Compound Tenses	
	Singular	**Plural**	**Singular**	**Plural**
Indicative	**Present**		**Present Perfect**	
	sirvo	servimos	he servido	hemos servido
	sirves	servís	has servido	habéis servido
	sirve	sirven	ha servido	han servido
	Preterit		**Preterit Perfect**	
	serví	servimos	hube servido	hubimos servido
	serviste	servisteis	hubiste servido	hubisteis servido
	sirvió	sirvieron	hubo servido	hubieron servido
	Imperfect		**Pluperfect**	
	servía	servíamos	había servido	habíamos servido
	servías	servíais	habías servido	habíais servido
	servía	servían	había servido	habían servido
	Future		**Future Perfect**	
	serviré	serviremos	habré servido	habremos servido
	servirás	serviréis	habrás servido	habréis servido
	servirá	servirán	habrá servido	habrán servido
	Conditional		**Conditional Perfect**	
	serviría	serviríamos	habría servido	habríamos servido
	servirías	serviríais	habrías servido	habríais servido
	serviría	servirían	habría servido	habrían servido
Subjunctive	**Present**		**Present Perfect**	
	sirva	sirvamos	haya servido	hayamos servido
	sirvas	sirváis	hayas servido	hayáis servido
	sirva	sirvan	haya servido	hayan servido
	Imperfect		**Pluperfect**	
	sirviera	sirviéramos	hubiera servido	hubiéramos servido
	sirvieras	sirvierais	hubieras servido	hubierais servido
	sirviera	sirvieran	hubiera servido	hubieran servido

Other High-Frequency -ir Verbs with e→i Stem Changes

Verb	English
competir	to compete
despedir	to say goodbye to
expedir	to send
gemir	to moan
impedir	to impede
medir	to measure
pedir	to request
repetir	to repeat
vestir	to clothe

-*GIR* VERBS WITH *E*→*I* STEM CHANGES

elegir ("to elect")

Gerund
eligiendo

Past Participle
elegido

Commands

Pronoun	Affirmative	Negative
Ud.	elija	no elija
Uds.	elijan	no elijan
tú	elige	no elijas
vosotros	elegid	no elijáis
nosotros	elijamos	no elijamos

Mood	Simple Tenses		Compound Tenses	
	Singular	*Plural*	*Singular*	*Plural*
Indicative	**Present**		**Present Perfect**	
	elijo	elegimos	he elegido	hemos elegido
	eliges	elegís	has elegido	habéis elegido
	elige	eligen	ha elegido	han elegido
	Preterit		**Preterit Perfect**	
	elegí	elegimos	hube elegido	hubimos elegido
	elegiste	elegisteis	hubiste elegido	hubisteis elegido
	eligió	eligieron	hubo elegido	hubieron elegido
	Imperfect		**Pluperfect**	
	elegía	elegíamos	había elegido	habíamos elegido
	elegías	elegíais	habías elegido	habíais elegido
	elegía	elegían	había elegido	habían elegido
	Future		**Future Perfect**	
	elegiré	elegiremos	habré elegido	habremos elegido
	elegirás	elegiréis	habrás elegido	habréis elegido
	elegirá	elegirán	habrá elegido	habrán elegido
	Conditional		**Conditional Perfect**	
	elegiría	elegiríamos	habría elegido	habríamos elegido
	elegirías	elegiríais	habrías elegido	habríais elegido
	elegiría	elegirían	habría elegido	habrían elegido
Subjunctive	**Present**		**Present Perfect**	
	elija	elijamos	haya elegido	hayamos elegido
	elijas	elijáis	hayas elegido	hayáis elegido
	elija	elijan	haya elegido	hayan elegido
	Imperfect		**Pluperfect**	
	eligiera	eligiéramos	hubiera elegido	hubiéramos elegido
	eligieras	eligierais	hubieras elegido	hubierais elegido
	eligiera	eligieran	hubiera elegido	hubieran elegido

Other High-Frequency -gir *Verbs with* e→i *Stem Changes*

Verb	English
colegir	to collect
corregir	to correct
regir	to rule

-*GUIR* VERBS WITH *I*→*IE* STEM CHANGES

seguir ("to follow")

Gerund
siguiendo

Past Participle
seguido

Commands

Pronoun	Affirmative	Negative
Ud.	siga	no siga
Uds.	sigan	no sigan
tú	sigue	no sigas
vosotros	seguid	no sigáis
nosotros	sigamos	no sigamos

Mood	Simple Tenses		Compound Tenses	
	Singular	*Plural*	*Singular*	*Plural*
Indicative	**Present**		**Present Perfect**	
	sigo	seguimos	he seguido	hemos seguido
	sigues	seguís	has seguido	habéis seguido
	sigue	siguen	ha seguido	han seguido
	Preterit		**Preterit Perfect**	
	seguí	seguimos	hube seguido	hubimos seguido
	seguiste	seguisteis	hubiste seguido	hubisteis seguido
	siguió	siguieron	hubo seguido	hubieron seguido
	Imperfect		**Pluperfect**	
	seguía	seguíamos	había seguido	habíamos seguido
	seguías	seguíais	habías seguido	habíais seguido
	seguía	seguían	había seguido	habían seguido
	Future		**Future Perfect**	
	seguiré	seguiremos	habré seguido	habremos seguido
	seguirás	seguiréis	habrás seguido	habréis seguido
	seguirá	seguirán	habrá seguido	habrán seguido
	Conditional		**Conditional Perfect**	
	seguiría	seguiríamos	habría seguido	habríamos seguido
	seguirías	seguiríais	habrías seguido	habríais seguido
	seguiría	seguirían	habría seguido	habrían seguido
Subjunctive	**Present**		**Present Perfect**	
	siga	sigamos	haya seguido	hayamos seguido
	sigas	sigáis	hayas seguido	hayáis seguido
	siga	sigan	haya seguido	hayan seguido
	Imperfect		**Pluperfect**	
	siguiera	siguiéramos	hubiera seguido	hubiéramos seguido
	siguieras	siguierais	hubieras seguido	hubierais seguido
	siguiera	siguieran	hubiera seguido	hubieran seguido

Other High-Frequency -guir *Verbs with* e→i *Stem Changes*

Verb	English
conseguir	to get
perseguir	to pursue
proseguir	to continue

Irregular Verbs

andar ("to walk")

Gerund
andando

Past Participle
andado

Commands

Pronoun	Affirmative	Negative
Ud.	ande	no ande
Uds.	anden	no anden
tú	anda	no andes
vosotros	andad	no andéis
nosotros	andemos	no andemos

Mood	Simple Tenses		Compound Tenses	
	Singular	*Plural*	*Singular*	*Plural*
Indicative	**Present**		**Present Perfect**	
	ando	andamos	he andado	hemos andado
	andas	andáis	has andado	habéis andado
	anda	andan	ha andado	han andado
	Preterit		**Preterit Perfect**	
	anduve	anduvimos	hube andado	hubimos andado
	anduviste	anduvisteis	hubiste andado	hubisteis andado
	anduvo	anduvieron	hubo andado	hubieron andado
	Imperfect		**Pluperfect**	
	andaba	andábamos	había andado	habíamos andado
	andabas	andabais	habías andado	habíais andado
	andaba	andaban	había andado	habían andado
	Future		**Future Perfect**	
	andaré	andaremos	habré andado	habremos andado
	andarás	andaréis	habrás andado	habréis andado
	andará	andarán	habrá andado	habrán andado
	Conditional		**Conditional Perfect**	
	andaría	andaríamos	habría andado	habríamos andado
	andarías	andaríais	habrías andado	habríais andado
	andaría	andarían	habría andado	habrían andado
Subjunctive	**Present**		**Present Perfect**	
	ande	andemos	haya andado	hayamos andado
	andes	andéis	hayas andado	hayáis andado
	ande	anden	haya andado	hayan andado
	Imperfect		**Pluperfect**	
	anduviera	anduviéramos	hubiera andado	hubiéramos andado
	anduvieras	anduvierais	hubieras andado	hubierais andado
	anduviera	anduvieran	hubiera andado	hubieran andado

caber ("to fit")

Gerund
cabiendo

Past Participle
cabido

Commands

Pronoun	Affirmative	Negative
Ud.	quepa	no quepa
Uds.	quepan	no quepan
tú	cabe	no quepas
vosotros	cabed	no quepáis
nosotros	quepamos	no quepamos

Mood	Simple Tenses		Compound Tenses	
	Singular	*Plural*	*Singular*	*Plural*
Indicative	**Present**		**Present Perfect**	
	quepo	cabemos	he cabido	hemos cabido
	cabes	cabéis	has cabido	habéis cabido
	cabe	caben	ha cabido	han cabido
	Preterit		**Preterit Perfect**	
	cupe	cupimos	hube cabido	hubimos cabido
	cupiste	cupisteis	hubiste cabido	hubisteis cabido
	cupo	cupieron	hubo cabido	hubieron cabido
	Imperfect		**Pluperfect**	
	cabía	cabíamos	había cabido	habíamos cabido
	cabías	cabíais	habías cabido	habíais cabido
	cabía	cabían	había cabido	habían cabido
	Future		**Future Perfect**	
	cabré	cabremos	habré cabido	habremos cabido
	cabrás	cabréis	habrás cabido	habréis cabido
	cabrá	cabrán	habrá cabido	habrán cabido
	Conditional		**Conditional Perfect**	
	cabría	cabríamos	habría cabido	habríamos cabido
	cabrías	cabríais	habrías cabido	habríais cabido
	cabría	cabrían	habría cabido	habrían cabido
Subjunctive	**Present**		**Present Perfect**	
	quepa	quepamos	haya cabido	hayamos cabido
	quepas	quepáis	hayas cabido	hayáis cabido
	quepa	quepan	haya cabido	hayan cabido
	Imperfect		**Pluperfect**	
	cupiera	cupiéramos	hubiera cabido	hubiéramos cabido
	cupieras	cupierais	hubieras cabido	hubierais cabido
	cupiera	cupieran	hubiera cabido	hubieran cabido

caer ("to fall")

Gerund
cayendo

Past Participle
caído

Commands

Pronoun	Affirmative	Negative
Ud.	caiga	no caiga
Uds.	caigan	no caigan
tú	cae	no caigas
vosotros	caed	no caigáis
nosotros	caigamos	no caigamos

Mood	Simple Tenses		Compound Tenses	
	Singular	*Plural*	*Singular*	*Plural*
Indicative	**Present**		**Present Perfect**	
	caigo	caemos	he caído	hemos caído
	caes	caéis	has caído	habéis caído
	cae	caen	ha caído	han caído
	Preterit		**Preterit Perfect**	
	caí	caímos	hube caído	hubimos caído
	caiste	caísteis	hubiste caído	hubisteis caído
	cayó	cayeron	hubo caído	hubieron caído
	Imperfect		**Pluperfect**	
	caía	caíamos	había caído	habíamos caído
	caías	caíais	habías caído	habíais caído
	caía	caían	había caído	habían caído
	Future		**Future Perfect**	
	caeré	caeremos	habré caído	habremos caído
	caerás	caeréis	habrás caído	habréis caído
	caerá	caerán	habrá caído	habrán caído
	Conditional		**Conditional Perfect**	
	caería	caeríamos	habría caído	habríamos caído
	caerías	caeríais	habrías caído	habríais caído
	caería	caerían	habría caído	habrían caído
Subjunctive	**Present**		**Present Perfect**	
	caiga	caigamos	haya caído	hayamos caído
	caigas	caigáis	hayas caído	hayáis caído
	caiga	caigan	haya caído	hayan caído
	Imperfect		**Pluperfect**	
	cayera	cayéramos	hubiera caído	hubiéramos caído
	cayeras	cayerais	hubieras caído	hubierais caído
	cayera	cayeran	hubiera caído	hubieran caído

dar ("to give")

Gerund
dando

Past Participle
dado

Commands

Pronoun	Affirmative	Negative
Ud.	dé	no dé
Uds.	den	no den
tú	da	no des
vosotros	dad	no deis
nosotros	demos	no demos

Mood	Simple Tenses		Compound Tenses	
	Singular	*Plural*	*Singular*	*Plural*
Indicative	**Present**		**Present Perfect**	
	doy	damos	he dado	hemos dado
	das	dáis	has dado	habéis dado
	da	dan	ha dado	han dado
	Preterit		**Preterit Perfect**	
	dí	dimos	hube dado	hubimos dado
	diste	disteis	hubiste dado	hubisteis dado
	dió	dieron	hubo dado	hubieron dado
	Imperfect		**Pluperfect**	
	daba	dábamos	había dado	habíamos dado
	dabas	dabais	habías dado	habíais dado
	daba	daban	había dado	habían dado
	Future		**Future Perfect**	
	daré	daremos	habré dado	habremos dado
	darás	daréis	habrás dado	habréis dado
	dará	darán	habrá dado	habrán dado
	Conditional		**Conditional Perfect**	
	daría	daríamos	habría dado	habríamos dado
	darías	daríais	habrías dado	habríais dado
	daría	darían	habría dado	habrían dado
Subjunctive	**Present**		**Present Perfect**	
	dé	demos	haya dado	hayamos dado
	des	deis	hayas dado	hayáis dado
	dé	den	haya dado	hayan dado
	Imperfect		**Pluperfect**	
	diera	diéramos	hubiera dado	hubiéramos dado
	dieras	dierais	hubieras dado	hubierais dado
	diera	dieran	hubiera dado	hubieran dado

decir ("to say," "to tell")

Gerund
diciendo

Past Participle
dicho

Commands

Pronoun	Affirmative	Negative
Ud.	diga	no diga
Uds.	digan	no digan
tú	di	no digas
vosotros	decid	no digáis
nosotros	digamos	no digamos

Mood	Simple Tenses		Compound Tenses	
	Singular	*Plural*	*Singular*	*Plural*
Indicative	**Present**		**Present Perfect**	
	digo	decimos	he dicho	hemos dicho
	dices	decís	has dicho	habéis dicho
	dice	dicen	ha dicho	han dicho
	Preterit		**Preterit Perfect**	
	dije	dijimos	hube dicho	hubimos dicho
	dijiste	dijisteis	hubiste dicho	hubisteis dicho
	dijo	dijeron	hubo dicho	hubieron dicho
	Imperfect		**Pluperfect**	
	decía	decíamos	había dicho	habíamos dicho
	decías	decíais	habías dicho	habíais dicho
	decía	decían	había dicho	habían dicho
	Future		**Future Perfect**	
	diré	diremos	habré dicho	habremos dicho
	dirás	diréis	habrás dicho	habréis dicho
	dirá	dirán	habrá dicho	habrán dicho
	Conditional		**Conditional Perfect**	
	diría	diríamos	habría dicho	habríamos dicho
	dirías	diríais	habrías dicho	habríais dicho
	diría	dirían	habría dicho	habrían dicho
Subjunctive	**Present**		**Present Perfect**	
	diga	digamos	haya dicho	hayamos dicho
	digas	digáis	hayas dicho	hayáis dicho
	diga	digan	haya dicho	hayan dicho
	Imperfect		**Pluperfect**	
	dijera	dijéramos	hubiera dicho	hubiéramos dicho
	dijeras	dijerais	hubieras dicho	hubierais dicho
	dijera	dijeran	hubiera dicho	hubieran dicho

estar ("to be")

Gerund
estando

Past Participle
estado

Commands

Pronoun	Affirmative	Negative
Ud.	esté	no esté
Uds.	estén	no estén
tú	está	no estés
vosotros	estad	no estéis
nosotros	estemos	no estemos

Mood	Simple Tenses		Compound Tenses	
	Singular	*Plural*	*Singular*	*Plural*
Indicative	**Present**		**Present Perfect**	
	estoy	estamos	he estado	hemos estado
	estás	estáis	has estado	habéis estado
	está	están	ha estado	han estado
	Preterit		**Preterit Perfect**	
	estuve	estuvimos	hube estado	hubimos estado
	estuviste	estuvisteis	hubiste estado	hubisteis estado
	estuvo	estuvieron	hubo estado	hubieron estado
	Imperfect		**Pluperfect**	
	estaba	estábamos	había estado	habíamos estado
	estabas	estabais	habías estado	habíais estado
	estaba	estaban	había estado	habían estado
	Future		**Future Perfect**	
	estaré	estaremos	habré estado	habremos estado
	estarás	estaréis	habrás estado	habréis estado
	estará	estarán	habrá estado	habrán estado
	Conditional		**Conditional Perfect**	
	estaría	estaríamos	habría estado	habríamos estado
	estarías	estaríais	habrías estado	habríais estado
	estaría	estarían	habría estado	habrían estado
Subjunctive	**Present**		**Present Perfect**	
	esté	estemos	haya estado	hayamos estado
	estés	estéis	hayas estado	hayáis estado
	esté	estén	haya estado	hayan estado
	Imperfect		**Pluperfect**	
	estuviera	estuviéramos	hubiera estado	hubiéramos estado
	estuvieras	estuvierais	hubieras estado	hubierais estado
	estuviera	estuvieran	hubiera estado	hubieran estado

haber ("to have")

Gerund
habiendo

Past Participle
habido

Commands

Pronoun	Affirmative	Negative
Ud.	haya	no haya
Uds.	hayan	no hayan
tú	hé	no hayas
vosotros	habed	no hayáis
nosotros	hayamos	no hayamos

Mood	Simple Tenses		Compound Tenses	
	Singular	*Plural*	*Singular*	*Plural*
Indicative	**Present**		**Present Perfect**	
	he	hemos	he habido	hemos habido
	has	habéis	has habido	habéis habido
	ha	han	ha habido	han habido
	Preterit		**Preterit Perfect**	
	hube	hubimos	hube habido	hubimos habido
	hubiste	hubisteis	hubiste habido	hubisteis habido
	hubo	hubieron	hubo habido	hubieron habido
	Imperfect		**Pluperfect**	
	había	habíamos	había habido	habíamos habido
	habías	habíais	habías habido	habíais habido
	había	habían	había habido	habían habido
	Future		**Future Perfect**	
	habré	habremos	habré habido	habremos habido
	habrás	habréis	habrás habido	habréis habido
	habrá	habrán	habrá habido	habrán habido
	Conditional		**Conditional Perfect**	
	habría	habríamos	habría habido	habríamos habido
	habrías	habríais	habrías habido	habríais habido
	habría	habrían	habría habido	habrían habido
Subjunctive	**Present**		**Present Perfect**	
	haya	hayamos	haya habido	hayamos habido
	hayas	hayáis	hayas habido	hayáis habido
	haya	hayan	haya habido	hayan habido
	Imperfect		**Pluperfect**	
	hubiera	hubiéramos	hubiera habido	hubiéramos habido
	hubieras	hubierais	hubieras habido	hubierais habido
	hubiera	hubieran	hubiera habido	hubieran habido

hacer ("to make," "to do")

Gerund
haciendo

Past Participle
hecho

Commands

Pronoun	Affirmative	Negative
Ud.	haga	no haga
Uds.	hagan	no hagan
tú	haz	no hagas
vosotros	haced	no hagáis
nosotros	hagamos	no hagamos

Mood	Simple Tenses		Compound Tenses	
	Singular	*Plural*	*Singular*	*Plural*
Indicative	**Present**		**Present Perfect**	
	hago	hacemos	he hecho	hemos hecho
	haces	hacéis	has hecho	habéis hecho
	hace	hacen	ha hecho	han hecho
	Preterit		**Preterit Perfect**	
	hice	hicimos	hube hecho	hubimos hecho
	hiciste	hicisteis	hubiste hecho	hubisteis hecho
	hizo	hicieron	hubo hecho	hubieron hecho
	Imperfect		**Pluperfect**	
	hacía	hacíamos	había hecho	habíamos hecho
	hacías	hacíais	habías hecho	habíais hecho
	hacía	hacían	había hecho	habían hecho
	Future		**Future Perfect**	
	haré	haremos	habré hecho	habremos hecho
	harás	haréis	habrás hecho	habréis hecho
	hará	harán	habrá hecho	habrán hecho
	Conditional		**Conditional Perfect**	
	haría	haríamos	habría hecho	habríamos hecho
	harías	haríais	habrías hecho	habríais hecho
	haría	harían	habría hecho	habrían hecho
Subjunctive	**Present**		**Present Perfect**	
	haga	hagamos	haya hecho	hayamos hecho
	hagas	hagáis	hayas hecho	hayáis hecho
	haga	hagan	haya hecho	hayan hecho
	Imperfect		**Pluperfect**	
	hiciera	hiciéramos	hubiera hecho	hubiéramos hecho
	hicieras	hicierais	hubieras hecho	hubierais hecho
	hiciera	hicieran	hubiera hecho	hubieran hecho

ir ("to go")

Gerund
yendo

Past Participle
ido

Commands

Pronoun	Affirmative	Negative
Ud.	vaya	no vaya
Uds.	vayan	no vayan
tú	ve	no vayas
vosotros	id	no vayáis
nosotros	vayamos	no vayamos

Mood	Simple Tenses		Compound Tenses	
	Singular	*Plural*	*Singular*	*Plural*
Indicative	**Present**		**Present Perfect**	
	voy	vamos	he ido	hemos ido
	vas	vais	has ido	habéis ido
	va	van	ha ido	han ido
	Preterit		**Preterit Perfect**	
	fui	fuimos	hube ido	hubimos ido
	fuiste	fuisteis	hubiste ido	hubisteis ido
	fue	fueron	hubo ido	hubieron ido
	Imperfect		**Pluperfect**	
	iba	íbamos	había ido	habíamos ido
	ibas	ibais	habías ido	habíais ido
	iba	iban	había ido	habían ido
	Future		**Future Perfect**	
	iré	iremos	habré ido	habremos ido
	irás	iréis	habrás ido	habréis ido
	irá	irán	habrá ido	habrán ido
	Conditional		**Conditional Perfect**	
	iría	iríamos	habría ido	habríamos ido
	irías	iríais	habrías ido	habríais ido
	iría	irían	habría ido	habrían ido
Subjunctive	**Present**		**Present Perfect**	
	vaya	vayamos	haya ido	hayamos ido
	vayas	vayáis	hayas ido	hayáis ido
	vaya	vayan	haya ido	hayan ido
	Imperfect		**Pluperfect**	
	fuera	fuéramos	hubiera ido	hubiéramos ido
	fueras	fuerais	hubieras ido	hubierais ido
	fuera	fueran	hubiera ido	hubieran ido

oír ("to hear")

Gerund
oyendo

Past Participle
oído

Commands

Pronoun	Affirmative	Negative
Ud.	oiga	no oiga
Uds.	oigan	no oigan
tú	oye	no oigas
vosotros	oíd	no oigáis
nosotros	oigamos	no oigamos

Mood	Simple Tenses		Compound Tenses	
	Singular	*Plural*	*Singular*	*Plural*
Indicative	**Present**		**Present Perfect**	
	oigo	oímos	he oído	hemos oído
	oyes	oís	has oído	habéis oído
	oye	oyen	ha oído	han oído
	Preterit		**Preterit Perfect**	
	oí	oímos	hube oído	hubimos oído
	oíste	oísteis	hubiste oído	hubisteis oído
	oyó	oyeron	hubo oído	hubieron oído
	Imperfect		**Pluperfect**	
	oía	oíamos	había oído	habíamos oído
	oías	oíais	habías oído	habíais oído
	oía	oían	había oído	habían oído
	Future		**Future Perfect**	
	oiré	oiremos	habré oído	habremos oído
	oirás	oiréis	habrás oído	habréis oído
	oirá	oirán	habrá oído	habrán oído
	Conditional		**Conditional Perfect**	
	oiría	oiríamos	habría oído	habríamos oído
	oirías	oiríais	habrías oído	habríais oído
	oiría	oirían	habría oído	habrían oído
Subjunctive	**Present**		**Present Perfect**	
	oiga	oigamos	haya oído	hayamos oído
	oigas	oigáis	hayas oído	hayáis oído
	oiga	oigan	haya oído	hayan oído
	Imperfect		**Pluperfect**	
	oyera	oyéramos	hubiera oído	hubiéramos oído
	oyeras	oyerais	hubieras oído	hubierais oído
	oyera	oyeran	hubiera oído	hubieran oído

oler ("to smell")

Gerund
oliendo

Past Participle
olido

Commands

Pronoun	Affirmative	Negative
Ud.	huela	no huela
Uds.	huelan	no huelan
tú	huele	no huelas
vosotros	oled	no oláis
nosotros	olamos	no olamos

Mood	Simple Tenses		Compound Tenses	
	Singular	*Plural*	*Singular*	*Plural*
Indicative	**Present**		**Present Perfect**	
	huelo	olemos	he olido	hemos olido
	hueles	oléis	has olido	habéis olido
	huele	huelen	ha olido	han olido
	Preterit		**Preterit Perfect**	
	olí	olimos	hube olido	hubimos olido
	oliste	olisteis	hubiste olido	hubisteis olido
	olió	olieron	hubo olido	hubieron olido
	Imperfect		**Pluperfect**	
	olía	olíamos	había olido	habíamos olido
	olías	olíais	habías olido	habíais olido
	olía	olían	había olido	habían olido
	Future		**Future Perfect**	
	oleré	oleremos	habré olido	habremos olido
	olerás	oleréis	habrás olido	habréis olido
	olerá	olerán	habrá olido	habrán olido
	Conditional		**Conditional Perfect**	
	olería	oleríamos	habría olido	habríamos olido
	olerías	oleríais	habrías olido	habríais olido
	olería	olerían	habría olido	habrían olido
Subjunctive	**Present**		**Present Perfect**	
	huela	olamos	haya olido	hayamos olido
	huelas	oláis	hayas olido	hayáis olido
	huela	huelan	haya olido	hayan olido
	Imperfect		**Pluperfect**	
	oliera	oliéramos	hubiera olido	hubiéramos olido
	olieras	olierais	hubieras olido	hubierais olido
	oliera	olieran	hubiera olido	hubieran olido

poder ("to be able")

Gerund
pudiendo

Past Participle
podido

Commands

Pronoun	Affirmative	Negative
Ud.	pueda	no pueda
Uds.	puedan	no puedan
tú	puede	no puedas
vosotros	poded	no podáis
nosotros	podamos	no podamos

Mood	Simple Tenses		Compound Tenses	
	Singular	*Plural*	*Singular*	*Plural*
Indicative	**Present**		**Present Perfect**	
	puedo	podemos	he podido	hemos podido
	puedes	podéis	has podido	habéis podido
	puede	pueden	ha podido	han podido
	Preterit		**Preterit Perfect**	
	pude	pudimos	hube podido	hubimos podido
	pudiste	pudisteis	hubiste podido	hubisteis podido
	pudo	pudieron	hubo podido	hubieron podido
	Imperfect		**Pluperfect**	
	podía	podíamos	había podido	habíamos podido
	podías	podíais	habías podido	habíais podido
	podía	podían	había podido	habían podido
	Future		**Future Perfect**	
	podré	podremos	habré podido	habremos podido
	podrás	podréis	habrás podido	habréis podido
	podrá	podrán	habrá podido	habrán podido
	Conditional		**Conditional Perfect**	
	podría	podríamos	habría podido	habríamos podido
	podrías	podríais	habrías podido	habríais podido
	podría	podrían	habría podido	habrían podido
Subjunctive	**Present**		**Present Perfect**	
	pueda	podamos	haya podido	hayamos podido
	puedas	podáis	hayas podido	hayáis podido
	pueda	puedan	haya podido	hayan podido
	Imperfect		**Pluperfect**	
	pudiera	pudiéramos	hubiera podido	hubiéramos podido
	pudieras	pudierais	hubieras podido	hubierais podido
	pudiera	pudieran	hubiera podido	hubieran podido

poner ("to put")

Gerund
poniendo

Past Participle
puesto

Commands

Pronoun	Affirmative	Negative
Ud.	ponga	no ponga
Uds.	pongan	no pongan
tú	pon	no pongas
vosotros	poned	no pongáis
nosotros	pongamos	no pongamos

Mood	Simple Tenses		Compound Tenses	
	Singular	*Plural*	*Singular*	*Plural*
Indicative	**Present**		**Present Perfect**	
	pongo	ponemos	he puesto	hemos puesto
	pones	ponéis	has puesto	habéis puesto
	pone	ponen	ha puesto	han puesto
	Preterit		**Preterit Perfect**	
	puse	pusimos	hube puesto	hubimos puesto
	pusiste	pusisteis	hubiste puesto	hubisteis puesto
	puso	pusieron	hubo puesto	hubieron puesto
	Imperfect		**Pluperfect**	
	ponía	poníamos	había puesto	habíamos puesto
	ponías	poníais	habías puesto	habíais puesto
	ponía	ponían	había puesto	habían puesto
	Future		**Future Perfect**	
	pondré	pondremos	habré puesto	habremos puesto
	pondrás	pondréis	habrás puesto	habréis puesto
	pondrá	pondrán	habrá puesto	habrán puesto
	Conditional		**Conditional Perfect**	
	pondría	pondríamos	habría puesto	habríamos puesto
	pondrías	pondríais	habrías puesto	habríais puesto
	pondría	pondrían	habría puesto	habrían puesto
Subjunctive	**Present**		**Present Perfect**	
	ponga	pongamos	haya puesto	hayamos puesto
	pongas	pongáis	hayas puesto	hayáis puesto
	ponga	pongan	haya puesto	hayan puesto
	Imperfect		**Pluperfect**	
	pusiera	pusiéramos	hubiera puesto	hubiéramos puesto
	pusieras	pusierais	hubieras puesto	hubierais puesto
	pusiera	pusieran	hubiera puesto	hubieran puesto

querer ("to wish," "to want")

Gerund
queriendo

Past Participle
querido

Commands

Pronoun	Affirmative	Negative
Ud.	quiera	no quiera
Uds.	quieran	no quieran
tú	quiere	no quieras
vosotros	quered	no queráis
nosotros	queramos	no queramos

Mood	Simple Tenses		Compound Tenses	
	Singular	*Plural*	*Singular*	*Plural*
Indicative	**Present**		**Present Perfect**	
	quiero	queremos	he querido	hemos querido
	quieres	queréis	has querido	habéis querido
	quiere	quieren	ha querido	han querido
	Preterit		**Preterit Perfect**	
	quise	quisimos	hube querido	hubimos querido
	quisiste	quisisteis	hubiste querido	hubisteis querido
	quiso	quisieron	hubo querido	hubieron querido
	Imperfect		**Pluperfect**	
	quería	queríamos	había querido	habíamos querido
	querías	queríais	habías querido	habíais querido
	quería	querían	había querido	habían querido
	Future		**Future Perfect**	
	querré	querremos	habré querido	habremos querido
	querrás	querréis	habrás querido	habréis querido
	querrá	querrán	habrá querido	habrán querido
	Conditional		**Conditional Perfect**	
	querría	querríamos	habría querido	habríamos querido
	querrías	querríais	habrías querido	habríais querido
	querría	querrían	habría querido	habrían querido
Subjunctive	**Present**		**Present Perfect**	
	quiera	queramos	haya querido	hayamos querido
	quieras	queráis	hayas querido	hayáis querido
	quiera	quieran	haya querido	hayan querido
	Imperfect		**Pluperfect**	
	quisiera	quisiéramos	hubiera querido	hubiéramos querido
	quisieras	quisierais	hubieras querido	hubierais querido
	quisiera	quisieran	hubiera querido	hubieran querido

reír ("to laugh")

Gerund
riendo

Past Participle
reído

Commands

Pronoun	Affirmative	Negative
Ud.	ría	no ría
Uds.	rían	no rían
tú	rie	no rías
vosotros	reíd	no riáis
nosotros	riamos	no riamos

Mood	Simple Tenses		Compound Tenses	
	Singular	*Plural*	*Singular*	*Plural*
Indicative	**Present**		**Present Perfect**	
	río	reímos	he reído	hemos reído
	ríes	reís	has reído	habéis reído
	ríe	ríen	ha reído	han reído
	Preterit		**Preterit Perfect**	
	reí	reímos	hube reído	hubimos reído
	reíste	reísteis	hubiste reído	hubisteis reído
	rió	rieron	hubo reído	hubieron reído
	Imperfect		**Pluperfect**	
	reía	reíamos	había reído	habíamos reído
	reías	reíais	habías reído	habíais reído
	reía	reían	había reído	habían reído
	Future		**Future Perfect**	
	reiré	reiremos	habré reído	habremos reído
	reirás	reiréis	habrás reído	habréis reído
	reirá	reirán	habrá reído	habrán reído
	Conditional		**Conditional Perfect**	
	reiría	reiríamos	habría reído	habríamos reído
	reirías	reiríais	habrías reído	habríais reído
	reiría	reirían	habría reído	habrían reído
Subjunctive	**Present**		**Present Perfect**	
	ría	riamos	haya reído	hayamos reído
	rías	riáis	hayas reído	hayáis reído
	ría	rían	haya reído	hayan reído
	Imperfect		**Pluperfect**	
	riera	riéramos	hubiera reído	hubiéramos reído
	rieras	rierais	hubieras reído	hubierais reído
	riera	rieran	hubiera reído	hubieran reído

saber ("to know")

Gerund
sabiendo

Past Participle
sabido

Commands

Pronoun	Affirmative	Negative
Ud.	sepa	no sepa
Uds.	sepan	no sepan
tú	sabe	no sepas
vosotros	sabed	no sepáis
nosotros	sepamos	no sepamos

Mood	Simple Tenses		Compound Tenses	
	Singular	*Plural*	*Singular*	*Plural*
Indicative	**Present**		**Present Perfect**	
	sé	sabemos	he sabido	hemos sabido
	sabes	sabéis	has sabido	habéis sabido
	sabe	saben	ha sabido	han sabido
	Preterit		**Preterit Perfect**	
	supe	supimos	hube sabido	hubimos sabido
	supiste	supisteis	hubiste sabido	hubisteis sabido
	supo	supieron	hubo sabido	hubieron sabido
	Imperfect		**Pluperfect**	
	sabía	sabíamos	había sabido	habíamos sabido
	sabías	sabíais	habías sabido	habíais sabido
	sabía	sabían	había sabido	habían sabido
	Future		**Future Perfect**	
	sabré	sabremos	habré sabido	habremos sabido
	sabrás	sabréis	habrás sabido	habréis sabido
	sabrá	sabrán	habrá sabido	habrán sabido
	Conditional		**Conditional Perfect**	
	sabría	sabríamos	habría sabido	habríamos sabido
	sabrías	sabríais	habrías sabido	habríais sabido
	sabría	sabrían	habría sabido	habrían sabido
Subjunctive	**Present**		**Present Perfect**	
	sepa	sepamos	haya sabido	hayamos sabido
	sepas	sepáis	hayas sabido	hayáis sabido
	sepa	sepan	haya sabido	hayan sabido
	Imperfect		**Pluperfect**	
	supiera	supiéramos	hubiera sabido	hubiéramos sabido
	supieras	supierais	hubieras sabido	hubierais sabido
	supiera	supieran	hubiera sabido	hubieran sabido

salir ("to go out")

Gerund
saliendo

Past Participle
salido

Commands

Pronoun	Affirmative	Negative
Ud.	salga	no salga
Uds.	salgan	no salgan
tú	sal	no salgas
vosotros	salid	no salgáis
nosotros	salgamos	no salgamos

Mood	Simple Tenses		Compound Tenses	
	Singular	*Plural*	*Singular*	*Plural*
Indicative	**Present**		**Present Perfect**	
	salgo	salimos	he salido	hemos salido
	sales	saléis	has salido	habéis salido
	sale	salen	ha salido	han salido
	Preterit		**Preterit Perfect**	
	salí	salimos	hube salido	hubimos salido
	saliste	salisteis	hubiste salido	hubisteis salido
	salió	salieron	hubo salido	hubieron salido
	Imperfect		**Pluperfect**	
	salía	salíamos	había salido	habíamos salido
	salías	salíais	habías salido	habíais salido
	salía	salían	había salido	habían salido
	Future		**Future Perfect**	
	saldré	saldremos	habré salido	habremos salido
	saldrás	saldréis	habrás salido	habréis salido
	saldrá	saldrán	habrá salido	habrán salido
	Conditional		**Conditional Perfect**	
	saldría	saldríamos	habría salido	habríamos salido
	saldrías	saldríais	habrías salido	habríais salido
	saldría	saldrían	habría salido	habrían salido
Subjunctive	**Present**		**Present Perfect**	
	salga	salgamos	haya salido	hayamos salido
	salgas	salgáis	hayas salido	hayáis salido
	salga	salgan	haya salido	hayan salido
	Imperfect		**Pluperfect**	
	saliera	saliéramos	hubiera salido	hubiéramos salido
	salieras	salierais	hubieras salido	hubierais salido
	saliera	salieran	hubiera salido	hubieran salido

ser ("to be")

Gerund

siendo

Past Participle

sido

Commands

Pronoun	Affirmative	Negative
Ud.	sea	no sea
Uds.	sean	no sean
tú	sé	no seas
vosotros	sed	no seáis
nosotros	seamos	no seamos

Mood	Simple Tenses		Compound Tenses	
	Singular	*Plural*	*Singular*	*Plural*
Indicative	**Present**		**Present Perfect**	
	soy	somos	he sido	hemos sido
	eres	sois	has sido	habéis sido
	es	son	ha sido	han sido
	Preterit		**Preterit Perfect**	
	fui	fuimos	hube sido	hubimos sido
	fuiste	fuisteis	hubiste sido	hubisteis sido
	fue	fueron	hubo sido	hubieron sido
	Imperfect		**Pluperfect**	
	era	éramos	había sido	habíamos sido
	eras	erais	habías sido	habíais sido
	era	eran	había sido	habían sido
	Future		**Future Perfect**	
	seré	seremos	habré sido	habremos sido
	serás	seréis	habrás sido	habréis sido
	será	serán	habrá sido	habrán sido
	Conditional		**Conditional Perfect**	
	sería	seríamos	habría sido	habríamos sido
	serías	seríais	habrías sido	habríais sido
	sería	serían	habría sido	habrían sido
Subjunctive	**Present**		**Present Perfect**	
	sea	seamos	haya sido	hayamos sido
	seas	seáis	hayas sido	hayáis sido
	sea	sean	haya sido	hayan sido
	Imperfect		**Pluperfect**	
	fuera	fuéramos	hubiera sido	hubiéramos sido
	fueras	fuerais	hubieras sido	hubierais sido
	fuera	fueran	hubiera sido	hubieran sido

tener ("to have")

Gerund
teniendo

Past Participle
tenido

Commands

Pronoun	Affirmative	Negative
Ud.	tenga	no tenga
Uds.	tengan	no tengan
tú	ten	no tengas
vosotros	tened	no tengáis
nosotros	tengamos	no tengamos

Mood	Simple Tenses		Compound Tenses	
	Singular	*Plural*	*Singular*	*Plural*
Indicative	**Present**		**Present Perfect**	
	tengo	tenemos	he tenido	hemos tenido
	tienes	tenéis	has tenido	habéis tenido
	tiene	tienen	ha tenido	han tenido
	Preterit		**Preterit Perfect**	
	tuve	tuvimos	hube tenido	hubimos tenido
	tuviste	tuvisteis	hubiste tenido	hubisteis tenido
	tuvo	tuvieron	hubo tenido	hubieron tenido
	Imperfect		**Pluperfect**	
	tenía	teníamos	había tenido	habíamos tenido
	tenías	teníais	habías tenido	habíais tenido
	tenía	tenían	había tenido	habían tenido
	Future		**Future Perfect**	
	tendré	tendremos	habré tenido	habremos tenido
	tendrás	tendréis	habrás tenido	habréis tenido
	tendrá	tendrán	habrá tenido	habrán tenido
	Conditional		**Conditional Perfect**	
	tendría	tendríamos	habría tenido	habríamos tenido
	tendrías	tendríais	habrías tenido	habríais tenido
	tendría	tendrían	habría tenido	habrían tenido
Subjunctive	**Present**		**Present Perfect**	
	tenga	tengamos	haya tenido	hayamos tenido
	tengas	tengáis	hayas tenido	hayáis tenido
	tenga	tengan	haya tenido	hayan tenido
	Imperfect		**Pluperfect**	
	tuviera	tuviéramos	hubiera tenido	hubiéramos tenido
	tuvieras	tuvierais	hubieras tenido	hubierais tenido
	tuviera	tuvieran	hubiera tenido	hubieran tenido

traer ("to bring")

Gerund

trayendo

Past Participle

traído

Commands

Pronoun	Affirmative	Negative
Ud.	traiga	no traiga
Uds.	traigan	no traigan
tú	trae	no traigas
vosotros	traed	no traigáis
nosotros	traigamos	no traigamos

Mood	Simple Tenses		Compound Tenses	
	Singular	*Plural*	*Singular*	*Plural*
Indicative	**Present**		**Present Perfect**	
	traigo	traemos	he traído	hemos traído
	traes	traéis	has traído	habéis traído
	trae	traen	ha traído	han traído
	Preterit		**Preterit Perfect**	
	traje	trajimos	hube traído	hubimos traído
	trajiste	trajisteis	hubiste traído	hubisteis traído
	trajo	trajeron	hubo traído	hubieron traído
	Imperfect		**Pluperfect**	
	traía	traíamos	había traído	habíamos traído
	traías	traíais	habías traído	habíais traído
	traía	traían	había traído	habían traído
	Future		**Future Perfect**	
	traeré	traeremos	habré traído	habremos traído
	traerás	traeréis	habrás traído	habréis traído
	traerá	traerán	habrá traído	habrán traído
	Conditional		**Conditional Perfect**	
	traería	traeríamos	habría traído	habríamos traído
	traerías	traeiríais	habrías traído	habríais traído
	traería	traerían	habría traído	habrían traído
Subjunctive	**Present**		**Present Perfect**	
	traiga	traigamos	haya traído	hayamos traído
	traigas	traigáis	hayas traído	hayáis traído
	traiga	traigan	haya traído	hayan traído
	Imperfect		**Pluperfect**	
	trajera	trajéramos	hubiera traído	hubiéramos traído
	trajeras	trajerais	hubieras traído	hubierais traído
	trajera	trajeran	hubiera traído	hubieran traído

valer ("to be worth")

Gerund
valiendo

Past Participle
valido

Commands

Pronoun	Affirmative	Negative
Ud.	valga	no valga
Uds.	valgan	no valgan
tú	val (vale)	no valgas
vosotros	valed	no valgáis
nosotros	valgamos	no valgamos

Mood	Simple Tenses		Compound Tenses	
	Singular	*Plural*	*Singular*	*Plural*
Indicative	**Present**		**Present Perfect**	
	valgo	valemos	he valido	hemos valido
	vales	valéis	has valido	habéis valido
	vale	valen	ha valido	han valido
	Preterit		**Preterit Perfect**	
	valí	valimos	hube valido	hubimos valido
	valiste	valisteis	hubiste valido	hubisteis valido
	valió	valieron	hubo valido	hubieron valido
	Imperfect		**Pluperfect**	
	valía	valíamos	había valido	habíamos valido
	valías	valíais	habías valido	habíais valido
	valía	valían	había valido	habían valido
	Future		**Future Perfect**	
	valdré	valdremos	habré valido	habremos valido
	valdrás	valdréis	habrás valido	habréis valido
	valdrá	valdrán	habrá valido	habrán valido
	Conditional		**Conditional Perfect**	
	valdría	valdríamos	habría valido	habríamos valido
	valdrías	valdríais	habrías valido	habríais valido
	valdría	valdrían	habría valido	habrían valido
Subjunctive	**Present**		**Present Perfect**	
	valga	valgamos	haya valido	hayamos valido
	valgas	valgáis	hayas valido	hayáis valido
	valga	valgan	haya valido	hayan valido
	Imperfect		**Pluperfect**	
	valiera	valiéramos	hubiera valido	hubiéramos valido
	valieras	valierais	hubieras valido	hubierais valido
	valiera	valieran	hubiera valido	hubieran valido

venir ("to come")

Gerund
viniendo

Past Participle
venido

Commands

Pronoun	Affirmative	Negative
Ud.	venga	no venga
Uds.	vengan	no vengan
tú	ven	no vengas
vosotros	venid	no vengáis
nosotros	vengamos	no vengamos

Mood	Simple Tenses		Compound Tenses	
	Singular	*Plural*	*Singular*	*Plural*
Indicative	**Present**		**Present Perfect**	
	vengo	venimos	he venido	hemos venido
	vienes	venís	has venido	habéis venido
	viene	vienen	ha venido	han venido
	Preterit		**Preterit Perfect**	
	vine	vinimos	hube venido	hubimos venido
	viniste	vinisteis	hubiste venido	hubisteis venido
	vino	vinieron	hubo venido	hubieron venido
	Imperfect		**Pluperfect**	
	venía	veníamos	había venido	habíamos venido
	venías	veníais	habías venido	habíais venido
	venía	venían	había venido	habían venido
	Future		**Future Perfect**	
	vendré	vendremos	habré venido	habremos venido
	vendrás	vendréis	habrás venido	habréis venido
	vendrá	vendrán	habrá venido	habrán venido
	Conditional		**Conditional Perfect**	
	vendría	vendríamos	habría venido	habríamos venido
	vendrías	vendríais	habrías venido	habríais venido
	vendría	vendrían	habría venido	habrían venido
Subjunctive	**Present**		**Present Perfect**	
	venga	vengamos	haya venido	hayamos venido
	vengas	vengáis	hayas venido	hayáis venido
	venga	vengan	haya venido	hayan venido
	Imperfect		**Pluperfect**	
	viniera	viniéramos	hubiera venido	hubiéramos venido
	vinieras	vinierais	hubieras venido	hubierais venido
	viniera	vinieran	hubiera venido	hubieran venido

ver ("to see")

Gerund
viendo

Past Participle
visto

Commands

Pronoun	Affirmative	Negative
Ud.	vea	no vea
Uds.	vean	no vean
tú	ve	no veas
vosotros	ved	no veáis
nosotros	veamos	no veamos

Mood	Simple Tenses		Compound Tenses	
	Singular	*Plural*	*Singular*	*Plural*
Indicative	**Present**		**Present Perfect**	
	veo	vemos	he visto	hemos visto
	ves	veis	has visto	habéis visto
	ve	ven	ha visto	han visto
	Preterit		**Preterit Perfect**	
	vi	vimos	hube visto	hubimos visto
	viste	visteis	hubiste visto	hubisteis visto
	vió	vieron	hubo visto	hubieron visto
	Imperfect		**Pluperfect**	
	veía	veíamos	había visto	habíamos visto
	veías	veíais	habías visto	habíais visto
	veía	veían	había visto	habían visto
	Future		**Future Perfect**	
	veré	veremos	habré visto	habremos visto
	verás	veréis	habrás visto	habréis visto
	verá	verán	habrá visto	habrán visto
	Conditional		**Conditional Perfect**	
	vería	veríamos	habría visto	habríamos visto
	verías	veríais	habrías visto	habríais visto
	vería	verían	habría visto	habrían visto
Subjunctive	**Present**		**Present Perfect**	
	vea	veamos	haya visto	hayamos visto
	veas	veáis	hayas visto	hayáis visto
	vea	vean	haya visto	hayan visto
	Imperfect		**Pluperfect**	
	viera	viéramos	hubiera visto	hubiéramos visto
	vieras	vierais	hubieras visto	hubierais visto
	viera	vieran	hubiera visto	hubieran visto

SPANISH VOCABULARY

The Family

Males		Females	
English	**Spanish**	**English**	**Spanish**
boyfriend	*novio*	girlfriend	*novia*
brother	*hermano*	sister	*hermana*
brother-in-law	*cuñado*	sister-in-law	*cuñada*
child	*niño*	child	*niña*
cousin	*primo*	cousin	*prima*
father	*padre*	mother	*madre*
father-in-law	*suegro*	mother-in-law	*suegra*
godfather	*padrino*	godmother	*padrina*
grandfather	*abuelo*	grandmother	*abuela*
grandson	*nieto*	granddaughter	*nieta*
husband	*esposo*	wife	*esposa*
nephew	*sobrino*	niece	*sobrina*
son	*hijo*	daughter	*hija*
son-in-law	*yerno*	daughter-in-law	*nuera*
stepbrother	*hermanastro*	stepsister	*hermanastra*
stepfather	*padrastro*	stepmother	*madrastra*
stepson	*hijastro*	stepdaughter	*hijastra*
uncle	*tío*	aunt	*tía*
great-grandfather	*bisabuelo*	great-grandmother	*bisabuela*

The House

Places

English	Spanish	English	Spanish
apartment	el apartamento	ground floor	la planta baja
apartment building	el edificio de apartamentos	hall	el pasillo
attic	el desván, el ático, el entretecho	house	la casa
backyard	el jardín	kitchen	la cocina
balcony	el balcón	laundry room	la lavandería
basement	el sótano	lawn	el césped
bathroom	el (cuarto de) baño	living room	la sala
bathtub	la bañera	owner	el dueño
bedroom	el dormitorio, la habitación	patio	el patio
ceiling	el techo	roof	el techo
closet	el armario	room	el cuarto, la habitación
courtyard	el patio	shower	la ducha
den	el estudio	sink (bathroom) (kitchen)	el lavabo el fregadero
dining room	el comedor	stair(s)	la(s) escalera(s)
door	la puerta	story (floor)	el piso
elevator	el ascensor	study	el estudio
fireplace	la chimenea	terrace	la terraza
floor	el suelo	wall	la pared
garage	el garaje	wardrobe	el armario
garden	el jardín	window	la ventana

Furnishings

English	Spanish	English	Spanish
armchair	el sillón	mirror	el espejo
bed	la cama	nightstand	el buró
bookcase	el librero	painting	el cuadro

English	Spanish	English	Spanish
carpet	*la moqueta*	picture	*la pintura*
chair	*la silla*	rug	*la alfombra*
clock	*el reloj*	sofa	*el sofá*
curtain	*la cortina*	table	*la mesa*
dresser	*el tocador, la cómoda*	wardrobe	*el guardarropa*
lamp	*la lámpara*		

Appliances and Electronics

English	Spanish	English	Spanish
camera	*la cámara, la máquina fotográfica*	monitor	*el monitor*
ceiling fan	*el ventilador de aspas, el ventilador hélice*	printer	*la impresora*
clothes dryer	*la secadora*	oven	*el horno*
computer	*el ordenador, la computadora*	refrigerator	*el refrigerador*
dishwasher	*el lavaplatos*	stereo	*el estéreo*
DVD player	*el lector de DVD*	stove	*la estufa*
fan	*el ventilador*	television set	*el televisor*
freezer	*el congelador*	VCR	*el video*
hair dryer	*el secador*	washing machine	*la lavadora*
microwave oven	*el horno de microondas*		

Household Chores

English	Spanish	English	Spanish
to babysit	*cuidar/guardar a los niños*	to mow the lawn	*cortar el césped*
to clean the house	*limpiar la casa*	to pay the bills	*pagar las cuentas*
to clear the table	*quitar la mesa*	to prepare the meals	*preparar las comidas*
to cook	*cocinar*	to repair	*reparar*

(continues)

Household Chores   *(continued)*

English	Spanish	English	Spanish
to do housework	*hacer los quehaceres doméstsicos*	to set the table	*poner la mesa*
to do laundry	*lavar la ropa*	to straighten	*ordenar*
to dust	*sacudir los muebles*	to take out garbage	*sacar la basura*
to go downtown	*ir al centro*	to vacuum	*pasar la aspiradora*
to go shopping	*ir de compras*	to wash the car	*lavar el coche*
to iron	*planchar la ropa*	to wash the dishes	*lavar los platos*
to make the bed	*hacer la camat ender la cama*		

Animals and Insects

English	Spanish	English	Spanish
bear	*el oso*	kangaroo	*el canguro*
bee	*la abeja*	leopard	*el leopardo*
bird	*el pájaro, el ave*	lion	*el león*
bull	*el toro*	monkey	*el mono*
cat	*el gato*	mosquito	*el mosquito*
chicken	*el pollo*	panther	*la pantera*
cow	*la vaca*	pig	*el cochino*
crocodile	*el cocodrilo*	rabbit	*el conejo*
deer	*el ciervo*	rooster	*el gallo*
dog	*el perro*	shark	*el tiburón*
dolphin	*el delfín*	sheep	*la oveja*
donkey	*el burro*	snake	*la serpiente*
duck	*el pato*	spider	*la araña*
elephant	*el elefante*	squirrel	*la ardilla*
fish	*el pez*	swan	*el cisne*
fox	*el zorro*	tiger	*el tigre*
giraffe	*la jirafa*	tortoise	*la tortuga*
goat	*la cabra*	turkey	*el pavo*
gorilla	*el gorila*	turtle	*la tortuga*

English	Spanish	English	Spanish
gnat	*el jején*	whale	*la ballena*
hen	*la gallina*	wolf	*el lobo*
horse	*el caballo*	zebra	*la cebra*

Foods

Meats

English	Spanish	English	Spanish
bacon	*el tocino*	pork	*el puerco*
beef	*la carne de vaca*	roast beef	*el rosbíf*
ham	*el jamón*	sausages	*las salchichas*
hamburger	*la hamburguesa*	steak	*el bistec*
lamb	*el cordero*	steak (BBQ)	*el churrasco*
liver	*el hígado*	stew	*el estofado, el guisado*
meat	*la carne*	veal	*la ternera*

Poultry

English	Spanish	English	Spanish
chicken	*el pollo*	goose	*el ganso*
duck	*el pato*	turkey	*el pavo*
fowl	*la carne de ave*	venison	*el venado*

Fish and Seafood

English	Spanish	English	Spanish
anchovy	*la anchoa*	red snapper	*el pargo colorado*
bass	*la merluza*	salmon	*el salmón*
clams	*las almejas*	sardines	*las sardinas*
codfish	*el bacalao*	scallops	*las vieiras*
crab	*el cangrejo*	seafood	*los mariscos*
fish	*el pescado*	shrimp	*los camarones, las gambas*
flounder	*la platija*	sole	*el lenguado*

(continues)

Fish and Seafood   *(continued)*

English	Spanish	English	Spanish
grouper	*el mero*	squid	*el calamar*
lobster	*la langosta*	swordfish	*el pez espada*
mussels	*los mejillones*	trout	*la trucha*
oysters	*las ostras*	tuna	*el atún*

Vegetables

English	Spanish	English	Spanish
artichoke	*la alcachofa*	onion	*la cebolla*
asparagus	*los espárragos*	peas	*las arvejas, los guisantes*
beans (green)	*las judías, las habichuelas*	pepper	*la pimienta*
beets	*las remolachas*	potato	*la papa, la patata*
broccoli	*el brócoli (el brécol)*	rice	*el arroz*
carrot	*la zanahoria*	salad	*la ensalada*
cauliflower	*la coliflor*	soy	*la soja*
celery	*el apio*	soybean	*la semila de soja*
corn	*el maíz*	spinach	*la espinaca*
cucumber	*el pepino*	sweet potato	*la papa dulce*
eggplant	*la berenjena*	tomato	*el tomate*
garlic	*el ajo*	turnip	*el nabo*
green beans (Mexico)	*los ejotes*	vegetable	*la verdura*
lettuce	*le lechuga*	zucchini	*el calabacín*
mushroom	*el champiñón*		

Fruits and Nuts

English	Spanish	English	Spanish
almond	*la almendra*	melon	*el melón*
apple	*la manzana*	olive	*la oliva/la aceituna*
apricot	*el albaricoque*	orange	*la naranja*
avocado	*el aguacate*	peach	*el melocotón*

English	Spanish	English	Spanish
banana	*la banana*	peanut	*el cacahuete* (Spain, Mexico); *el maní* (Latin America)
blueberry	*el mirtilo, el arándano azul*	pear	*la pera*
cashew	*el anacardo*	pecan	la pacana
cherry	*la cereza*	pineapple	*la piña*
chestnut	*la castaña*	plantain	*el plátano*
coconut	*el coco*	plum	*la ciruela*
cranberry	*el arándano rojo y agrio*	prune	*la ciruela pasa*
fruit	*la fruta*	raisin	*la pasa, la uva seca*
grape	*la uva*	raspberry	*la frambuesa, la mora*
grapefruit	*la toronja, el pomelo*	strawberry	*la fresa*
hazelnut	*la avellana*	tangerine	*la mandarina*
lemon	*el limón*	walnut	*la nuez*
lime	*la lima*	watermelon	*la sandía*

Dairy Products and Condiments

English	Spanish	English	Spanish
butter	*la mantequilla*	mayonnaise	*la mayonesa*
cheese	*el queso*	mustard	*la mostaza*
cream	*la crema*	oil	*el aceite*
eggs	*los huevos*	oregano	*el orégano*
flour	*la harina*	pepper (black) (red)	*la pimienta el pimiento, el ají*
garlic	*el ajo*	saccharin	*la sacarina*
honey	*la miel*	salt	*la sal*
jam, jelly	*la mermelada*	sugar	*el azúcar*
ketchup	*la salsa de tomate*	vinegar	*el vinagre*
maple syrup	*el jarabe de arce*	yogurt	*el yogur*

Eggs

English	Spanish	English	Spanish
fried	*huevos fritos*	scrambled	*huevos revueltos*
hard-boiled	*huevos duros*	soft-boiled	*huevos pasados por agua*
poached	*huevos escalfados*	with spicy sausage	*huevos con chorizo*
an omelette	*una tortilla*	with spicy tomato sauce (fried)	*huevos rancheros*

Breads and Desserts

English	Spanish	English	Spanish
caramel custard	*el flan*	meringue	*el merengue*
cracker	*la galleta*	pie	*el pastel*
bread	*el pan*	pudding	*la natilla, el pudín*
bun	*el bollo*	rice pudding	*el arroz con leche*
cake	*el pastel, la torta*	rolls	*los panecillos*
cookie	*la galletita*	sandwich	*el sándwich*
dessert	*el postre*	sponge cake	*el bizcocho*
gelatin	*la gelatina*	sundae	*el helado con frutas, jarabes or nueces; la copa de helado*
ice cream	*el helado*	tart	*la tarta*
marzipan	*el marzapán*		

Beverages

English	Spanish	English	Spanish
beer	*la cerveza*	lemonade	*la limonada*
champagne	*el champán*	milk	*la leche*
(hot) chocolate	*el chocolate*	milkshake	*la batida, la licuada*
cider	*la sidra*	soda	*la gaseosa*
coffee	*el café*	soup	*la sopa*
decaffeinated coffee	*el café descafeinado*	tea	*el té*
herbal tea	*el té herbario*	(mineral) water (carbonated) water (noncarbonated) water	*el agua (mineral)* *el agua (con gas)* *el agua (sin gas)*
juice (orange)	*el jugo (de naranja)*	wine	*el vino*

Meals

English	Spanish	English	Spanish
breakfast	*el desayuno*	lunch	*el almuerzo*
dinner	*la cena*	snack	*la merienda*

Table Setting

English	Spanish	English	Spanish
bowl	*el tazón*	pepper shaker	*el pimentero*
carafe	*la garrafa*	place setting	*el cubierto*
cup	*la taza*	salt shaker	*el salero*
dinner plate	*el plato*	saucer	*el platillo*
fork	*el tenedor*	soup dish	*la sopera*
glass	*el vaso*	soup spoon	*la cuchara*
knife	*el cuchillo*	tablecloth	*el mantel*
menu	*el menú*	teaspoon	*la cucharita*
napkin	*la servilleta*	wine glass	*la copa*
pepper mill	*el molinillo de pimienta*		

Quantities

English	Spanish	English	Spanish
a bag of	*un saco de*	a half pound of	*doscientos gramos de, una media libra de*
a bar of	*una tableta de, una barra de*	a jar of	*un pomo de, un frasco de*
a bottle of	*una botella de*	a package of	*un paquete de*
a box of	*una caja de*	a pound of	*quinientos gramos de, una libra de*
a can of	*una lata de*	a quart of	*un litro de*
a dozen of	*una docena de*	a slice of	*un trozo de*

Parts of the Body

English	Spanish	English	Spanish
ankle	el tobillo	heart	el corazón
arm	el brazo	hip	la cadera
back	la espalda	knee	la rodilla
beard	la barba	leg	la pierna
blood	la sangre	lip	el labio
body	el cuerpo	liver	el hígado
brain	el cerebro	lung	el pulmón
calf	la pantorrilla	mouth	la boca
cheek	la mejilla	muscle	el músculo
chest	el pecho	mustache	el bigote, el mostacho
chin	la barbilla	nail	la uña
ear	la oreja	neck	el cuello
elbow	el codo	nose	la nariz
eye	el ojo	shoulder	el hombro
eyebrow	la ceja	skin	la piel
eyelash	la pastaña	stomach	el estómago
eyelid	el párpado	thigh	el muslo
face	la cara	throat	la garganta
finger	el dedo	toe	el dedo del pie
foot	el pie	tongue	la lengua
forehead	la frente	tooth	el diente
hair	el cabello, el pelo	waist	la cintura, la talle
hand	la mano	wrist	la muñeca
head	la cabeza		

Places in Town

English	Spanish	English	Spanish
airport	el aeropuerto	monument	el monumento
avenue	la avenida	movie theater	el cine

English	Spanish	English	Spanish
bakery	*la panadería*	museum	*el museo*
bank	*el banco*	neighborhood	*el barrio*
bookstore	*la librería*	newsstand	*el quiosco de periódicos*
boulevard	*el bulevar; el zócalo* (Mexico)	park	*el parque*
building	*el edificio*	pastry shop	*la pastelería*
butcher shop	*la carnicería*	police station	*la comisaría*
cafe	*el café*	post office	*el correo*
camera shop	*la tienda del fotógrafo*	record store	*la tienda de discos*
cathedral	*la catedral*	restaurant	*el restaurante*
church	*la iglesia*	road	*el camino*
clothing store	*la tienda de ropa*	school	*la escuela*
courthouse	*el palacio de justicia*	sidewalk	*la acera*
department store	*el almacén*	skyscraper	*el rascacielos*
downtown	*el centro*	souvenir shop	*la tienda de recuerdos*
drugstore	*la farmacia*	square	*la plaza*
dry cleaner's	*la tintorería*	stadium	*el estadio*
factory	*la fábrica*	station	*la estación*
florist	*la florería*	statue	*la estatua*
gas station	*la gasolinera*	store	*la tienda*
grocery store	*la bodega*	street	*la calle*
gym	*el gimnasio*	suburb	*el suburbio*
highway	*la carretera*	supermarket	*el supermercado*
hospital	*el hospital*	swimming pool	*la piscina*
hotel	*el hotel*	theater	*el teatro*
jewelry store	*la joyería*	tobacco store	*la tabaquería*
laundry	*la lavandería*	town	*el pueblo*
leather goods store	*la marroquinería*	town hall	*el ayuntamiento*
library	*la biblioteca*	toy store	*la juguetería*
mall	*el centro comercial*	university	*la universidad*
market	*el mercado*	youth center	*el centro juvenil*

School and the Classroom

English	Spanish	English	Spanish
academy	el colegio	middle school	la escuela intermedia entre la primaria y la secundaria
answer	la respuesta	notebook	el cuaderno
backpack	la mochila	notes	los apuntes
ballpoint pen	el bolígrafo	page	la página
bell	el timbre	paper	el papel
bench	el banco	pen (ballpoint)	la pluma (el bolígrafo)
book	el libro	pencil	el lápiz
cafeteria	la cantina	poetry	la poesía
calculator	la calculadora	principal	el director
calendar	el calendario	professor	el profesor, la profesora
chalk	la tiza	pupil	el alumno, el estudiante
chalkboard	la pizarra	question	la pregunta
class	la clase	quiz	la prueba
classroom	la sala de clase	reading	la lectura
computer	el ordenador, la computadora	recess	la hora de recreo
counselor	el consejero	rule	la regla
crayon	el creyón	ruler	la regla
(student) desk	el pupitre	schedule	el horario
dictionary	el diccionario	school	la escuela
elementrary school	la escuela elemental, la primaria	school supplies	los útiles
eraser	la goma	scissors	las tijeras
error	la falta	sentence	la frase, la oración
exercise	el ejercicio	student	el (la) alumno(a), el (la) estudiante
explanation	la explicación	subject	la materia

English	Spanish	English	Spanish
grade	*la nota*	summary	*el resumen*
grammar	*la gramática*	teacher	*el (la) profesor(a)*
gym	*el gimnasio*	test	*el examen*
high school	*la escuela de segunda enseñanza, la secundaria*	tutor	*el profesor, la profesora particular*
homework	*la tarea*	vocabulary	*el vocabulario*
laboratory	*el laboratorio*	word	*la palabra*
lesson	*la lección*	work	*el trabajo*
map	*el mapa*		

School Subjects and Activities

English	Spanish	English	Spanish
algebra	*el álgebra*	geometry	*la geometría*
art	*el arte*	gym	*la educación física*
arts and crafts	*la artesanía*	historia	*la historia*
band	*la banda*	Latin	*el latín*
biology	*la biología*	math	*las matemáticas*
calculus	*el cálculo*	music	*la música*
chemistry	*la química*	orchestra	*la orquesta*
chorus	*el coro*	physics	*la física*
club	*el círculo*	science	*la ciencia*
computer science	*la informática*	shop	*las artes industriales*
drawing	*el diseño*	Spanish	*el español*
English	*el inglés*	team	*el equipo*
French	*el francés*	technology	*la tecnología*
geography	*la geografía*		

Professions

English	Male	Female
accountant	*el contable (el contador)*	*la contable (la contadora)*
actor/actress	*el actor*	*la actriz*
artist	*el artista*	*la artista*
athlete	*el atleta*	*la atleta*
baker	*el panadero*	*la panadera*
barber	*el peluquero*	*la peluquera*
businessperson	*el hombre de negocios*	*la mujer de necocios*
butcher	*el carnicero*	*la carnicera*
cashier	*el cajero*	*la cajera*
cook	*el cocinero*	*la cocinera*
dentist	*el dentista*	*la dentista*
designer	*el diseñador*	*la diseñadora*
doctor	*el médico*	*la médica*
electrician	*el electricista*	*la electricista*
engineer	*el ingeniero*	*la ingeniera*
farmer	*el campesino*	*la campesina*
firefighter	*el bombero*	*la bombera*
flight attendant	*el aeromozo*	*la aeromoza, la azafata*
government employee	*el empleado del gobierno*	*la empleada del gobierno*
hairstylist	*el peluquero*	*la peluquera*
jeweler	*el joyero*	*la joyera*
judge	*el juez*	*la juez*
laborer	*el obrero*	*la obrera*
lawyer	*el abogado*	*la abogada*
mail carrier	*el cartero*	*la cartera*
manager	*el director, el gerente*	*la directora, la gerente*
mechanic	*el mecánico*	*la mecánica*
merchant	*el comerciante*	*la comerciante*

English	Male	Female
musician	*el músico*	*la música*
nurse	*el enfermero*	*la enfermera*
painter	*el pintor*	*la pintora*
pharmacist	*el farmacéutico*	*la farmacéutica*
pilot	*el piloto*	*la pilota*
poet	*el poeta*	*la poetisa*
police officer	*el policía*	*la policía*
president	*el presidente*	*la presidenta*
programmer	*el programador*	*la programadora*
researcher	*el investigador*	*la investigadora*
salesperson	*el dependiente*	*la dependiente*
scientist	*el científico*	*la científica*
secretary	*el secretario*	*la secretaria*
server	*el mozo, el mesero*	*la moza, la mesera*
soldier	*el soldado*	*la soldada*
teacher	*el profesor*	*la profesora*
waiter/waitress	*el camarero, el mesero, el mozo*	*la camarera, la mesera, la moza*
writer	*el escritor*	*la escritora*

Leisure Time

Hobbies and Other Leisure Activities

English	Spanish	English	Spanish
ballet	*el ballet*	movies	*el cine*
beach	*la playa*	opera	*la ópera*
cards	*los naipes*	parade	*el desfile*
concert	*el concierto*	picnic	*el picnic*
country	*el campo*	play	*la obra teatral*
dance	*el baile*	show	*la exposición*

(continues)

Hobbies and Other Leisure Activities   (continued)

English	Spanish	English	Spanish
fair	*la feria*	theater	*el teatro*
hike	*la caminata*	walk	*el paseo*
holiday	*la fiesta*	zoo	*el parque zoológico*
mountain	*la montaña*		

Computer Terms

English	Spanish	English	Spanish
to boot	*arrancar*	joystick	*el control*
byte	*el byte, el coteto*	key	*la tecla*
CD	*el CD*	keyboard	*el teclado*
to click	*chascar*	laptop	*la computadora portátil*
computer	*la computadora, el ordenador*	memory	*la memoria*
computer science	*la informática*	to merge	*fusionar*
CPU	*la unidad central*	modem	*el modem*
cursor	*el cursor*	monitor	*el monitor*
cyberspace	*el ciberespacio*	motherboard	*la carta-madre*
database	*la base de datos*	mouse	*el ratón*
disk drive	*la disquetera*	network	*la red*
to download	*bajar, descargar*	to press	*apretar*
DVD	*el DVD*	to scan	*barrer*
e-mail	*el correo electrónico*	scanner	*el scanner*
e-mail address	*la diréccion de correo electrónico*	screen	*la pantalla*
hard disk	*el disco duro*	search engine	*el buscador*
hardware	*el hardware equipo, el soporte físico*	software	*el logicial*
home page	*la página inicial*	tape backup	*la cinta de seguridad*
icon	*el icono*	Web	*la teleraña*
instant message	*el recado instantáneo*	word processor	*el procesador de textos*
Internet	*el internet*		

Musical Instruments

English	Spanish	English	Spanish
accordion	*el acordeón*	horn	*el cuerno*
cello	*el violoncelo*	oboe	*el oboe*
clarinet	*el clarinete*	piano	*el piano*
drum	*el tambor*	piccolo	*el piccolo*
drum set	*la batería*	saxophone	*el saxofón*
flute	*la flauta*	trombone	*el trombón*
guitar	*la guitarra*	trumpet	*la trompeta*
harp	*la arpa*	violin	*el violín*

Sports

English	Spanish	English	Spanish
aerobics	*los aeróbicos*	jai alai	*el jai alai*
athletics	*el atletismo*	jogging	*el trotar (el footing)*
auto racing	*las carreras de coches*	mountain climbing	*el alpinismo*
baseball	*el béisbol*	Ping-Pong	*el ping-pong*
body-building	*el culturismo*	roller skating	*el patinaje sobre ruedas*
bowling	*los bolos*	sailing	*la navegación*
canoeing	*el piragüismo*	scuba diving	*el buceo*
cycling	*el ciclismo*	skateboarding	*el patinaje sobre plancha, el monopatín*
deep-sea fishing	*la pesca de altura*	skiing	*el esquí*
diving	*el buceo*	soccer	*el fútbol*
fishing	*la pesca*	surfing	*el surf*
football	*el fútbol americano*	swimming	*la natación*
golf	*el golf*	tennis	*el tenis*
hockey	*el hockey*	track	*la carrera*
hunting	*la caza*	volleyball	*el volibol*
horse racing	*las carreras de caballos*	waterskiing	*el esquí acuático*
horseback riding	*la equitación*	windsurfing	*el windsurf*
ice skating	*el patinaje sobre hielo*		

Playing Fields

English	Spanish	English	Spanish
beach	la playa	park	el parque
course (golf)	el campo	pool	la piscina
court	la cancha	rink	la pista
field	el campo	sea	el mar
gymnasium	el gimnasio	slope	la pista
mountain	la montaña	stadium	el estadio
ocean	el océano	track	la pista

Equipment

English	Spanish	English	Spanish
ball (football, soccer)	la bola	jogging shoes	los tenis
ball (baseball, jai alai, tennis)	la pelota	jogging suit	el traje de trotar
ball (basketball)	el balón	knee pads	las rodilleras
bat	el bate	mitt	el guante
bathing suit	el traje de baño	net	la red
bicycle	la bicicleta	poles (ski)	los palos
boat	el barco	puck	el puck, el disco
boots (ski)	las botas	racket	la raqueta
canoe	la canoa	rifle	el fusil, el rifle
diver's helmet	el yelmo	sailboard	la plancha de vela
diving suit	la escafandra	skateboard	la plancha de ruedas, el monopatín
fishing rod	la caña de pesca	skates	los patines
flippers	las aletas	ski bindings	las ataduras
goggles (ski)	las gafas de esquí	skis	los esquís
goggles (swimming)	las gafas submarinas	water-skis	los esquís acuáticos
golf clubs	los palos de golf	surfboard	el acuaplano
helmet	el casco	wet suit	la escafandra

Nature

English	Spanish	English	Spanish
bay	*la bahía, el golfo*	ocean	*el océano*
beach	*la playa*	ozone layer	*la capa de ozono*
cloud	*la nube*	planet	*el planeta*
coast	*la costa*	plant	*la planta*
country, field	*el campo*	pond	*la charca*
desert	*el desierto*	rain	*la lluvia*
earth	*la tierra*	river	*el río*
flower	*la flor*	sand	*la arena*
fog	*la niebla*	sea	*el/la mar*
forest	*la selva*	sky	*el cielo*
grass	*la hierba*	snow	*la nieve*
island	*la isla*	star	*la estrella*
hill	*la colina*	stream	*el arroyo*
lagoon	*la laguna*	sun	*el sol*
lake	*el lago*	tree	*el árbol*
landscape	*el paisaje*	waterfall	*la cáscada*
leaf	*la hoja*	wind	*el viento*
moon	*la luna*	woods	*el bosque*
mountain	*la montaña*	world	*el mundo*

Apparel

Articles of Clothing

English	Spanish	English	Spanish
bathing suit	*el traje de baño*	pullover	*el jersey*
belt	*el cinturón*	raincoat	*el impermeable, la gabardina*
blouse	*la blusa*	robe	*la bata*
boots	*las botas*	sandals	*las sandalias*

(continues)

Articles of Clothing   *(continued)*

English	Spanish	English	Spanish
clothing	*la ropa*	scarf	*la bufanda*
coat	*el abrigo*	shirt	*la camisa*
dress	*el vestido*	shoe	*el zapato*
evening gown	*el traje de noche*	shorts	*los pantalones cortos*
gloves	*los guantes*	skirt	*la falda*
handkerchief	*el pañuelo*	slip (half) (full)	*el faldellín* *la combinación*
hat	*el sombrero*	sneakers	*los tenis*
jacket	*la chaqueta*	socks	*los calcetines*
jeans	*los vaqueros (los jeans)*	sports coat	*la chaqueta de esport*
lingerie	*la ropa interior feminina*	stockings	*las medias*
mittens	*los mitones*	suit	*el traje*
night shirt	*la camisa de dormir*	sweater	*el suéter*
overcoat	*el abrigo*	tie	*la corbata*
pajamas	*las pijamas/piyamas*	T-shirt	*la camiseta*
pants	*el pantalón*	umbrella	*el paraguas*
pantsuit	*el traje de pantalones*	underwear	*la ropa interior*
pantyhose	*las pantimedias*	vest	*el chaleco*
pocket	*el bolsillo*	wallet	*la cartera*
pocketbook	*la bolsa*	windbreaker	*el abrigo contra el viento*

Materials

English	Spanish	English	Spanish
alpaca	*lla alpaca*	leather	*el cuero*
angora	*la angora*	linen	*el lino*
cashmere	*la cachemira*	microfiber	*la microfibra*
corduroy	*la pana*	nylon	*el nilón*
cotton	*el algodón*	polyester	*el sintético*

English	Spanish	English	Spanish
denim	*la tela tejana*	rubber	*la goma, el caucho, el hule* (Latin America), *el jebe* (Colombia, Peru)
flannel	*la franela*	satin	*el raso*
fleece	*el forro polar*	silk	*la seda*
fur	*la piel*	suede	*la gamusa*
gabardine	*la gabardina*	taffeta	*el tafetán*
knit	*el tejido de punto*	velvet	*el terciopelo*
lace	*el encaje*	wool	*la lana*

Parts of Clothing

English	Spanish	English	Spanish
back	*el atrás, la espalda*	lining	*el forro*
back pocket	*el bolsillo anterior*	pleat	*el pliegue, la pinza*
button	*el botón*	pocket	*el bolsillo*
collar	*el cuello*	shoelaces	*los cordones*
cuff (shirt) (pants)	*el puño* *la vuelta, el doblez*	side pocket	*el bolsillo de lado*
fly	*la bragueta*	sleeve	*la manga*
front	*el frente*	snap	*el broche de presión*
heel	*el tacón*	waist	*la cintura*
hem	*el bajo, el ruedo*	zipper	*el cierre*

Clothing Descriptions

English	Spanish	English	Spanish
baggy	*holgado(a)*	modest	*modesto(a)*
casual	*casual*	narrow	*estrecho(a)*
dressy	*elegante*	short	*corto(a)*
formal	*etiquetero(a)*	small	*pequeño(a)*

(continues)

Clothing Descriptions   *(continued)*

English	Spanish	English	Spanish
long	*largo(a)*	sporty	*deportivo(a)*
loose (shoes)	*hogado(a), suelto(a) apretado(a)*	tight (clothing)	*estrecho(a)*
loud	*chillón(ona)*	wide	*ancho(a)*
low-cut	*escotado(a)*		

Colors

English	Spanish	English	Spanish
beige	*beige*	olive green	*verde oliva*
black	*negro*	orange	*anaranjado(a)*
blue (navy blue)	*azul (azul marino)*	pink	*rosado*
brown	*café, marrón, pardo*	purple	*morado*
burgundy	*granate*	red	*rojo*
chestnut	*marrón*	salmon	*color salmón*
coffee	*color café*	tan	*marrón claro*
gray	*gris*	violet	*violeta*
green	*verde*	white	*blanco*
khaki	*caqui*	yellow	*amarillo*
maroon	*rojo oscuro*		

Jewelry

English	Spanish	English	Spanish
bracelet	*la pulsera*	pin	*el broche*
chain	*la cadena*	ring (jeweled)	*la sortija*
earring	*el arete*	ring (plain)	*el anillo*
gold	*el oro*	silver	*la plata*
necklace	*el collar*	watch	*el reloj*

Jewels

English	Spanish	English	Spanish
amethyst	*la amatista*	onyx	*el ónix*
aquamarine	*el aguamarina*	opal	*el ópalo*
diamond	*el diamante*	pearls	*las perlas*
emerald	*la esmeralda*	ruby	*el rubí*
garnet	*la granate*	sapphire	*el zafiro*
ivory	*el marfíl*	topaz	*el topacio*
jade	*el jade*	turquoise	*la turquesa*

Travel and Transportation

English	Spanish	English	Spanish
airplane	*el avión*	rocket	*el cohete*
airport	*el aeropuerto*	route	*la ruta*
bicycle	*la bicicleta*	sedan	*el sedán*
boat	*el barco*	ship	*la nave, el buque, el barco*
bus	*el autobús*	space shuttle	*el transbordador espacial*
bus terminal	*el terminal de autobuses*	subway	*el metro*
car (sports)	*el automóvil, el coche, el carro (deportivio)*	taxi	*el taxi*
convertible	*el convertible, el descapotable*	ticket	*el boleto, el billete*
flight	*el vuelo*	ticket window	*la ventanilla*
freeway	*la autopista*	toll	*el peaje*
gate	*la puerta*	trailer truck	*un camión articulado*
highway	*la carretera*	train	*el tren*
minivan	*una minicamioneta*	train station	*la estación*
motorcycle	*la motocicleta, la moto*	traveler	*el viajero*
passenger	*el pasajero*	trip	*el viaje*
pickup truck	*la furgoneta*	truck	*el camión*
pier	*el muelle*	van	*la camioneta*
railroad	*el ferrocarril*	wheel	*la rueda*
road	*el camino*		

Car Parts

English	Spanish	English	Spanish
accelerator	el acelerador	hood	la capota
air bag	la bolsa de aire	horn	la bocina
air conditioner	el acondicionador de aire	ignition	el contacto
anti-lock brakes	los frenos anti-bloqueantes	license plate	la placa de matrícula
battery	la batería	motor	el motor
brake light	la luz de freno	oil	el aceite
brakes	los frenos	radiator	el radiador
bumper	el parachoques	roof rack	el portaequipajes
carburetor	el carburador	steering wheel	el volante
clutch pedal	el embrague	stereo	el esterio
door handle	el tirador de puerta	sunroof	el techo corredizo
fan	el ventilador	taillight	el faro trasero
fender	el guardafango	tire	la goma, la llanta
gasoline	la gasolina	transmission	la tansmisión
gas tank	el tanque	trunk	el baúl
gear shift	el cambio de velocidades	turn signal	el direccional
glove compartment	la guantera	wheel	la rueda
hand brake	el freno de mano	windshield wiper	el limpia parabrisas
headlight	el faro delantero		

Countries

English	Spanish	English	Spanish
Algeria	Argelia	Ireland	Irlanda
Argentina	la Argentina	Israel	Israel
Austria	Austria	Italy	Italia
Belgium	Bélgica	Japan	el Japón
Belize	Bélice	Lebanon	Líbano

English	Spanish	English	Spanish
Bolivia	*Bolivia*	Mexico	*México (Méjico)*
Brazil	*el Brasil*	Morocco	*el Marruecos*
Canada	*el Canadá*	the Netherlands	*los Países Bajos*
Chile	*Chile*	Nicaragua	*Nicaragua*
China	*China*	Norway	*Noruega*
Colombia	*Colombia*	Panama	*Panamá*
Costa Rica	*Costa Rica*	Paraguay	*Paraguay*
Cuba	*Cuba*	Peru	*el Perú*
Denmark	*Dinamarca*	Poland	*Polonia*
Dominican Republic	*la República Dominicana*	Portugal	*Portugal*
Ecuador	*el Ecuador*	Puerto Rico	*Puerto Rico*
Egypt	*Egipto*	Romania	*Rumanía*
El Salvador	*El Salvador*	Russia	*Rusia*
England	*Inglaterra*	Scotland	*Escocia*
Finland	*Finlandia*	Spain	*España*
France	*Francia*	Sweden	*Suecia*
Germany	*Alemania*	Switzerland	*Suiza*
Greece	*Grecia*	Tunisia	*Túnez*
Guatemala	*Guatemala*	Turkey	*Turquía*
Haiti	*Haití*	United States	*los Estados Unidos*
Honduras	*Honduras*	Uruguay	*el Uruguay*
Hungary	*Hungría*	Venezuela	*Venezuela*
India	*India*		

The Continents

English	Spanish	English	Spanish
Africa	*África*	Europe	*Europa*
Antarctica	*la Antártica*	North America	*Norte América, La América del Norte*
Asia	*Asia*	South America	*Sud América, la América del Sur*
Australia	*Australia*		

The Weather

English	Spanish	English	Spanish
It's bad weather.	*Hace mal tiempo.*	It's overcast.	*Está cubierto.*
It's beautiful weather	*Hace buen tiempo.*	It's pouring.	*Hay lluvias torrenciales.*
It's cloudy.	*Está cubierto.* or *Está nubloso.*	It's raining.	*Llueve. Está lloviendo.*
It's cold.	*Hace frío.*	It's showery.	*Está lluvioso.*
It's cool.	*Hace fresco.*	It's snowing.	*Nieva. Está nevando.*
It's hailing.	*Hay granizo.*	It's sunny.	*Hace sol.*
It's hot.	*Hace calor.*	It's thundering.	*Truena.*
It's humid.	*Hay humedad.*	It's windy.	*Hace viento.*
It's lightning.	*Hay relámpagos.*		

Index